Franz Ahn

Ahn-Henn's second Latin reader

Selections from the writings of Justinus Caesar

Franz Ahn

Ahn-Henn's second Latin reader
Selections from the writings of Justinus Caesar

ISBN/EAN: 9783337278199

Printed in Europe, USA, Canada, Australia, Japan

Cover: Foto ©Paul-Georg Meister /pixelio.de

More available books at **www.hansebooks.com**

Steiger's Latin Series.

AHN-HENN'S
SECOND LATIN READER.

Selections from the Writings of

JUSTINUS, CAESAR, CICERO, and PHAEDRUS.

With Notes, Vocabulary, and References to Ahn-Henn's *Latin Grammar*.

NEW YORK:

E. STEIGER & CO.

1882.

PREFACE.

This *Second Latin Reader* is intended to be used in connection with AHN-HENN's *Third Latin Book.* It comprises Selections from JUSTIN, CAESAR, CICERO and PHAEDRUS, **Notes** with references to the *Grammar*, and a very full and accurate **Vocabulary.**

Though strictly classical in all important respects, the *First Latin Reader,* which omits the more difficult constructions and parenthetical clauses of the original author, is, of course, but a preparation for what ought to be the next step in the learner's progress — the perusal of the undiminished text of classic authors appropriate for early tuition. The books used for this purpose should at first be as easy as possible, and they are all the better if their contents are cut up into short extracts complete in themselves. With this in view, the selections have been made for the *Second Latin Reader.* To the specimens of the simple narrative style of CAESAR and CICERO it is impossible to take any exception, while JUSTIN whose history was, at one time, extensively in use on account of his purity and propriety of diction, is sufficiently easy to begin with. The fables selected from PHAEDRUS are such as have become familiar to many, in English, and this previous acquaintance has a wondrous effect of smoothing the learner's way through the difficulties which he encounters when first set to read Latin poetry.

In preparing the **Notes** the editor has endeavored to give such assistance as may help a pupil in making out his text, and to point out the usages and idioms of grammar so as to enable him to answer the questions of an intelligent instructor. At this stage it is, of course, a careful study of the **Notes** that must be strongly insisted upon. It is likewise essential to consult the passages in the *Grammar* to which the numerous references are made.

The **Vocabulary** may seem too elaborate, but in reality it is not so. In a book for beginners, every thing should be as clear as

III

possible, and written in such a way that a pupil of fair abilities should be able to make it out without the assistance of a master. Accordingly every word occurring in the text, should have its English equivalent given in the Vocabulary. The special references, however, by page and line (as in the Vocabulary to the *First Reader*) have been discarded, since the pupil must now be able to get for himself the particular shade of meaning which a word has in the given context.

In the preparation of the *Readers* as well, as of all the other books of this series it has been the author's constant endeavor *to facilitate the thorough study of the Latin language* and to make it, at the same time, so practical that when a pupil has mastered these two *Readers* he will be able to read authors of average difficulty (Caesar, Cicero, etc.) *at sight* and thus be fully prepared for the study of Latin at College.

TABLE of CONTENTS.

M. JUSTINIANUS JUSTINUS.

		Text.	Notes.
1.	*The Assyrians*	1	53
2.	*Astyages and Cyrus*	2	55
3.	*The Athenians. Battle of Marathon*	5	60
4.	*Xerxes. Third Invasion of Greece*	9	65
5.	*Sparta and Lycurgus*	15	74
6.	*Sicily. Invasion of the Athenians*	16	76
7.	*Character of Philip and Alexander*	20	81
8.	*The death of Alexander*	21	83
9.	*The earliest history of Carthage*	23	85

C. JULIUS CAESAR.

10.	*First landing in Britain*	28	91
11.	*On the habits of the Germans*	31	96

M. TULLIUS CICERO.

12.	*Solon*	33	99
13.	*Leonidas*	34	101
14.	*Themistocles*	34	101
15.	*Alexander the Great*	35	103
16.	*Dionysius, Tyrant of Syracuse*	36	104
17.	*Socrates*	39	107
18.	*Demosthenes*	42	110
19.	*The best sauce*	43	112
20.	*Burial service at Athens*	44	112
21.	*Aratus of Sicyon*	45	113
22.	*A remarkable dream*	46	114

PHAEDRUS.

		Text.	Notes.
23	*The wolf and the lamb*	47	115
24.	*The frogs and their king*	47	116
25.	*The wolf and the crane*	48	116
26.	*The ass and the lion in partnership*	49	117
27.	*The fox and the crow*	49	117
28.	*The aged lion*	49	118
29.	*The kite and the doves*	50	118
30.	*The two mules*	50	119
31.	*The dog and the wolf*	51	119
32.	*The fox and the sour grapes*	52	120
33.	*The ungrateful snake*	52	120
34.	*The discontented stag*	52	120
	Vocabulary	121	

1. The Assyrians.

I. Principĭo rerum gentĭum nationumque imperĭum penes reges erat, quos ad fastigĭum hujus majestātis non ambitĭo popŭlāris, sed spectāta inter bonos moderatĭo provehēbat. Po- 5 pŭlus nullis legĭbus tenebātur: arbitrĭa princĭpum pro legĭbus erant. Fines imperĭi tuēri magis quam proferre mos erat: intra suam cuīque patrĭam regna finiebantur. Primus omnĭum Ninus, rex Assyriōrum, vetĕrem et quasi avītum gentĭbus morem nova imperĭi cupiditāte mutāvit. Hic primus intŭlit 10 bella finitĭmis et rudes adhuc resistendi popŭlos termĭnos usque Libўae perdomŭit. Magnitudĭnem quaesītae dominatiōnis continŭa possessiōne firmāvit. Domĭtis igĭtur proxĭmis cum accessiōne virĭum fortĭor ad alĭos transīret et proxĭma quaeque victorĭa instrumentum sequentis esset, totīus orientis 15 popŭlos subēgit. Postrēmum bellum illi fuit cum Zoroastre, rege Bactrianōrum, qui primus dicĭtur artes magĭcas invenisse et mundi principĭa siderumque motus diligentissĭme spectasse. Hoc occīso et ipse decessit, relicto adhuc impubĕre filĭo Ninўa et uxōre Semiramĭde.   20

II. Haec Babylonĭam condĭdit murumque urbi cocto latĕre circumdĕdit, harēnae vice bitumĭne interstrāto, quae materĭa in illis locis passim invenītur et e terra exaestŭat. Multa et alĭa praeclāra hujus regīnae fuēre: siquĭdem non contenta regni termĭnos tuēri, Aethiopĭam quoque imperĭo adjēcit. Sed 25 et Indis bellum intŭlit, quos praeter illam et Alexandrum Magnum nemo intrāvit. Postrēmo a filĭo interfecta est, duo et XXX annos post Ninum regno potīta. Filīus ejus Ninўa contentus elaborāto a parentĭbus imperĭo belli studĭa deposŭit et vel̮ŭti̮ sexum cum matre mutasset, raro a viris visus in feminārvm turba̮ c̮onsenŭit. Postĕri quoque ejus id exemplum

5 secūti̮ responsa. gentĭbus per internuntĭos dabant. Imperĭum A̮s̮s̮yrĭ̮i̮, qui·postĕa. Syri dicti sunt, mille trecentos annos tenuĕre.

III. Postrĕmus apud eos regnāvit Sardanapallus, vir muliĕre corrŭptĭor. Ad hunc videndum (quod nemĭni ante eum

10 permissum fuĕrat) praefectus ipsīus Medis praepositus, nomĭne Arbactus, cum admitti aegre obtinuisset, invĕnit eum inter feminārum greges purpŭras colo nentem et muliĕbri habĭtu pensa inter virgĭnes partientem. Quibus visis indignātus, tali femĭnae tot viros tractantes ferrum et arma habentes pa-

15 rēre, progressus ad socĭos quid vidĕrit refert: negat se ei parēre posse, qui se femĭnam malit esse quam virum. Fit igĭtur conjuratĭo; bellum Sardanapallo infertur. Quo ille audīto non ut vir regnum defensūrus, sed, ut metu mortis muliĕres solent, primo latĕbras circumspĭcit, mox deinde cum

20 paucis et inconposĭtis in bellum progredĭtur. Victus in regĭam se recēpit, ubi exstructa incensāque pyra et se et divitĭas suas in incendĭum mittit, hoc solo imitātus virum. Post hunc rex constituĭtur interfector ejus Arbactus, qui praefectus Medōrum fuĕrat. Is imperĭum ab Assyrĭis ad Medos transfert.

25 ## 2. Astyages and Cyrus.

I. Post multos deinde reges per ordĭnem successiōnis regnum ad Astyāgem descendit. Hic per somnum vidit ex filĭa, quam unĭcam habēbat, vitem enātam, cujus palmĭte omnis Asĭa obumbrarĕtur. Consulti hariŏli ex eādem filĭa nepōtem

30 ei futūrum, cujus magnitūdo praenuntiĕtur, regnīque ei amissiōnem portendi respondērunt. Hoc responso exterrĭtus neque claro viro neque civi filĭam suam, ne paterna maternāque

nobilĭtas nepōti anĭmos extollĕret, sed ex gente obscūra tum tempŏris Persārum Cambȳsi, mediŏcri viro, in matrimonĭum tradĭdit. Ne sic quidem somnĭi metu deposĭto filĭam, cum puĕrum peperisset, ad se arcessit, ut sub avi ocŭlis nepos necarētur. Infans datur occidendus Harpăgo, regis arcanō- 5 rum particĭpi. Is verĭtus, si ad filĭam mortŭo rege venisset imperĭum, quia nullum Astyăges filĭum habēbat, ne illa necāti infantis ultiōnem, quam a patre non potuisset, a ministro exigĕret, pastōri regĭi pecŏris puĕrum exponendum tradit.

II.   Forte eōdem tempŏre et ipsi pastōri natus filĭus erat. 10 Ejus igĭtur uxor audīta regis infantis expositiōne summis precĭbus rogat, ut sibi puer ostenderētur.   Cujus precĭbus fatigātus pastor, reversus in silvam, invēnit juxta infantem canem femĭnam parvŭlo ubĕra praebentem et a feris alitĭbusque defendentem.   Motus et ipse misericordĭa, qua motam etĭam 15 canem vidĕrat, puĕrum defert ad stabŭla, eādem cane anxĭe prosequente.   Quem ubi in manum mulĭer accēpit, velŭti ad notam adlūsit, tantusque in illo vigor et dulcis quidam blandientis infantis risus apparŭit, ut pastōrem ultro rogāret, permittĕret sibi puĕrum nutrīre.   Atque ita permutāta sorte 20 parvulōrum hic pro filĭo pastōris educātur, ille pro nepōte regis exponĭtur.   Nutrīci postĕa nomen Spaco fuit, quia canem Persae sic vocant.   ˌ

III.   Puĕr deinde cum inter pastōres esset, Cyri nomen accēpit.   Mox rex inter ludentes sorte delectus cum per lasci- 25 vĭam contumāces flagellis cecidisset, a parentĭbus puerōrum querella regi delāta, indignantĭbus a servo regĭo ingenŭos homĭnes servilĭbus verberĭbus adfectos: ille arcessīto puĕro et interrogāto, cum nihil mutāto vultu fecisse se ut regem respondisset, admirātus constantĭam in memorĭam somnĭi responsĭque 30 revocātur.   Atque ita cum et vultus similitūdo et expositiōnis tempŏra et pastōris confessĭo convenīrent, nepōtem agnōvit. Et quonĭam defunctus sibi somnĭo viderētur agitāto inter

pastōres regno, anĭmum minācem in illo fregit. Cetĕrum Harpăgo amīco suo infestus in ultiōncm servāti nepōtis fĭlĭum ejus
interfēcit cpulandumque patri tradĭdit. Sed Harpăgus ad
praesens tempus dissimulāto dolōre odĭum regis in vindictae
5 occasiōnem distŭlit.

IV. Interjecto deinde tempŏre cum adolevisset Cyrus, dolōre orbitātis admonĭtus scribit ei, ut ablegātus ab avo in
Persas fuĕrit; ut occīdi cum parvŭlum avus jussĕrit; ut bene-
ficĭo suo servātus sit; ut regem offendĕrit; ut fĭlĭum amisĕrit.
10 Hortātur, exercĭtum paret et pronam ad regnum viam ingre-
diātur, Medōrum transitiōncm pollicĭtus. Epistŭla quia palam
ferri nequībat, regis custodĭbus omnes adĭtus obsidentĭbus,
exinterāto lepŏri inserĭtur lepusque in Persas Cyro ferendus
fido servo tradĭtur; addĭta retĭa, ut sub specĭe venatōris dolus
15 latēret.

V. Lectis ille epistŭlis eādem somnĭo adgrĕdi jussus est,
sed praemonĭtus, ut quem primum postĕro die obvĭum habuisset, socĭum cocptis adsumĕret. Antelucāno igĭtur tempŏre ruri
iter ingressus obvĭum habŭit servum de ergastŭlo cujusdam
20 Medi, nomĭne Soebāren. Hujus requisīta origĭne ut in Persis
genĭtum audīvit, demptis conpedĭbus adsumptōque comĭte
Persepŏlim regredĭtur. Ibi convocāto popŭlo jubet omnes
praesto cum securĭbus esse et silvam viae circumdātam ex-
cidĕre. Quod cum strenŭe fecissent, eosdem postĕro die appa-
25 rātis epŭlis invītat; dein cum alacriōres ipso convivĭo factos
vidēret, rogat: si condicĭo ponātur, utrīus vitae sortem legant,
hesterni labōris an praesentĭum epulārum? Praesentĭum ut
adclamavĕre omnes, ait hesterno simĭlem labōri omnem vitam
actūros, quoad Medis parĕant: se secūtos, hodiernis epŭlis.
30 Lactis omnĭbus bellum Medis infert.

VI. Astyăges merĭti sui in Harpăgo oblītus summam belli
eīdem committit: qui exercĭtum acceptum statim Cyro per
deditiōnem tradĭdit regisque crudelitātem perfūdĭa defectiōnis

ulciscĭtur. Quod ubi Astyăgcs audīvit, contractis undīque
auxilĭis ipse in Persas proficiscĭtur: et repetīto alacrĭus certamĭne pugnantĭbus suis partcm exercĭtus de tergo ponit et
tergiversantcs ferro agi in hostes jubet ac denuntĭat suis, ni
vincĕrent, non minus fortes post terga inventūros quam a fron- 5
tĭbus viros: proinde vidĕant, fugientĭbus hacc an illa pugnantĭbus acĭes rumpcnda sit. Ingcns post necessitātcm pugnandi
anĭmus exercitŭi ejus accessit; pulsatăque cum Persārum acĭes
paulātim cedĕret, matres et uxōres cōrum obvĭam occurrunt;
orant in proelĭum revertantur. Hac repressi castigatiōnc in 10
proelĭum redĕunt et facta inpressiōnc quos fugiēbant, fugĕre
conpellunt. In co proelĭo Astyăgcs capĭtur; cui Cyrus nihil
alĭud quam regnum abstŭlit nepōtemque in illo magis quam
victōrcm egit, cumque ducem genti Hyrcanōrum praeposŭit;
nam in Medos reverti ipse nolŭit. Hic finis imperĭi Medōrum 15
fuit; regnavērunt annis CCCL.

3. The Athenians. Battle of Marathon.

I. Ante Deucaliōnis tempŏra Athenienses regem habuēre
Cecrŏpem, quem, ut omnis antiquĭtas fabulōsa est, biformem
tradidēre. Huic successit Cranăus, cujus filĭa Atthis nomen 20
regiōni dedit. Post hunc Amphictўon regnāvit, qui primus
Minervae urbem sacrāvit et nomen civitāti Athēnas dedit.
Hujus temporĭbus aquārum inluvĭes majōrem partem populō-
rum Graecĭae absumpsit. Superfuērunt, quos refugĭa montĭum
recepērunt, aut ad regcm Thessalĭac Deucaliōnem ratĭbus 25
evecti sunt, a quo proptcrĕa genus homĭnum condĭtum dicĭtur.
Per ordĭnem deinde successiōnis regnum ad Erechthĕum descendit, sub quo frumenti satĭo est Eleusīne a Triptolĕmo re-
perta, in cujus munĕris honōrem noctes initiōrum sacrātae.
Tenŭit et Aegēus Athēnis regnum, post Aegĕum patrem The- 30
sēus ac deinceps Thescĭ filĭus, Demophŏon, qui auxilĭum Graecis adversus Trojānos tulit, regnum possēdit.

II. Erant inter Athenienses et Dorienses simultatĭum vetĕres offensae, quas vindicatūri bello Dorienses de eventu proelĭi oracŭla consuluĕrunt. Responsum, superiōres fore, ni regem Atheniensĭum occidissent. Cum ventum esset in bel-
5 lum, militĭbus ante omnĭa custodĭa regis praecipĭtur. Athenicnsĭbus eo tempŏre rex Codrus erat, qui et responso dei et praeceptis hostĭum cognĭtis permutāto regis habĭtu pannōsus, sarmenta collo gerens castra hostĭum ingredĭtur: ibi in turba obsistentĭum a milĭte, quem falce astu convulneravĕrat, inter-
10 ficĭtur. Cognĭto regis corpŏre Dorienses sine proelĭo discēdunt. Atque ita Athenienses virtūte ducis pro salūte patrĭae morti se offerentis bello liberantur.

III. Post Codrum nemo Athēnis regnāvit, quod memorĭae nomĭnis ejus tribūtum est. Administratĭo rei publĭcae annŭa
15 magistratĭbus permissa. Sed civitāti nullae tunc leges erant, quia libīdo regum pro legĭbus habebātur. Legĭtur ităque Solon, vir justitĭae insignis, qui velut novam civitātem legĭbus condĕret: qui tanto temperamento inter plebem senātumque egit (cum, si quid pro altĕro ordĭne tulisset, altĕri displicitū-
20 rum viderētur), ut ab utrisque parem gratĭam trahĕret.

IV. Hujus viri inter multa egregĭa illud memorabĭle fuit. Inter Athenienses et Megarenses de proprietāte Salamīnis insūlae prope usque interĭtum armis dimicātum fuĕrat. Post multas clades capitāle esse apud Athenienses coepit, si quis
25 legem de vindicanda insŭla tulisset. Sollicĭtus igĭtur Solon, ne aut tacendo parum rei publĭcae consulĕret aut censendo offendĕret sibi, subĭtam dementĭam simŭlat, cujus venĭa non dictūrus modo prohibĭta, sed et factūrus erat. Deformis habĭtu more vaecordĭum in publĭcum evŏlat factōque concursu
30 homĭnum, quo magis consilĭum dissimulāret, insolĭtis sibi versĭbus suadēre popŭlo coepit, quod vetabātur, omnĭumque animos ita cepit, ut extemplo bellum adversus Megarenses decernerētur insulāque devictis hostĭbus Atheniensĭum fiĕret.

V. Interea Megarenses memores inlāti Atheniensĭbus belli et verĭti, ne frustra arma movisse viderentur, matrōnas Atheniensĭum in Eleusinĭis sacris noctu oppressūri naves conscendunt. Qua re cognĭta dux Atheniensĭum Pisistrătus juventūtem in insidiis locat, jussis matrōnis solĭto clamōre ac 5 strepĭtu etĭam in accessu hostĭum, ne intellectos se sentĭant, sacra celebrāre: egressosque navĭbus Megarenses inopinantes· adgressus delēvit ac protĭnus classe captīva intermixtis mulierĭbus, ut specĭem captārum matronārum praebērent, Megăra contendit. Illi cum et narĭum formam et petītam praedam 10 cognoscērent, obvĭi ad portum procēdunt, quibus caesis Pisistrătus paulum a capienda urbe afūit. Ita Dorienses suis dolis hosti victorĭam dedēre.

VI. Sed Pisistrătus, quasi sibi, non patrĭae vicisset, tyrannĭdem per dolum occŭpat: quippe voluntarĭis verberĭbus 15 domi adfectus laceratōque corpŏre in publĭcum progredĭtur, advocāta contiōne vulnĕra popŭlo ostendit, de crudelitāte princĭpum, e quibus haec se passum simulābat, querĭtur; adduntur vocĭbus lacrĭmae et invidiōsa oratiōne multitūdo credŭla accendĭtur: amōre plebis invĭsum se senatŭi simŭlat: 20 obtĭnet ad custodĭam corpŏris sui satellĭtum auxilĭum, per quos occupāta tyrannĭde per annos XXXIII regnāvit.

VII. Post hujus mortem Hipparchus, alter ex filĭis interficĭtur, alter, Hippĭas nomĭne, cum imperĭum paternum tenēret, interfectōrem fratris conprehendi jubet, qui cum per 25 tormenta conscĭos caedis nomināre cogerētur, omnes amīcos tyranni nomināvit, quibus interfectis quaerenti tyranno, an adhuc alĭqui conscĭi essent, nemĭnem ait superesse, quem amplĭus mori gestĭat, quam ipsum tyrannum. Qua voce ejusdem se tyranni victōrem ostendit. Hujus virtūte cum admo- 30 nĭta civĭtas libertātis esset, tandem Hippĭas regno pulsus in exsilĭum agĭtur, qui profectus in Persas ducem se Darēo inferenti Atheniensĭbus bellum adversus patrĭam suam offert.

VIII. Athenienses igĭtur audīto Darēi advēntu auxilĭum a Lacedaemonĭis, socĭa tum civitāte, petivērunt, quos ubi vidērunt quadridŭi tenēri religiōne, non expectāto, instructis decem milĭbus civĭum et Plataeensĭbus auxiliarĭbus mille ad-
5 versus sescenta milĭa hostĭum in campis Marathonĭis in proc-
lĭum egrediuntur. Miltiādes et dux belli erat et auctor non exspectandi auxilĭi: quem tanta fiducĭa cepērat, ut plus prae-sidĭi in celeritāte quam in socĭis ducēret. Magna igĭtur in pugnam euntĭbus animōrum alacrĭtas fuit, adĕo ut, cum mille
10 passus inter duas acĭes essent, citāto cursu ante jactum sagit-tārum ad hostem venīrent. Nec audacĭae ejus eventus defŭit: pugnātum est enim tanta virtūte, ut hinc viros, inde pecŭdes putāres. Victi Persae in naves confugērunt, ex quibus multae suppressae, multae captae sunt. In eo proelĭo tanta virtus
15 singulōrum fuit, ut, cujus laus prima esset, difficĭle judicĭum vidērētur.

IX. Inter cetĕros tamen Themistŏclis adulescentis glorĭa emicŭit, in quo jam indŏles futūrae imperatorĭae dignitātis apparŭit. Cynegĭri quoque milĭtis Atheniensis glorĭa magnis
20 scriptōrum laudĭbus celebrāta est, qui post proelii innumĕras caedes cum fugientes hostes ad naves egisset, onustam navem dextra manu tenŭit nec prius dimīsit quam manum amittĕret: tum quoque amputāta dextĕra navem sinistra conprehendit, quam et ipsam cum amisisset, ad postrēmum morsu navem de-
25 tinŭit. Tantam in eo virtūtem fuisse, ut non tot caedĭbus fatigātus, non duābus manĭbus amissis victus, truncus ad po-strēmum et velut rabĭda fera dentĭbus dimicāret. Ducenta milĭa Persae seu proelĭo sive naufragĭo amisēre. Cecĭdit et Hippĭas, tyrannus Atheniensis, auctor et concĭtor ejus belli, dis patrĭae
30 ultorĭbus poenas repetentĭbus.

4. Xerxes. Third invasion of Greece.

I. Interĕa et Darēus, cum bellum restaurāret, in ipso apparātu decēdit, relictis multis filīis et in regno et ante regnum susceptis. Ex his Ariaemĕnes maxĭmus natu actātis privilegĭo regnum sibi vindicābat, quod jus et ordo nascendi et 5 natūra ipsa gentĭbus dedit. Porro Xerxes controversĭam non de ordĭne, sed de nascendi felicitāte referēbat: nam Ariaemĕnem primum quidem Darēo, sed privāto provenisse: se regi primum natum. Ităque fratres suos, qui ante genĭti essent, privātum patrimonĭum, quod eo tempŏre Darēus habuisset, 10 non regnum vindicāre sibi posse: se esse, quem primum in regno jam rex pater sustulĕrit. Huc accedĕre, quod Ariaemĕnes non patre tantum, sed et matre privātae adhuc fortūnae, avo quoque materno privāto procreātus sit: se vero et matre regīna natum et patrem non nisi regem vidisse: avum 15 quoque maternum Cyrum se regem habuisse, non herēdem, sed conditōrem tanti regni: et si in aequo jure utrumque fratrem pater reliquisset, materno tamen se jure et avīto vincĕre.

II. Hoc certāmen concordi anĭmo ad patrŭum suum Artaphernen velŭti ad domestĭcum judĭcem deferunt, qui domi 20 cognĭta causa Xerxem praeposŭit: adeōque fraterna contentĭo fuit, ut nec victor insultāret nec victus dolēret ipsōque litis tempŏre munĕra invĭcem mittĕrent, jucunda quoque inter se non solum, sed credŭla convivĭa habērent, judicĭum quoque ipsum sine arbĭtris, sine convicĭo esset. Tanto moderatĭus tum 25 fratres inter se maxĭma regna dividēbant, quam nunc exigŭa patrimonĭa partiuntur. Xerxes igĭtur bellum a patre coeptum adversus Graecĭam quinquennĭum instruxit.

III. Quod ubi primum didĭcit Demarātus, rex Lacedaemoniōrum, qui apud Xerxen exsulābat, amicĭor patrĭae post 30 fugam quam regi post beneficĭa, ne inopināto bello opprimerentur, omnĭa in tabellis ligneĭs magistratĭbus perscrĭbit easdemque cera superindūcit delīta, ne aut scriptūra sine tegmĭne

indicĭum darct aut recens ccra dolum prodĕret: fido dcindc
servo pcrfcrendas tradit, jusso magistratĭbus Spartanōrum
tradĕrc. Quibus perlātis Lacedaemŏnc quaestiōni res diu fuit,
quod ncquc scriptum alĭquid vidērent nec frustra missas suspi-
5 carentur, tantōquc rem majōrcm, quanto esset occultĭor, putābant. Haercntĭbus in conjectūra viris soror regis Leonĭdae
consilĭum scribcntis invēnit. Erāsa igĭtur ccra belli consilĭa
dctcguntur.

IV. Jam Xerxes scptingenta milĭa dc regno armavĕrat ct
10 trecénta milĭa dc auxilĭis, ut non inmerĭto prodĭtum sit, flumĭna ab cxcrcĭtu cjus siccāta Gracciamquc omncm vix capĕre
cxcrcĭtum cjus potuissc. Navcs quoquc decĭens ccntum milĭum
numĕro habuissc dicĭtur. Huic tanto agmĭni dux defŭit. Cetĕrum si regcm spcctcs, divitĭas, non duccm laudcs: quarum
15 tanta copĭa in regno cjus fuit, ut, cum flumĭna multitudĭne
consumerentur, opcs tamen regĭac supcrcsscnt. Ipsc autcm
primus in fuga, postrēmus in proelĭo sempcr visus cst; in pcri-
cŭlis timĭdus: sicŭbi mctus abcsset, inflātus; denĭquc antc cx-
perimcntum belli fiducĭa virĭum velŭti natūrac ipsĭus domĭnus·
20 ct montes in planum deducēbat et convexa vallĭum acquābat
et quaedam marĭa pontĭbus sternēbat, quacdam ad navigatiōnis commŏdum pcr conpendĭum ducēbat.

V. Cujus introĭtus in Gracciam quam tcrribĭlis, tam turpis
ac focdus discessus fuit. Namquc cum Leonĭdas, rex Sparta-
25 nōrum cum IIII milĭbus milĭtum angustĭas Thermopylārum
occupasset, Xcrxcs contcmptu paucitātis cos pugnam capcssĕrc
jubet, quorum cognāti Marathonĭa pugna interfecti fuĕrant:
qui dum ulcisci suos quaerunt, principĭum cladis fuēre; succe-
dcntc dein inutĭli turba major caedes edĭtur. Tridŭo ibi cum
30 dolōrc et indignatiōnc Persārum dimicātum: quarta dic cum
nuntiātum csset Leonĭdae, a XX milĭbus hostĭum summum ca-
cūmcn tenēri, tum hortātur socĭos, recēdant ct se ad meliōra
patrĭae tempŏra rescrvent: sibi cum Spartānis fortūnam

experiendam: plura se patrĭae quam vitae debēre: cetĕros ad
praesidĭa Graecĭae servandos.

VI. Audīto regis imperĭo discessēre cetĕri, soli Lacedaemonĭi remansērunt. Initĭo hujus belli sciscitantĭbus Delphis
oracŭla responsum fuĕrat, aut regi Spartanōrum aut urbi 5
cadendum. Et idcirco rex Leonĭdas, cum in bellum proficiscerētur, ita suos firmavĕrat, ut ire se parāto ad moriendum
anĭmo scirent. Angustĭas proptereă occupavĕrat, ut cum
paucis aut majōre glorĭa vincĕret aut minōre damno rei publĭcae cadĕret. Dimissis igĭtur socĭis hortātur Spartānos, memi- 10
nĕrint qualitercumque procliātis cadendum esse; cavērent, ne
fortĭus mansisse quam dimicasse viderentur; nec expectan-
dum, ut ab hoste circumvenirentur, sed dum nox occasiōnem
daret, secūris et laetis superveniendum: nusquam victōres
honestĭus quam in castris hostĭum peritūros. 15

VII. Nihil erat difficĭle persuadēre persuāsis mori: statim
arma capĭunt et sescenti viri castra quingentōrum milĭum in-
rumpunt statimque regis praetorĭum petunt, aut cum illo aut,
si ipsi oppressi essent, in ipsīus potissĭmum sede moritūri.
Tumultus totis castris orĭtur. Spartāni, postquam regem non 20
invenĭunt, per omnĭa castra victōres vagantur; caedunt ster-
nuntque omnĭa, ut qui sciunt, se pugnāre non spe victorĭae,
sed in mortis ultiōnem. Proelĭum a principĭo noctis in majōrem partem diĕi tractum. Ad postrēmum non victi, sed vincendo fatigāti inter ingentes stratōrum hostĭum catervas occi- 25
dērunt. Xerxes duōbus vulnerĭbus terrestri proelĭo acceptis
experīri maris fortūnam statŭit.

VIII. Sed Atheniensĭum dux Themistŏcles cum animadvertisset Iōnas, propter quos bellum Persārum suscepērunt, in
auxilĭum regis classe venisse, sollicitāre eos in partes suas 30
statŭit, et cum colloquendi copĭam non habēret, symbŏlos pro-
pōn‘ et saxis proscrībi curat: ‘‘Quae vos, Iōnes, dementĭa
tenet? Quod facĭnus agitātis? Bellum inferre olim conditorĭbus

vestris, nuper etĭam vindicĭbus cogitātis? An idĕo moenĭa vestra condidĭmus, ut essent qui nostra delērent? Quid si non haec Darēo prius et nunc Xerxi belli causa nobiscum foret, quod vos rebellantes non destituĭmus? Quin vos in haec 5 castra vestra ex ista obsidiōne transĭtis? Aut si hoc parum tutum est, at vos commisso proelĭo ite cessim, inhibēte remis et a bello discedĭte."

IX. Ante navālis proelĭi congressiōnem misĕrat Xerxes IIII milĭa milĭtum armatōrum Delphos ad templum Apollĭnis 10 diripiendum, prorsus quasi non cum Graecis tantum, sed et cum dis inmortalĭbus bellum gerĕret: quae manus tota imbrĭbus et fulminĭbus delēta est, ut intellegĕret, quam nullae essent homĭnum adversum deos vires. Post haec Thespĭas et Plataeas et Athēnas vacŭas hominĭbus incendit, et quonĭam ferro 15 in homĭnes non potĕrat, in aedificĭa igne grassātur. Namque Athenienses post pugnam Marathonĭam praemonente Themistŏcle, victorĭam illam de Persis non finem, sed causam majōris belli fore, CC naves fabricavērunt. Adventante igĭtur Xerxe (consulentĭbus Delphis oracŭlum responsum fuĕrat, salūtem 20 muris lignĕis tuerentur) Themistŏcles, navĭum praesidĭum demonstrātum ratus, persuādet omnĭbus, patrĭam municĭpes esse, non moenĭa, civitātemque non in aedificĭis, sed in civĭbus posĭtam: ităque melĭus salūtem navĭbus quam urbi commissūros; hujus sententĭae etĭam deum auctōrem esse.

25 X. Probāto consilĭo conjŭges liberosque cum pretiosissĭmis rebus abdĭtis insŭlis relicta urbe demandant; ipsi naves armāti conscendunt. Exemplum Atheniensĭum et alĭae urbes imitātae. Ităque cum adunāta omnis sociōrum classis et intenta in bellum navāle esset angustĭasque Salaminĭi freti, ne 30 circumvenīri a multitudĭne posset, occupassent, dissensĭo inter civitātum princĭpes orītur: qui cum deserto bello ad sua tuenda dilābi vellent, timens Themistŏcles, ne discessu sociōrum vires minuerentur, per servum fidum Xerxi nuntĭat, uno in

loco cum contractam Graeciam capĕre facillĭme posse. Quod si civitātes, quae jam abīre vellent, dissiparentur, majōre labōre ei singŭlas consectandas. Hoc dolo impellit regem signum pugnae dare. Graeci quoque adventu hostĭum occupāti proelĭum collātis virĭbus capessunt.   5

XI. Interĕa rex velut spectātor pugnae cum parte navĭum in litŏre remănet. Artemisĭa autem, regīna Halicarnāsi, quae in auxilĭum Xerxi venĕrat, inter primos duces bellum acerrĭme ciēbat, ut in viro muliēbrem timōrem, ita in muliĕre virīlem audacĭam cernĕres. Cum anceps proelĭum esset, Iōnes juxta 10 praeceptum Themistŏclis pugnae se paulātim subtrahĕre coepērunt: quorum defectĭo anĭmos ceterōrum fregit. Ităque circumspicientes fugam pelluntur Persae et mox proelĭo victi in fugam vertuntur. In qua trepidatiōne multae captae naves, multae mersae; plures tamen non minus saevitĭam regis quam 15 hostem timentes domum dilabuntur.

XII. Hac clade perculsum et dubĭum consilĭi Xerxem Mardonĭus adgredītur. Hortātur ut in regnum abĕat, ne quid seditiōnis movĕat fama adversi belli et in majus, sicŭti mos est, omnĭa extollens: sibi CCC milĭa armatōrum lecta ex omnĭ- 20 bus copĭis relinquat, qua manu aut cum glorĭa ejus perdomitūrum se Graecĭam aut, si alĭter eventus fuĕrit, sine ejusdem infamĭa hostĭbus cessūrum. Probāto consilĭo Mardonĭo exercĭtus tradītur: relĭquas copĭas rex ipse deducĕre in regnum parat. Sed Graeci audīta regis fuga consilĭum incŭnt pontis 25 interrumpendi, quem ille Abȳdi velŭti victor maris fecĕrat, ut interclūsus redītu aut cum exercĭtu delerētur aut desperatiōne rerum pacem victus petĕre cogerētur.

XIII. Sed Themistŏcles timens, ne interclūsi hostes desperatiōnem in virtūtem vertĕrent et iter, quod alĭter non patēret, 30 ferro patefacĕrent: satis multos hostes in Graecĭa remanēre dictĭtans, nec augēri numĕrum retinendo oportēre, cum vincĕre consilĭo cetĕros non posset, eundem servum ad Xerxem

mittit certiōremque consilii facit et occupāre transītum maturāta fuga jubet. Ille perculsus nuntīo tradit ducībus milītes
perducendos: ipse cum paucis Abÿdum contendit. Ubi cum
solūtum pontem hibernis tempestatībus offendisset, piscatorīa
5 scapha trepīdus trajēcit. Erat res spectacŭlo digna et aesti-
matiōne sortis humānae rerum varietāte miranda, in exigŭo
latentem vidēre navigīo quem paulo ante vix aequor omne capiēbat, carentem omni etiam servōrum ministerīo, cujus exercītus propter multitudīnem terris graves erant. Nec pedestrībus
10 copīis, quas ducībus adsignavĕrat, felicīus iter fuit, siquīdem
cotidiāno labōri (neque enim ulla est metuentībus quies) etiam
fames accessĕrat. Multōrum deinde diērum inopīa contraxĕrat
et pestem, tantāque foedītas morientīum fuit, ut viae cadaverī-
bus implerentur alītesque et bestīae escae inlecĕbris sollici-
15 tātae exercītum sequerentur.

XIV. Intĕrim Mardonīus in Graecīa Olynthum expugnat.
Athenienses quoque in spem pacis amicitiamque regis sollicī-
tat, spondens incensae eōrum urbis etiam in majus restitutiōnem. Postquam nullo pretīo libertātem his venālem videt,
20 incensis quae aedificāre coepĕrant, copīas in Boeotīam transfert. Eo et Graecōrum exercītus, qui centum milīum fuit,
secūtus est ibīque proelīum commissum. Sed fortūna regis
cum duce mutāta non est. Nam victus Mardonīus velūti ex
naufragīo cum paucis profūgit. Castra referta regālis opu-
25 lentīae capta. Unde primum Graecos divīso inter se auro
Persīco divitiārum luxurīa cepit.

XV. Eōdem forte die, quo Mardonīi copīae delētae sunt,
etiam navāli proelīo in Asīa sub monte Mycāle adversus Persas dimicātum est. Ibi ante congressiōnem, cum classes ex
30 adverso starent, fama ad utrumque exercītum venit, vicisse
Graecos et Mardonīi copīas occidiōne cecidisse. Tantam
famae velocitātem fuisse, ut, cum matutīno tempŏre proelīum
in Boeotīa commissum sit, meridiānis horis in Asīam per tot

marĭa et tantum spatĭi tam brevi horārum momento de victorĭa nuntiātum sit. Confecto bello, cum de praemĭis civitatĭum agerētur, omnĭum judicĭo Athen}ensĭum virtus cetĕris praclāta. Inter duces quoque Themistŏcles princeps civitātum testimonĭo judicātus glorĭam patrĭae suae auxit.   5

5. Sparta and Lycurgus.

I. Graecĭa omnis ducĭbus Lacedaemonĭis et Athenĭensĭbus in duas divīsa partes ab externis bellis velut in viscĕra sua arma convertit. Fiunt igĭtur de uno popŭlo duo corpŏra, et eorundem castrōrum homĭnes in duos hostīles exercĭtus divi- 10 duntur. Hinc Lacedaemonĭi communĭa quondam civitatĭum auxilĭa ad vires suas trahĕre: inde Athenĭenses et vetustāte gentis et gestis rebus inlustres proprĭis virĭbus confidēbant. Atque ita duo potentissĭmi Graecĭae popŭli institūtis Solōnis et Lycurgi legĭbus pares ex aemulatiōne virĭum in bellum ruēbant. 15

II. Namque Lycurgus, cum fratri suo Polydectae, Sparta-nōrum regi, successisset regnumque sibi vindicāre potuisset, Charillo, filĭo ejus, qui natus postŭmus erat, cum ad aetātem adultam pervenisset, regnum summa fide restitūit, ut intelle-gĕrent omnes, quanto plus apud bonos pietātis jura quam 20 omnes opes valērent. Medĭo igĭtur tempŏre, dum infans con-valescit tutēlamque ejus administrat, non habentĭbus Spartānis leges institūit, non inventiōne cārum magis quam exemplo clarĭor: siquĭdem nihil lege ulla in alĭos sanxit, cujus non ipse primus in se documentum daret. Popŭlum in obsequĭa prin- 25 cĭpum, princĭpes ad justitĭam imperiōrum firmāvit. Parsimo-nĭam omnĭbus suāsit, existĭmans labōrem militĭae adsidŭa frugalitātis consuetudĭne faciliōrem fore. Emi singŭla non pe-cunĭa, sed compensatiōne mercĭum jussit. Auri argentīque usum ut omnĭum scelĕrum materĭam sustŭlit.   30

III. Administratiōnem rei publĭcae per ordĭnes divīsit: regĭbus potestātem bellōrum, magistratĭbus judicĭa et annŭos

successōres, senatŭi custodĭam legum, popŭlo sublegendi senātum vel creandi quos vellet magistrātus potestātem permīsit.
Fundos omnĭum aequalĭter inter omnes divīsit, ut aequāta patrimonĭa nemĭnem potentiōrem altĕro reddĕrent. Convivāri
5 omnes publĭce jussit, ne cujus divitĭae vel luxurĭa in occulto
essent. Juvenĭbus non amplĭus una veste uti toto anno permissum, nec quemquam cultĭus quam altĕrum progrĕdi nec
epulāri opulentĭus, ne imitatĭo in luxurĭam verterētur. Puĕros
pubĕres non in forum, sed in agrum dedūci praecēpit, ut
10 primos annos non in luxurĭa, sed in opĕre et in laborĭbus agĕ-
rent. Nihil eos somni causa substernĕre et vitam sine pul-
mento degĕre neque prius in urbem redīre, quam viri facti
essent, statŭit.

IV. Virgĭnes sine dote nubĕre jussit, ut uxōres eligerentur,
15 non pecunĭae, severiusque matrimonĭa sua viri coërcērent,
cum nullis frenis dotis tenerentur. Maxĭmum honōrem non
divītum et potentĭum, sed pro gradu aetātis senum esse volŭit,
nec sane usquam terrārum locum honoratiōrem senectus habet.
Haec quonĭam primo solūtis antĕa morĭbus dura vidēbat esse,
20 auctōrem cōrum Apollĭnem Delphĭcum fingit et inde se ea ex
praecepto numĭnis detulisse, ut consuescendi taedĭum metus
religiōnis vincat. Dein ut aeternitātem legĭbus suis daret,
jure jurando oblĭgat civitātem, nihil eos de ejus legĭbus muta-
tūros, priusquam reverterētur, et simŭlat se ad oracŭlum Del-
25 phĭcum proficisci, consultūrum quid addendum mutandumque
legĭbus viderētur. Proficiscĭtur autem Cretam ibīque perpetŭum exsilĭum egit abjicīque in mare ossa sua morĭens jussit,
ne relātis Lacedaemŏnem solūtos se Spartāni religiōne juris
jurandi in dissolvendis legĭbus arbitrarentur.

30 ## 6. Sicily. Invasion of the Athenians.

I. Sicilĭam ferunt angustis quondam faucĭbus Italĭae adhaesisse diremptamque velut a corpŏre majōre impĕtu supĕri

maris, quod toto undārum onēre illuc vehītur. Est autem terra
ipsa tenŭis ac fragĭlis et cavernis quibusdam fistŭlisque ita
penetrabĭlis, ut ventōrum tota fermc flatĭbus patĕat; nec non
et ignĭbus generandis nutriendisque soli ipsīus naturālis materĭa: quippe intrinsĕcus stratum sulphŭre et bitumĭne tradĭtur: 5
quae res facit, ut spirītu cum igne in matcrīa luctante frequenter et complurĭbus locis nunc flammas, nunc vapōrem,
nunc fumum eructet. Et ubi acrĭor per spiramenta cavernā-
rum ventus incubŭit, harenārum moles egeruntur. Proxĭmum
Italīae promuntorīum Regīum dicĭtur, idĕo quia Graece 'ab- 10
rupta' hoc nomĭne pronuntiantur.

II. Nec mirum, si fabulōsa est loci hujus antiquĭtas, in
quem res tot coiĕre mirae: primum quod nusquam latīus torrens fretum, nec solum citāto impĕtu, verum etĭam saevo; neque experientĭbus modo terribĭle, verum etĭam procul visentĭ- 15
bus. Undārum porro in se concurrentīum tanta pugna est, ut
alīas velŭti terga dantes in imum desidĕre, alīas quasi victrīces
in sublīme ferri vidĕas; nunc hic fremĭtum ferventis aestus,
nunc illic gemĭtum in voragĭnem desidentis exaudīas. Accē-
dunt vicīni et perpetŭi Aetnae montis ignes et insulārum 20
Aeolĭdum, velŭti ipsis in undis alātur incendīum: neque enim
in tam angustis termĭnis alĭter durāre tot saecŭlis tantus ignis
potuisset, nisi humōris nutrimentis alerētur.

III. Hinc igĭtur fabŭlae Scyllam et Charybdin peperēre;
hinc latrātus audītus; hinc monstri credĭta simulacra, dum na- 25
vigantes magnis verticĭbus pelăgi desidentis exterrĭti latrāre
putant undas, quas sorbentis aestus vorāgo conlīdit. Eādem
causa etĭam Aetnae montis perpetŭos ignes facit. Nam aquārum ille concursus raptum secum spirĭtum in imum fundum
trahit atque ibi suffocātum tam diu tenet, donec per spira- 30
menta terrae diffūsus nutrimenta ignis incendat. Jam ipsa
Italīae Sicilīaeque vicinĭtas, jam promuntoriōrum altitūdo ipsa
ita simīlis est, ut quantum nunc admiratiōnis, tantum antīquis

terrōris dedĕrit, credentĭbus, coëuntĭbus in se promuntorĭis
ac rursum discedentĭbus solĭda intercĭpi absumĭque navigĭa.
Neque hoc ab antīquis in dulcedĭnem fabŭlae conposĭtum, sed
metu et admiratiōne transeuntĭum. Ea est enim procul inspi-
5 cientĭbus natūra loci, ut sinum maris, non transĭtum putes:
quo cum accessĕris, discedĕre ac sejungi promuntorĭa, quae
ante juncta fuĕrant, arbitrēre.

IV. Sicilĭae primo Trinacrĭae nomen fuit; postĕa Sicanĭa
cognomināta est. Haec a principĭo patrĭa Cyclōpum fuit, qui-
10 bus exstinctis Cocălus regnum insŭlae occupāvit. Post quem
singŭlae civitātes in tyrannōrum imperĭum concessērunt, quorum nulla terra feracĭor fuit. Horum ex numĕro Anaxilăus
justitĭa cum ceterōrum crudelitāte certābat, cujus moderatiōnis
haud mediŏcrem fructum tulit: quippe decēdens cum filĭos par-
15 vŭlos reliquisset tutēlamque cōrum Micÿtho, spectātae fidĕi
servo, commisisset, tantus amor memorĭae ejus apud omnes
fuit, ut parĕre servo quam deserĕre regis filĭos mallent prin-
cĭpesque civitātis oblīti dignitātis suae regni majestātem ad-
ministrāri per servum paterentur. Imperĭum Sicilĭae etĭam
20 Carthaginienses temptavēre, diūque varĭa victorĭa cum tyrannis dimicātum. Ad postrēmum amisso amilcăre imperatōre
cum exercĭtu aliquantisper quievēre victi.

V. Medĭo tempŏre cum Regīni discordĭa laborārent civĭ-
tasque per dissensiōnem divīsa in duas partes esset, veterāni
25 ex altĕra parte ab Himĕra in auxilĭum vocāti, pulsis civitāte
contra quos implorāti fuĕrant et mox caesis quibus tulĕrant
auxilĭum, urbem cum conjugĭbus et libĕris sociōrum occupa-
vēre, ausi facĭnus nulli tyranno comparandum, ut Regīnis
melĭus fuĕrit vinci quam vicisse. Nam sive victorĭbus captivi-
30 tātis jure servissent sive amissa patrĭa exsulāre eos necesse
fuisset, non tamen inter aras et patrĭos lares trucidāti crude-
lissĭmis tyrannis patrĭam cum conjugĭbus ac libĕris praedam
reliquissent.

VI. Catinienses quoque, cum Syracusānos graves paterentur diffīsi virĭbus suis auxilĭum ab Athcnicnsĭbus petivēre:
qui seu studĭo majōris imperĭi, quod Asĭam Graecĭamque penī-
tus occupavĕrant, seu metu factae pridem a Syracusānis classis, nc Laccdacmonĭis illac vires accedĕrent, Lamponĭum ducem 5
cum classe in Sicilĭam misēre, ut sub specĭe ferendi Catinicn-
sĭbus auxilĭi temptārent Sicilĭac imperĭum. Et quonĭam prima
initĭa frequenter caesis hostĭbus prospēra fuērant, majōre denŭo classe et robustiōre exercĭtu Lachēte et Chariǎde ducĭbus
Sicilĭam petivēre: sed Catinienses sive metu Athenicnsĭum 10
sive taedĭo belli pacem cum Syracusānis remissis Athcnicnsĭum
auxilĭis fecĕrant.

VII. Interjecto deinde tempŏre, cum fides pacis a Syracusānis non servarētur, denŭo legātos Athēnas mittunt, qui sordīda veste, capillo barbāque promissis et omni squalōris habĭtu 15
ad miscricordĭam commovendam adquisīto contiōnem deformes
adĕunt: adduntur precĭbus lacrĭmae, et ita miscricordem popŭlum supplĭces movent, ut damnarentur duces, qui ab his
auxilĭa deduxĕrant. Classis igĭtur ingens decernĭtur: creantur
duces Nicĭas et Alcibiǎdes et Lamǎchus, tantisque virĭbus Si- 20
cilĭa repetītur, ut ipsis terrōri essent, in quorum auxilĭa mitte-
bantur. Brevi post tempŏre revocāto ad reātum Alcibiǎde
duo proelĭa pedestrĭa secunda Nicĭas et Lamǎchus facĭunt;
munitionĭbus deinde circumdǎtis hostes etĭam marīnis com-
meatĭbus in urbe clausos intercludunt.   25

VIII. Quibus rebus fracti Syracusāni auxilĭum a Laccdacmonĭis petivērunt. Ab his mittītur Gylippus solus, sed qui
instar omnĭum auxiliōrum erat. Is audīto genĕre belli jam
inclināto statu auxilĭis partim in Graecĭa, partim in Sicilĭa
contractis opportūna bello loca occŭpat. Duōbus deinde proc- 30
lĭis victus, congressus tertĭo occīso Lamǎcho et hostes in
fugam compŭlit et socĭos obsidiōne liberāvit. Sed cum Athenienses a bello terrestri in navāle se transtulissent, Gylippus

classem Lacedaemŏne cum auxilĭis arcessit. Quo cognĭto et ipsi Athenienses in locum amissi ducis Demosthĕnen et Eurymedonta cum supplemento copiārum mittunt. Peloponnesĭi quoque communi civitatĭum decrēto ingentĭa Syracusānis au-
5 xilĭa misēre, et quasi Graeciae bellum in Sicilĭam translātum esset, ita ex utrāque parte summis virībus dimicabātur.

IX. Prima igĭtur congressiōne navālis certamĭnis Athenienses vincuntur, castra quoque cum omni publĭca ac privāta pecunĭa amittunt. Super haec mala cum etĭam terrestri
10 proelĭo victi essent, tunc Demosthĕnes censēre coepit, ut abīrent Sicilĭa, dum res quamvis adflictae nondum tamen perdītae forent: neque in bello male auspicāto amplĭus perseverandum: esse domi gravĭora et forsĭtan infelicĭōra bella, in quae servāre hos urbis apparātus oportēret. Nicĭas seu pudōre male actae
15 rei seu metu destitūtae spei civĭum seu impellente fato manēre contendit. Reparātur igĭtur navāle bellum et anĭmi a priōris fortūnae procella ad spem certamĭnis revocantur: sed inscitĭa ducum inter angustĭas maris tuentes se Syracusānos adgressi facĭle vincuntur. Eurymĕdon dux in prima acĭe fortissĭme
20 dimĭcans primus cadit: XXX naves, quibus praefuĕrat, incenduntur. Demosthĕnes et Nicĭas et ipsi victi exercĭtum in terra depōnunt, tutiōrem fugam rati itinĕre terrestri. Ab his relictas centum XXX naves Gylippus invāsit: ipsos deinde insequĭtur: fugientes partim capit, partim caedit. Demosthĕnes amisso
25 exercĭtu a captivitāte gladĭo et voluntarĭa morte se vindĭcat: Nicĭas autem ne Demosthĕnis quidem exemplo ut sibi consulēret admonītus cladem suōrum auxit dedecōre captivitātis.

7. *Character of Philip and Alexander.*

I. Decessit Philippus XL et septem annōrum, cum annis
30 XXV regnasset. Fuit rex armōrum quam conviviōrum apparatībus studiosĭor, cui maxĭme opus erant instrumenta bellōrum: divitiārum quaestus quam custodĭa sollertĭor. Ităque inter

cotidĭānas rapĭnas semper inops erat. Misericordĭa in eo et
perfĭdĭa pari jure dilectae. Nulla apud eum turpis ratĭo vincendi. Blandus parĭter et insidiōsus, alloquĭo qui plura promittĕret quam praestāret; in serĭa et jocos artĭfex. Amicitĭas
utilitāte, non fide colēbat. Gratĭam fingĕre in odĭo, instruĕre 5
inter concordantes odĭa, apud utrumque gratĭam quaerēre
sollemnis illi consuetūdo. Inter haec eloquentĭa et insignis
oratĭo, acumĭnis et sollertĭae plena, ut nec ornatūi facilĭtas nec
facilitāti inventiōnum deesset ornātus.

II. Huic Alexander filĭus successit et virtūte et vitĭis patre 10
major. Ităque vincendi ratĭo utrīque diversa. Hic aperta
vi, ille artĭbus bella tractābat. Deceptis ille gaudēre hostĭbus,
hic palam fusis. Prudentĭor ille consilĭo, hic anĭmo magnificentĭor. Iram pater dissimulāre, plerumque etĭam vincĕre:
hic ubi exarsisset, nec dilatĭo ultiōnis nec modus erat. Vini 15
nimis uterque avĭdus: sed ebrietātis diversa vitĭa. Patri mos
erat etĭam de convivĭo in hostem procurrĕre, manum conserĕre,
pericŭlis se temĕre offerre: Alexander non in hostem, sed in
suos saevĭēbat. Quam ob rem saepe Philippum vulnerātum
proelĭa remiscēre: hic amicōrum interfector convivĭo frequenter 20
excessit. Regnāre ille cum amīcis nolēbat, hic in amīcos regna
exercēbat. Amāri pater malle, hic metŭi. Litterārum cultus
utrīque simĭlis. Sollertĭae pater majōris, hic fidĕi. Verbis atque
oratiōne Philippus, hic rebus moderatĭor. Parcendi victis filĭo
anĭmus et promptĭor et honestĭor. Frugalitāti pater, luxurĭae 25
filĭus magis dedĭtus erat. Quibus artĭbus orbis imperĭi fundamenta pater jecit, opĕris totīus glorĭam filĭus consummāvit.

8. The death of Alexander.

I. Quarto die Alexander indubitātam mortem sentĭens
agnoscĕre se fatum domus majōrum suōrum ait: nam plerosque 30
Acacidārum intra tricesĭmum annum defunctos. Tumultuantes
deinde milĭtes insidiisque perīre regem suspicantes ipse sedāvit

eosque omnes, cum prolātus in editissĭmum urbis locum esset,
ad conspectum suum admīsit osculandamque dextram suam
flentĭbus porrexit. Cum lacrimārent omnes, ipse non sine
lacrĭmis tantum, verum sine ullo tristiōris mentis argumento
5 fuit, ut quosdam impatientĭus dolentes consolarētur, quibusdam mandāta ad parentes cōrum daret: adĕo sicut in hostem,
ita et in mortem invictus anĭmus fuit. Dimissis militĭbus cir-
cumstantes amīcos percontātur, videanturne simīlem sibi
repertūri regem? Tacentĭbus cunctis tum ipse, se hoc quidem
10 nescīre, at illud scire vaticinarīque se ac paene ocŭlis vidēre
dixit, quantum sit in hoc certamĭne sanguĭnis fusūra Macedonĭa, quantis caedĭbus, quo cruōre mortŭo sibi parentatūra.
Ad postrēmum corpus suum in Ammōnis templum condi jubet.

II. Cum deficĕre eum amīci vidērent, quaerunt, quem im-
15 perĭi faciat herēdem. Respondit: dignissĭmum. Tanta illi
magnitūdo anĭmi fuit, ut, cum Hercŭlem fīlĭum, cum fratrem
Aridaeum, cum Roxānen uxōrem relinquĕret, oblītus necessi-
tudĭnum dignissĭmum nuncupāret herēdem: prorsus quasi
nefas esset viro forti alĭum quam virum fortem succedĕre, aut
20 tanti regni opes alĭis quam probātis relinqui. Hac voce velŭti
bellĭcum inter amīcos cecinisset aut malum discordĭae misisset,
ita omnes in aemulatiōnem consurgunt et ambitiōne vulgi tacĭ-
tum favōrem milĭtum quaerunt. Sexto die praeclūsa voce
exemptum digĭto anŭlum Perdiccae tradĭdit, quae res gliscen-
25 tem amicōrum dissensiōnem sedāvit. Nam etsi non voce nun-
cupātus heres, judicĭo tamen electus videbātur.

III. Decessit Alexander mense Junĭo annos tres et XXX
natus, vir supra humānam potentĭam magnitudĭne anĭmi praedĭtus. Prodigĭa magnitudĭnis ejus ipso ortu nonnulla apparuēre.
30 Nam eo die, quo natus est, duae aquĭlae tota die perpĕtes
supra culmen domus patris ejus sedērunt, omen duplĭcis imperĭi Eurōpae Asiaeque praeferentes. Eōdem quoque die
nuntĭum pater ejus duārum victoriārum accēpit: altĕra belli

Illyrĭci, altĕra certamĭnis Olympĭci, in quod quadrigārum currus misĕrat: quod omen universārum terrārum victorĭam infanti portendēbat. Puer acerrĭmis litterārum studĭis erudĭtus fuit. Exacta pueritĭa per quinquennĭum sub Aristotĕle doctōre, inclitissĭmo omnĭum philosophōrum, crēvit. Accepto 5 deinde imperĭo regem se terrārum omnĭum ac mundi appellāri jussit tantamque fiducĭam sui militĭbus fecit, ut illo praesente nullĭus hostis arma nec inermes timērent. Ităque cum nullo hostĭum umquam congressus est, quem non vicĕrit; nullam urbem obsēdit, quam non expugnavĕrit; nullam gentem adĭit, 10 quam non calcavĕrit. Victus denĭque ad postrēmum est non virtūte hostīli sed insidĭis suōrum et fraude civīli.

IV. Exstincto in ipso aetātis ac victoriārum flore Alexandro Magno triste apud omnes tota Babylōne silentĭum fuit. Sed nec devictae gentes fidem nuntĭo habuērunt, quod ut in- 15 victum regem ita immortālem esse credidĕrant, recordantes quotĭens praesenti morte ereptus esset, quam saepe pro amisso repente se non sospĭtem tantum suis, verum etĭam victōrem obtulisset. Ut vero mortis ejus fides adfūit, omnes barbărae gentes paulo ante ab eo devictae non ut hostem, sed ut paren- 20 tem luxērunt. Mater quoque Darēi regis, quam amisso filĭo a fastigĭo tantae majestātis in captivitātem redacta indulgentĭa victōris in eam diem vitae non paenituĕrat, audīta morte Alexandri mortem sibi ipsa conscĭvit, non quod hostem filĭo praeferret, sed quod pietātem filii in eo, quem ut hostem timuĕrat, 25 experta esset. Contra Macedŏnes versa vice non ut civem ac tantae majestātis regem, verum ut hostem amissum gaudēbant et severitātem nimĭam et adsidŭa belli pericŭla exsecrantes.

9. The earliest history of Carthage.

I. Quonĭam ad Carthaginiensĭum mentiōnem ventum est, 30 de origĭne eōrum pauca dicenda sunt, repetītis Tyriōrum paulo altĭus rebus, quorum casus etĭam dolendi fuērunt. Tyriōrum

gens condĭta a Phoenicĭbus fuit, qui terrae motu vexāti relicto
patrĭae solo Assyrĭum stagnum primo, mox mari proxĭmum
litus incoluērunt, condĭta ibi urbe, quam a piscĭum ubertāte
Sidōna appellavērunt: nam piscem Phoenīces sidon vocant.
5 Post multos deinde annos a rege Ascaloniōrum expugnāti,
navĭbus appulsi Tyron urbem ante annum Trojānae cladis con-
didērunt. Ibi Persārum bellis diu variēque fatigāti victōres
quidem fuēre, sed attrītis virĭbus a servis suis multitudĭne
abundantĭbus indigna supplicĭa perpessi sunt: qui conspira-
10 tiōne facta omnem libĕrum popŭlum cum domĭnis interficĭunt
atque ita potīti urbe lares dominōrum occŭpant, rem publĭcam
invādunt, conjŭges ducunt et, quod ipsi non erant, libĕros
procrĕant.

II. Unus ex tot millĭbus servōrum fuit, qui miti ingenĭo
15 senis domĭni parvulīque filĭi ejus fortūna moverētur dominos-
que non truci feritāte, sed pia misericordĭae humanitāte respicĕret. Ităque cum velut occīsos alienasset servisque de statu
rei publĭcae deliberantĭbus placuisset regem ex corpŏre suo
creāri cumque potissĭmum quasi acceptissĭmum dis, qui solem
20 orientem primus vidisset, rem ad Stratōnem (hoc enim ei
nomen erat) domĭnum occulte latentem detŭlit. Ab eo formā-
tus, cum medĭo noctis omnes in unum campum processissent,
cetĕris in orientem spectantĭbus solus occidentis regiōnem in-
tuebātur. Id primum alĭis vidēri furor, in occidente solis
25 ortum quaerĕre. Ubi vero dies adventāre coepit editissimis-
que culminĭbus urbis orĭens splendēre, spectantĭbus alĭis, ut
ipsum solem aspicĕrent, hic primus omnĭbus fulgōrem solis in
summo fastigĭo civitātis ostendit. Non servīlis ingenĭi ratĭo
visa; requirentĭbus auctōrem de domĭno confitētur.

30 III. Tunc intellectum est, quantum ingenŭa servilĭbus
ingenĭa praestārent, malitiāque servos, non sapientĭa vincĕre.
Venĭa igĭtur seni filiōque data est, et velut numĭne quodam
reservātos arbitrantes regem Stratōnem creavērunt. Post

cujus mortem regnum ad filium ac deinde ad nepōtes transiit.
Celĕbre hoc servōrum facĭnus metuendumque exemplum toto
orbe terrārum fuit. Ităque Alexander Magnus, cum interjecto
tempŏre in oriente bellum gerĕret, velut ultor publĭcae securi-
tātis, expugnāta cōrum urbe omnes, qui proclĭo superfuĕrant, 5
ob memorĭam vetĕris caedis crucĭbus adfixit: genus tantum
Stratōnis inviolātum servāvit regnumque stirpi ejus restitŭit,
ingenŭis et innoxĭis incŏlis insŭlae attribŭtis, ut exstirpāto
servīli germĭne genus urbis ex intĕgro conderētur.

IV. Hoc igĭtur modo Tyrĭi Alexandri auspicĭis condĭti 10
parsimonĭa et labōre quaerendi cito convaluĕre. Ante cladem
dominōrum cum et opĭbus et multitudĭne abundārent, missa in
Afrĭcam juventūte Utĭcam condidĕre: cum intĕrim Mutto rex
Tyri decēdit filĭo Pygmaliōne et Elissa filĭa, insignis formae
virgĭne heredĭbus institūtis. Sed popŭlus Pygmaliōni admŏ- 15
dum puĕro regnum tradĭdit. Elissa quoque Acerbae avuncŭlo
suo, sacerdōti Hercŭlis, qui honos secundus a rege erat, nubit.
Huic magnae, sed dissimulātae opes erant, aurumque metu
regis non tectis, sed terrae credidĕrat: quam rem etsi homĭnes
ignorābant, fama tamen loquebātur. 20

V. Qua incensus Pygmalĭon oblītus juris humāni avun-
cŭlum suum eundemque genĕrum sine respectu pictātis occīdit.
Elissa diu fratrem propter scelus aversāta ad postrēmum dissimulāto odĭo mitigatŏque intĕrim vultu fugam tacīto molītur
adsumptis quibusdam principĭbus in societātem, quibus par 25
odĭum in regem esse eandemque fugiendi cupiditātem arbitrabātur. Tunc fratrem dolo adgredĭtur: fingit se ad eum migrāre
velle, ne amplĭus ei cupĭdae obliviōnis marīti domus gravem
luctus imagĭnem renŏvet neve ultra amāra admonitĭo ocŭlis
ejus occurrat. Non invītus Pygmalĭon verba sorōris audīvit 30
existĭmans cum ea et aurum Acerbae ad se ventūrum.

VI. Sed Elissa ministros migratiōnis a rege missos navĭbus
cum omnĭbus opĭbus suis prima vespĕra impōnit provectăque

in altum compellit eos onĕra harēnae pro pecunĭa involū-
cris involūta in mare dejicĕre. Tunc deflens ipsa lugubrīque
voce Acerbam ciet: orat, ut libens opes suas recipĭat,
quas reliquĕrat, habĕatque inferĭas, quas habuĕrat causam
5 mortis. Tunc ipsos ministros adgredītur: sibi quidem ait
optātam olim mortem, sed illis acerbos cruciātus et dira supplicĭa imminēre, qui Acerbae opes, quarum spe parricidĭum
rex fecĕrit, avaritĭae tyranni subtraxĕrint. Hoc metu omnĭbus
injecto comĭtes fugae accēpit. Junguntur et senatōrum in eam
10 noctem praeparāta agmĭna atque ita sacris Hercŭlis, cujus
sacerdos Acerbas fuĕrat, repetītis exsilĭo sedes quaerunt.

VII. Primus illis appulsus terrae Cyprus insŭla fuit, ubi
sacerdos Jovis cum conjŭge et libĕris deōrum monĭtu comĭtem
se Elissae socĭumque praebŭit, pactus sibi postĕrisque perpe-
15 tŭum honōrem sacerdotĭi. Condicĭo pro manifesto omĭne
accepta. Virgĭnes LXXX admŏdum Cyprĭas raptas navĭbus
impōni Elissa jubet, ut et juventus matrimonĭa et urbs subŏ-
lem habēre posset. Dum haec aguntur, Pygmalĭon cognĭta
sorōris fuga, cum impĭo bello fugientem persĕqui parasset,
20 aegre precĭbus matris deōrumque minis victus quiĕvit: cui
cum inspirāti vates canĕrent, non impūne incrementa urbis
toto orbe auspicatissĭmae interpellatūrum esse, hoc modo spatĭum respirandi fugientĭbus datum. Ităque Elissa delāta in
Afrĭcae sinum incŏlas ejus loci adventu peregrinōrum mutu-
25 arumque rerum commercĭo gaudentes in amicitĭam sollicĭtat:
dein empto loco, qui corĭo bovis tegi posset, in quo fessos
longa navigatiōne socĭos, quoad proficiscerētur, reficĕre posset, corĭum in tenuissĭmas partes secāri jubet atque ita majus
loci spatĭum, quam petiĕrat, occŭpat: unde postĕa ei loco
30 Byrsae nomen fuit.

VIII. Confluentĭbus deinde vicīnis locōrum, qui spe lucri
multa hospitĭbus venalĭa inferēbant, sedesque ibi statuentĭbus
ex frequentĭa homĭnum velut instar civitātis effectum est.

Uticensĭum quoque legāti dona ut consanguinĕis attulērunt hortatīque sunt, urbem sibi condĕrent, ubi sedes sortīti essent. Sed et Afros detinendi advĕnas amor cepit. Ităque consentientĭbus omnĭbus Carthāgo condĭtur statūto annŭo vectigāli pro solo urbis. In primis fundamentis caput bubŭlum inven- 5 tum est, quod auspicĭum fructuōsae quidem, sed laboriōsae perpetuōque servae urbis fuit; propter quod in alĭum locum urbs translāta. Ibi quoque equi caput repertum, bellicōsum potentemque popŭlum futūrum significans, urbi auspicātam sedem dedit. Tunc ad opiniōnem novae urbis concurrentĭbus 10 gentĭbus brevi et popŭlus et civĭtas magna facta.

IX. Condĭta est haec urbs LXXII annis ante quam Roma: cujus virtus sicut bello clara fuit, ita rei publĭcae status varĭis discordiārum casĭbus agitātus est. Cum inter cetĕra mala etĭam peste laborārent, cruenta sacrōrum religiōne et scelĕre 15 pro remedĭo usi sunt: quippe homĭnes ut victĭmas immolābant et impubĕres, quae aetas etĭam hostĭum misericordĭam provŏcat, aris admovēbant, pacem deōrum sanguĭne eōrum exposcentes, pro quōrum vita di rogāri maxĭme solent.

10. First landing in Britain.

I. Exigŭa parte aestātis relĭqua Caesar, etsi in his locis,
quod omnis Gallĭa ad septentriōnes vergit, matūrae sunt hiĕ-
5 mes, tamen in Britannĭam proficisci contendit, quod omnĭbus
fere Gallĭcis bellis hostĭbus nostris inde subministrāta auxilĭa
intelligēbat: et, si tempus anni ad bellum gerendum deficĕret,
tamen magno sibi usŭi fore arbitrabātur, si modo insŭlam
adisset, genus homĭnum perspexisset, loca, portus, adĭtus
10 cognovisset: quae omnĭa fere Gallis erant incognĭta. Neque
enim temĕre praeter mercatōres illo adit quisquam, neque iis
ipsis quicquam praeter oram maritĭmam atque eas regiōnes,
quae sunt contra Gallĭas, notum est. Ităque evocātis ad se
undĭque mercatorĭbus neque quanta esset insŭlae magnitūdo,
15 neque quae aut quantae natiōnes incolĕrent, neque quem
usum belli habērent aut quibus institūtis uterentur, neque qui
essent ad majōrum navĭum multitudĭnem idonĕi portus, reperīre potĕrat.

II. Ad haec cognoscenda, priusquam pericŭlum facĕret,
20 idonĕum esse arbitrātus Gajum Volusēnum cum navi longa
praemittit. Huic mandat, uti explorātis omnĭbus rebus ad se
quam primum revertātur: ipse cum omnĭbus copĭis in Morĭnos
proficiscĭtur, quod inde erat brevissĭmus in Britannĭam tra-
jectus. Huc naves undĭque ex finitĭmis regionĭbus et, quam
25 superiōre aestāte ad Venetĭcum bellum fecĕrat, classem jubet
convenīre. Intĕrim consilĭo ejus cognĭto et per mercatōres
perlāto ad Britannos a complurĭbus ejus insŭlae civitatĭbus ad

eum legāti venĭunt, qui polliceantur obsĭdes dare atque imperĭo popŭli Romāni obtemperāre. Quibus audītis, liberalĭter
pollicĭtus hortātusque, ut in ea sententĭa permanērent, eos
domum remittit et cum his una Commĭum, quem ipse Atreba-
tĭbus superātis regem ibi constituěrat, cujus et virtūtem et 5
consilĭum probābat et quem sibi fidēlem arbitrabātur, cujusque auctorĭtas in iis regionĭbus magni habebātur, mittit. Huic
impěrat, quas possit, aděat civitātes hortēturque ut popŭli
Romāni fidem sequantur; seque celerĭter eo ventūrum nuntĭet.
Volusēnus perspectis regionĭbus quantum ei facultātis dari 10
potŭit, quī navi egrědi ac se barbăris committěre non audēret,
quinto die ad Caesărem revertītur; quaeque ibi perspexisset
renuntĭat.

III. Dum in his locis Caesar navĭum parandārum causa
morātur, ex magna parte Morinōrum ad eum legāti venērunt, 15
qui se de superiōris tempŏris consilĭo excusārent, quod homĭnes barbări et nostrae consuetudĭnis imperīti bellum popŭlo
Romāno fecissent, seque ea, quae imperasset, factūros pollicerentur. Hoc sibi satis opportūne Caesar accidisse arbitrātus,
quod neque post tergum hostem relinquěre volēbat, neque belli 20
gerendi propter anni tempus facultātem habēbat, neque has
tantulārum rerum occupatiōnes sibi Britannĭae anteponendas
judicābat, magnum iis numěrum obsĭdum impěrat. Quibus
adductis eos in fidem recēpit. Navĭbus circĭter octoginta
onerarĭis coactis contractisque, quod satis esse ad duas 25
transportandas legiōnes existimābat, quod praeterěa navĭum
longārum habēbat, quaestōri, legātis praefectisque distribŭit.
Huc accedēbant octoděcim onerarĭae naves, quae ex eo loco
ab milĭbus passŭum octo vento tenebantur, quo minus in eundem portum pervenīre possent. Has equitĭbus distribŭit; re- 30
lĭquum exercĭtum Quinto Titurĭo Sabīno et Lucĭo Auruncŭlejo
Cottae legātis in Menapĭos atque in eos pagos Morinōrum,
ab quibus ad eum legāti non veněrant, deducendum dedit.

Publĭum Sulpicĭum Rufum legātum cum eo praesidĭo, quod satis esse arbitrabātur, portum tenēre jussit.

IV. His constitūtis rebus nactus idonĕam ad navigandum tempestātem tertĭa fere vigilĭa solvit equĭtesque in ⁵ ulteriōrem portum progrĕdi et naves conscendĕre et se sequi jussit: a quibus cum id paulo tardĭus esset administrātum, ipse hora circĭter diēi quarta cum primis navĭbus Britannĭam attĭgit atque ibi in omnĭbus collĭbus expositas hostĭum copĭas armātas conspexit. Cujus loci haec erat natūra, atque ita mon-¹⁰ tĭbus angustis mare continebātur, uti ex locis superiorĭbus in littus telum adjĭci posset. Hunc ad egrediendum nequāquam idonĕum locum arbitrātus, dum relĭquae naves eo convenīrent, ad horam nonam in ancŏris exspectāvit. Intĕrim legātis tribunisque milĭtum convocātis et quae ex Volusēno cognosset, ¹⁵ et quae fĭĕri vellet, ostendit monuitque (ut rei militāris ratĭo, maxĭme ut maritĭmae res postulārent, ut quae celĕrem atque instabĭlem motum habērent), ad nutum et ad tempus omnes res ab iis administrarentur. His dimissis et ventum et aestum uno tempŏre nactus secundum dato signo et sublātis ancŏris ²⁰ circĭter milĭa passūum septem ab eo loco progressus aperto ac plano littŏre naves constitŭit.

V. At barbari consilĭo Romanōrum cognĭto praemisso equitātu et essedarĭis, quo plerumque genĕre in proelĭis uti consuērunt, relĭquis copĭis subsecūti nostros navĭbus egrĕdi ²⁵ prohibēbant. Erat ob has causas summa difficultas, quod naves propter magnitudĭnem nisi in alto constitŭi non potĕrant, milĭtĭbus autem ignōtis locis, impedītis manĭbus magno et gravi armōrum onĕre oppressis simul et de navĭbus desiliendum et in fluctĭbus consistendum et cum hostĭbus erat ³⁰ pugnandum, cum illi aut ex arĭdo aut paulŭlum in aquam progressi omnĭbus membris expedītis notissĭmis locis audacter tela conjicĕrent et equos insuefactos incitārent. Quibus rebus nostri perterrĭti atque hujus omnīno genĕris pugnae imperīti non eādem alacritāte ac studĭo, quo in pedestrĭbus uti proelĭis consuevĕrant, utebantur.

VI. Quod ubi Caesar anĭmum advertit, naves longas, quarum et specĭes erat barbăris inusitatĭor et motus ad usum expeditĭor, paulum removēri ab onerarĭis navĭbus et remis ; incitāri et ad latus apertum hostĭum constitŭi atque inde fundis, sagittis, tormentis hostes propelli ac submovēri jussit: quae res magno usŭi nostris fuit. Nam et navĭum figūra et remōrum motu et inusitāto genĕre tormentōrum permōti barbări constitērunt ac paulum modo pedem retulērunt. Atque 10 nostris militĭbus cunctantĭbus, maxĭme propter altitudĭnem maris, qui decĭmae legiōnis aquĭlam ferēbat, contestātus deos, ut ea res legiōni felicĭter evenīret: "Desilīte", inquit, "commilitōnes, nisi vultis aquĭlam hostĭbus prodĕre: ego certe meum reipublĭcae atque imperatōri officĭum praestitĕro". Hoc 15 cum magna voce dixisset, se ex navi projēcit atque in hostes aquĭlam ferre coepit. Tum nostri cohortāti inter se, ne tantum dedĕcus admitterētur, universi ex navi desiluērunt: hos item ex proxĭmis navĭbus cum conspexissent, subsecūti hostĭbus appropinquārunt.   20

11. On the habits of the Germans.

I. Germāni multum ab consuetudĭne Gallōrum diffĕrunt: nam neque druĭdes habent, qui rebus divīnis praesint, neque sacrificĭis student. Deōrum numĕro eos solos ducunt, quos cernunt et quorum aperte opĭbus juvantur, Solem et Vulcānum 25 et Lunam: relĭquos ne fama quidem accepērunt. Vita omnis in venationĭbus atque in studĭis rei militāris consistit. Agricultūrae non student; majorque pars victus eōrum in lacte, casĕo, carne consistit: neque quisquam agri modum certum aut fines habet proprĭos; sed magistrātus ac princĭpes in annos 30 singŭlos gentĭbus cognationibusque homĭnum, qui una coiĕrunt, quantum et quo loco visum est agri attribŭunt atque anno post alĭo transĭre cogunt. Ejus rei multas affĕrunt causas: ne adsidŭa consuetudĭne capti studĭum belli gerendi agricultūra commŭtent; ne latos fines parāre studĕant, potentioresque humiliōres possessionĭbus expellant; ne accuratĭus ad frigŏra

5 atque aestus vitandos aedifĭcent; ne qua oriātur pecunĭae cupidĭtas, qua ex re factiōnes dissensionesque nascuntur; ut anĭmi aequitāte plebem contĭneant, cum suas quisque opes cum potentissĭmis aequāri vidĕat.

II. Civitatĭbus maxĭma laus est quam latissĭmas circum
10 se vastātis finĭbus solitudĭnes habēre. Hoc proprĭum virtūtis existĭmant, expulsos agris finitĭmos cedĕre, neque quemquam prope audēre consistĕre: simul hoc se fore tutiōres arbitrantur, repentīnae incursiōnis timōre sublāto. Cum bellum civĭtas aut illātum defendit aut infert; magistrātus, qui ei bello prae-
15 sint, ut vitae necisque habĕant potestātem, deliguntur. In pace nullus est commūnis magistrātus, sed princĭpes regiōnum atque pagōrum inter suos jus dicunt controversiasque minŭunt. Latrocinĭa nullam habent infamĭam, quae extra fines cujusque civitātis fiunt, atque ea juventūtis exercendae ac de-
20 sidĭae minuendae causa fĭeri praedĭcant. Atque ubi quis ex princĭpĭbus in concilĭo dixit se ducem fore, qui sequi velint, profiteantur, consurgunt ii, qui et causam et homĭnem probant, suumque auxilĭum pollicentur atque ab multitudĭne collaudantur: qui ex iis secūti non sunt, in desertōrum ac prodi-
25 tōrum numĕro ducuntur, omniumque his rerum postĕa fides derogātur. Hospĭtes violāre fas non putant; qui quaque de causa ad eos venērunt, ab injurĭa prohĭbent, sanctos habent, hisque omnĭum domus patent victusque communicātur.

12. Solon.

I. Prudentissĭma civĭtas Athenĭensĭum, dum ea rerum potīta est, fuisse tradītur. Ejus civitātis sapientissĭmum Solōnem dicunt fuisse, eum qui leges quibus hodĭe quoque utuntur scripsĕrit. Cujus imprīmis versūtum et callĭdum factum est quod, quo et tutĭor vita ejus esset et plus aliquando rei publĭcae prodesset furĕre se simulavĕrit. Idem cum interrogarētur, cur nullum supplicĭum constituisset in eum qui parentem necasset, respondit se id nemĭnem factūrum putasse. Sapienter fecisse dicĭtur cum de eo nihil sanxĕrit, quod antĕa commissum non erat, ne non tam prohibēre quam admonēre viderētur. Idem continēri rem publĭcam duābus rebus dixit: praemĭo et poena. Idem capĭte sanxit, si qui in seditiōne non alterīus utrīus partis fuisset.

II. Honestum illud Solōnis est quod ait versicŭlo quodam: "senescĕre se multa in dies addiscentem"; qua voluptāte anĭmi nulla certe potest esse major. Prudentĭbus enim et bene institūtis studĭa doctrīnae parĭter eum aetāte crescunt.

Animosĭor etĭam interdum senectus est quam adulescentĭa et fortĭor. Hoc illud est quod Pisistrăto — cujus orientem tyrannĭdem multo ante prospexĕrat vir prudens in re publĭca exercitātus — a Solōne responsum est, cum illi quaerenti, qua tandem spe fretus sibi tam audacĭter obsistĕret, respondisse tradītur: Senectūte. — Ejusdem Solōnis elogĭum est, quo se negat velle suam mortem dolōre amicōrum et lamentis vacāre:

Mors mea ne carĕat lacrĭmis; linquāmus amīcis
Maerōrem, ut*) celĕbrent funĕra cum gemĭtu.

---

*) Maerōrem, ut — *to be read*, maerōr' ut.

13. Leonidas.

I. Praeclārae sunt mortes imperatoriae. Leonĭdas, rex Lacedaemoniōrum, se in Thermopўlis trecentosque eos quos eduxĕrat Sparta, cum esset proposĭta aut fuga turpis aut glo-
⁵riōsa mors, opposŭit hostĭbus. — Idem Leonĭdas: "Prandēte", inquit, "anĭmo forti, Lacedaemonĭi, hodĭe apud infĕros fortasse cenabĭmus". — Ibi alăcri magnōque anĭmo occidērunt omnes, in quos Simonĭdes:

"Dic, hospes, Spartae nos te vidisse jacentes,
10   Dum sanctis patriae legĭbus obsequĭmur".

II. Fuit haec gens fortis dum Lycurgi leges vigēbant. E quibus unus, cum Perses hostis in colloquĭo dixisset glorĭans: "Solem prae jaculōrum multitudĭne et sagittārum non videbĭtis", — "In umbra igĭtur", inquit, "pugnabĭmus". Viros
15 commemŏro; qualis tandem Lacaena? quae cum filĭum in proclĭum misisset et interfectum audisset: "Idcirco", inquit, "genuĕram, ut esset qui pro patriā mortem non dubitāret occumbĕre". Esto: fortes et duri Spartiātae; magnam habet vim rei publĭcae disciplīna.

20 ## 14. Themistocles.

I. Themistŏcles post victoriam ejus belli quod cum Persis fuit dixit in contiōne se habēre consilĭum rei publĭcae salutāre, sed id sciri non opus esse: postulāvit, ut alĭquem popŭlus daret quocum communicāret. Datus est Aristīdes. Huic ille,
25 classem Lacedaemoniōrum quae subducta esset ad Gythēum clam incendi posse, quo facto frangi Lacedaemoniōrum opes necesse esset. Quod Aristīdes cum audisset, in contiōnem magna exspectatiōne venit dixitque perutĭle esse consilĭum quod Themistŏcles adferret, sed minĭme honestum. Ităque
30 Athenienses, quod honestum non esset, id ne utĭle quidem putavērunt totamque eam rem, quam ne audiĕrant quidem, auctōre Aristīde repudiavērunt.

II. Apud Graecos fertur incredibĭli quadam magnitudĭne consilĭi atque ingenĭi Atheniensis ille fuisse Themistŏcles: ad quem quidam doctus homo atque in primis crudĭtus accessisse dicĭtur eĭque artem memorĭae, quae tum primum proferebātur, pollicĭtus esse se traditūrum; cum ille quaesisset, quidnam illa ars efficĕre posset, dixisse illum doctōrem: ut omnĭa meminisset; et ei Themistŏclem respondisse, gratĭus sibi illum esse factūrum, si se oblivisci quae vellet quam si meminisse docuisset.

III. Noctu ambulābat in publĭco Themistŏcles, quod somnum capĕre non posset; quaerentĭbus respondēbat, Miltiădis tropaeis se e somno suscitāri.

Themistŏcles fertur Seriphĭo cuĭdam in jurgĭo respondisse, cum ille dixisset non eum sua, sed patrĭae glorĭa splendōrem adsecūtum: "Nec hercŭle", inquit, "si ego Scriphĭus essem, nec tu, si Atheniensis esses, clarus umquam fuisses".

Idem cum consulerētur utrum bono viro paupĕri an minus probāto divĭti filĭam collocāret: "Ego vero", inquit, "malo virum, qui pecunĭa egĕat, quam pecunĭam, quae viro".

15. Alexander the Great.

I. Qua nocte templum Ephesĭae Diānae deflagrāvit, eādem constat ex Olympiăde natum esse Alexandrum; atque ubi lucēre coepisset, clamitasse Magos pestem ac pernicĭem Asĭae proxĭma nocte natam. Concinne Timaeus in historĭa adjunxit, minĭme id esse mirandum quod Diāna, cum Olympiădi adesse voluisset, abfuisset domo.

II. Quam multos scriptōres rerum suārum magnus ille Alexander secum habuisse dicĭtur! Atque is tamen, cum in Sigēo ad Achillis tumŭlum adstitisset: "O fortunāte", inquit, "adulescens, qui tuae virtūtis Homērum praecōnem invenĕris!" Et vero. Nam nisi Ilĭas illa exstitisset, idem tumŭlus qui corpus ejus contexĕrat nomen etĭam obruisset.

III. Cum Ptolemaeus familiāris Alexandri in proelĭo telo
venenāto ictus esset eōque vulnĕre summo cum dolōre morcrē-
tur, rex adsīdens somno est consopītus. Tum secundum quiētem visus ei dicītur draco is, quem mater Olympĭas alēbat,
5 radicŭlam ore ferre et simul dicĕre quo illa loco nascerētur —
neque is longe abĕrat ab eo loco, — ejus autem esse vim tantam ut Ptolcmacum facĭle sanāret. Cum Alexander experrec-
tus narrasset amīcis somnĭum, emisisse qui illam radicŭlam
quaerĕrent: qua inventa, et Ptolcmaeus sanātus dicītur et
10 multi milītes qui erant eōdem genĕre teli vulnerāti.

IV. Est profecto quiddam etĭam in barbăris gentĭbus praesentĭens atque divīnans, siquīdem ad mortem proficiscens
Calānus Indus, — indoctus et barbărus, in radicĭbus Caucăsi
natus, — cum inscendĕret in rogum ardentem quo sua volun-
15 tāte vivus comburerētur: "O praeclārum discessum", inquit,
"e vita, cum, ut Hercŭli contĭgit, mortāli corpŏre cremāto in
lucem anĭmus excesscrit!" Cumque Alexander eum rogāret,
si quid vellet ut dicĕret: "Optĭme", inquit, "propedĭem te vi-
dēbo". Quod ita contĭgit. Nam Babylōne paucis post diēbus
20 Alexander est mortŭus.

16. Dionysius, Tyrant of Syracuse.

I. Duodequadraginta annos tyrannus Syracusanōrum fuit
Dionysĭus, cum quinque et viginti natus annos dominātum
occupavisset. Qua pulchritudĭne urbem, quibus autem opĭbus
25 praedĭtam servitūte oppressam tenŭit civitātem! Atqui de
hoc homĭne a bonis auctorĭbus sic scriptum accepĭmus, summam fuisse ejus in victu temperantĭam in rebusque gerundis
virum acrem et industrĭum, eundem tamen malefĭcum natūra
et injustum. Ex quo omnĭbus bene veritātem intuentĭbus
30 vidēri necesse est miserrĭmum. Ea enim ipsa quae concu-
piĕrat ne tum quidem, cum omnĭa se posse censēbat, conse-
quebātur.

II. Qui cum esset bonis parentĭbus atque honesto loco natus, — etsi id quidem alĭus alĭo modo tradĭdit, — abundārctque aequalĭum familiaritatĭbus et consuetudĭne propinquōrum, credēbat eōrum nemĭni, sed eis, quos ex familĭis locupletĭum servos delegērat, quibus nomen servitūtis ipse 5 detraxěrat, et quibusdam convěnis et feris barbărĭs corpŏris custodĭam committěbat. Ita propter injustam dominātus cupiditātem in carcěrem quodam modo ipse se inclusěrat. Quin etĭam ne tonsōri collum committěret, tondēre filĭas suas docŭit. Ita sordĭdo atque ancillări artificĭo regĭae virgĭnes ut tonstri- 10 cŭlae tondēbant barbam et capillum patris. Et tamen ab eis ipsis, cum jam essent adultae, ferrum remōvit instituĭtque ut candentĭbus juglandĭum putaminĭbus barbam sibi et capillum adurěrent.

III. Cumque duas uxōres habēret, Aristomăchen civem 15 suam, Dorĭdem autem Locrensem, sic ad eas ventitābat ut omnĭa specularētur et perscrŭtarētur ante. Et cum fossam latam cubiculāri lecto circumdedisset ejusque fossae transĭtum pontĭculo lignĕo conjunxisset, eum ipsum, cum forem cubicŭli clausěrat, detorquēbat. Idemque cum in communĭbus sug- 20 gestis consistěre non audēret, contionāri ex turri alta solēbat. Atque is cum pila luděre vellet, — studiōse enim id factitābat, — tunĭcamque poněret, adulescentŭlo quem amābat tradidisse gladĭum dicĭtur. Hic cum quidam familiāris jocans dixisset: "Huic quidem certe vitam tuam committis", adrisissetque 25 adulescens, utrumque jussit interfĭci: altěrum quia viam demonstravisset interimendi sui, altěrum quia dictum id risu approbavisset. Atque eo facto sic dolŭit, nihil ut tulěrit gravĭus in vita: quem enim vehementer amārat occiděrat. Sic distrahuntur in contrarĭas partes impotentĭum cupiditātes. 30

IV. Quamquam hic quidem tyrannus ipse judicāvit quam esset beātus. Nam cum quidam ex ejus adsentatorĭbus, Damŏcles, commemorāret in sermōne copĭas ejus, opes, majestātem

dominātus, rerum abundantĭam, magnificentĭam aedĭum re-
giārum, negāretque unquam beatĭōrem quemquam fuissc:
"Visnc igĭtur", inquit, "o Damŏclc, quonĭam te haec vita
delcctat, ipsc candcm degustāre et fortūnam experĭri meam?"
5 Cum se ille cupĕrc dixissct, collocāri jussit homĭnem in aurĕo
lecto strato pulchcrrĭmo textīli stragŭlo, magnifĭcis operĭbus
picto, abăcosquc complūrcs ornāvit argcnto aurōque caelāto.
Tum ad mensam eximĭa forma puĕros delcctos jussit consistĕre
cosquc nutum illīus intucntcs diligentcr ministrāre. Adĕrant
10 unguenta, corōnac; incendcbautur odōres; mensae conquisitis-
sīmis cpŭlis cxstrucbantur.

V. Fortunātus sibi Damŏcles vidcbātur. In hoc medĭo
apparātu fulgentcm gladĭum c lacunāri saeta equīna aptum
demitti jussit, ut impendĕrct illīus beāti cervicĭbus. Ităque
15 nec pulchros illos ministratōres aspiciēbat ncc plenum artis
argcntum ncc manum porrigēbat in mensam; jam ipsac de-
fluēbant corōnac: denĭquc exorāvit tyrannum, ut abīre licērct,
quod jam beātus nollct cssc. Satisnc vidētur declarasse Dionysĭus, nihil cssc ci beātum cui scmper alĭqui terror im-
20 pendĕat?

VI. Damōncm et Phintĭam Pythagorēos ferunt hoc anĭmo
inter se fuissc ut, cum cōrum altĕri Dionysĭus tyrannus diem
nccis dcstinavissct et is qui morti addictus cssct paucos sibi
dies commendandōrum suōrum causa postulavisset, vas factus
25 sit alter cjus sistcndi, ut, si ille non revertissct, moriendum
essct ipsi. Qui cum ad dicm se rcccpisset, admirātus eōrum
fidem tyrannus petīvit, ut se ad amicitĭam tertĭum adscri-
bĕrent.

VII. Dionysĭus cum fanum Proserpĭnac Locris cxpila-
30 vissct, navigābat Syracūsas; isquc cum sccundissĭmo vento
cursum tenēret, ridens: "Vidctisnc", inquit, 'amīci, quam
bona a dis immortalĭbus navigatĭo sacrilēgis detur?" Idque
homo acūtus cum bene planēquc percepisset, in eādem sententĭa

perseverābat: qui cum ad Peloponnēsum classem appulis-
set et in fanum venisset Jovis Olympĭi, aurĕum ei detraxit
amicŭlum grandi pondĕre, quo Jovem ornārat e manubĭis
Carthaginiensĭum tyrannus Gelo, atque in eo etĭam cavillātus
est, aestāte grave esse aurĕum amicŭlum, hiĕme frigĭdum, 5
eīque lanĕum pallĭum injēcit, cum id esse aptum ad omne anni
tempus dicĕret. Idemque Aesculapĭi Epidauri barbam aurĕam
demi jussit; neque enim convenīre barbātum esse filĭum, cum
in omnĭbus fanis pater imberbis esset.

VIII. Idem mensas argentĕas de omnĭbus delūbris jussit 10
auferri, in quibus quod more vetĕris Graecĭae inscriptum esset
"Bonōrum Deōrum", uti se eōrum bonitāte velle dicēbat.
Idem Victorĭŏlas aurĕas et patĕras et corōnas, quae simulacrōrum porrectis manĭbus sustinebantur, sine dubitatiōne
tollēbat eāque se accipĕre, non auferre dicēbat: esse enim 15
stultitĭam, a quibus bona precarēmur, ab eis porrigentĭbus et
dantĭbus nolle sumĕre. Eumdemque ferunt haec quae dixi
sublāta de fanis in forum protulisse et per praecōnem vendi-
disse exactāque pecunĭa edixisse ut, quod quisque a sacris
habēret, id ante diem certam in suum quidque fanum referret. 20
Ita ad impietātem in deos in homĭnes adjunxit injurĭam.

17. Socrates.

I. De Socrāte accepĭmus et ab ipso in libris Socraticōrum
saepe dicĭtur, esse divīnum quiddam (quod daemonĭum appellat) cui semper ipse parŭerit, numquam impellenti, saepe 25
revocanti. Et Socrātes quidem — quo quem auctōrem meliōrem quaerĭmus? — Xenophonti consulenti sequereturne
Cyrum, postĕa quam exposŭit quae ipsi videbantur: "Et nostrum quidem", inquit, "humānum est consilĭum, sed de rebus
et obscūris et incertis ad Apollĭnem censĕo referendum"; ad 30
quem etĭam Athenienses publĭce de majorĭbus rebus semper
rettulērunt. — Scriptum est item, cum Critōnis sui familiāris

ocŭlum adligātum vidisset, quaesivisse quid esset; cum autem
illo respondisset in agro ambulanti ramŭlum adductum, ut
remissus esset in ocŭlum suum recidisse, tum Socrātes: "Non
enim paruisti mihi revocanti, cum utĕrer qua solĕo praesagi-
5 tiōne divīna". — Idem etĭam Socrātes, cum apud Delĭum malo
pugnātum esset Lachēte praetōre fugĕretque cum ipso Lachēte,
ut ventum est in trivĭum, cādem qua cetĕri fugĕre nolŭit.
Quibus quaerentĭbus cur non cādem via pergĕret, deterrēri se
a deo dixit. Tum quidem ei qui alĭa via fugĕrant in hostĭum
10 equitātum incidĕrunt.

II. Memorĭam Plato, Socrătem secūtus magistrum, recor-
datiōnem esse vult superiōris vitae. Nam in illo libro qui
inscribĭtur Meno pusiōnem quemdam Socrātes interrŏgat quaedam de dimensiōne quadrāti. Ad ea sic ille respondit ut
15 puer, et tamen ita facĭles interrogatiōnes sunt ut gradātim
respondens cōdem pervenĭat quo si geometrĭca didicisset. Ex
quo effĭci vult Socrātes, ut discĕre nihil alĭud sit nisi recordāri.

III. Socrātes, cum esset ex eo quaesītum Archelāum,
Perdiccae filĭum, qui tum fortunatissĭmus haberētur, nonne
20 beātum putāret: "Haud scio", inquit, "numquam enim cum
eo collocūtus sum". — "Ain tu? An tu alīter id scire non
potes?" — "Nullo modo". — "Tu igītur ne de Persārum quidem rege magno potes dicĕre beatusne sit?" — "An ego
possim, cum ignōrem quam sit doctus, quam vir bonus?" —
25 "Quid? tu in eo sitam vitam beātam putas?" — "Ita prorsus
existĭmo: bonos beātos, imprŏbos misĕros". — "Miser ergo
Archelāus?" — "Certe, si injustus".

IV. Socrătes, cum omnĭum sapientissĭmus esset sanctis-
simēque vixisset, ita in judicĭo capĭtis pro se ipse dixit, ut non
30 supplex aut reus, sed magister aut domĭnus viderētur judĭcum.
Quin etĭam cum ei scriptam oratiōnem disertissĭmus orātor
Lysĭas attulisset, quam si ei viderētur eddiscĕret, ut ea pro se
in judicĭo uterētur, non invītus legit et commŏde scriptam esse

dixit; "sed", inquit, "ut si mihi calcĕos Sicyonĭos attulisses,
non utĕrer, quamvis essent habĭles et apti ad pedem, quia non
essent virīles: sic illam oratiōnem disertam sibi et oratorīam
vidēri, fortem et virīlem non vidēri". Ergo ille quoque dam-
nātus est; neque solum primis sententĭis, quibus tantum sta- 5
tuēbant judĭces, damnārent an absolvĕrent, sed etĭam illis quas
itĕrum legĭbus ferre debēbant. Erat enim Athēnis reo damnāto,
si fraus non capitālis esset, quasi poenae aestimatĭo; et sententĭa cum judicĭbus darētur, interrogabātur reus, quam quasi
aestimatiōnem commeruisse se maxĭme confiterētur. Quod 10
cum interrogātus Socrătes esset, respondit sese meruisse ut
amplissĭmis honorĭbus et praemĭis decorarētur et ut ei victus
cotidiānus in Prytanēo publĭce praebērētur, qui honos apud
Graecos maxĭmus habētur. Cujus responso judĭces sic exar-
sērunt, ut capĭtis homĭnem innocentissĭmum condemnārent. 15
 V. Est apud Platōnem Socrătes, cum esset in custodĭa
publĭca, dicens Critōni suo familiāri sibi post tertĭum diem
esse moriendum: vidisse se in somnis pulchritudĭne eximĭa
femĭnam, quae se nomĭne appellans dicĕret Homerĭcum quemdam ejus modi versum: 20
 "Tertĭa te Phthĭae tempestas laeta locābit."
Quod ut est dictum, sic scribĭtur contigisse.
 VI. Et suprēmo vitae die de anĭmi immortalitāte multa
disserŭit et paucis ante diēbus, cum facĭle posset edūci e custodĭa, nolŭit et tum paene in manu jam mortifĕrum illud 25
tenens pocŭlum locūtus ita est, ut non ad mortem trudi, verum
in caelum viderētur adscendĕre. Ita enim censēbat itāque
disserŭit: duas esse vias duplĭcesque cursus animōrum e corpŏre excedentĭum. Nam qui se humānis vitĭis contaminavis-
sent et se totos libidinĭbus dedissent, quibus caecāti vel 30
domestĭcis vitĭis atque flagitĭis se inquinavissent vel re publĭca
violanda fraudes inexpiabĭles concepissent, eis devĭum quoddam iter esse, seclūsum a concilĭo deōrum; qui autem se

intĕgros castosque servavissent quibusque fuisset minĭma cum corporĭbus contagĭo sesēque ab eis semper sevocavissent essentque in corporĭbus humānis vitam imitāti deōrum, eis ad illos, a quibus essent profecti, redĭtum facĭlem patēre. Ităque 5 commemŏrat, ut cycni, qui non sine causa Apollĭni dicāti sint sed quod ab eo divinatiōnem habēre videantur qua providentes quid in morte boni sit cum cantu et voluptāte moriantur, — sic omnĭbus bonis et doctis esse faciendum.

VII. His et talĭbus fere verbis cum de immortalitāte ani- 10 mōrum disputavisset et jam moriendi tempus urgēret, rogātus a Critōne quem ad modum sepelīri vellet: "Multam vero", inquit, "opĕram, amīci, frustra consumpsi. Critōni enim nostro non persuāsi me hinc avolatūrum neque mei quidquam relictūrum. Verum tamen, Crito, si me adsēqui potuĕris aut 15 sicŭbi nactus eris, ut tibi videbĭtur, sepelīto. Sed, mihi crede, nemo me vestrum, cum hinc excessĕro, consequĕtur." Prae- clāre id quidem, qui et amīco permisĕrit et se ostendĕrit de hoc toto genĕre nihil laborāre.

18. Demosthenes.

20   I. In Atheniense Demosthēne tantum studĭum fuisse tan- tusque labor dicĭtur, ut primum impedimenta natūrae dili- gentĭa industriāque superāret; cumque ita balbus esset, ut ejus ipsīus artis cui studēret primam litĕram non posset dicĕre, perfēcit meditando, ut nemo planĭus esse locūtus putarētur. 25 Deinde cum spirĭtus ejus esset angustĭor, tantum continenda anĭma in dicendo est adsecūtus, ut una continuatiōne ver- bōrum, id quod ejus scripta declārant, binae ei contentiōnes vocis et remissiōnes continerentur; qui etĭam, ut memorĭae prodĭtum est, conjectis in os calcŭlis, summa voce versus 30 multos uno spirĭtu pronuntiāre consuescēbat; neque is con- sistens in loco, sed inambŭlans atque adscensu ingredĭens ardŭo.

In Phalericum portum descendēre ibīque ad fluctum ajunt declamāre solītum Demosthēnem, ut fremītum maris adsuescēret voce vincēre.

II. Demosthēnes illo susurro delectāri se dicēbat aquam ferentis muliercŭlae, ut mos in Graecĭa est, insusurrantisque 5 altēri: "Hic est ille Demosthēnes!" — Quid hoc levĭus? At quantus orātor!

Sine actiōne summus orātor esse in numĕro nullo potest, mediŏcris hac instructus summos saepe superāre. Huic primas dedisse Demosthēnes dicītur, cum rogarētur quid in di-10 cendo esset primum; huic secundas, huic tertĭas. Quo mihi melĭus etĭam illud ab Aeschĭne dictum vidēri solet; qui cum propter ignominĭam judicĭi cessisset Athēnis et se Rhodum contulisset, rogātus a Rhodĭis legisse fertur oratiōnem illam egregĭam quam in Ctesiphontem contra Demosthēnem dixĕrat; 15 qua perlecta petītum est ab eo postridĭe, ut legĕret illam etĭam quae erat contra a Demosthēne pro Ctesiphonte edĭta. Quam cum suavissĭma et maxĭma voce legisset admirantĭbus omnĭbus: "Quanto", inquit, "magis miraremĭni si audissētis ipsum!" — Ex quo satis significāvit quantum esset in actiōne, 20 qui oratiōnem eamdem alĭam fore putārit actōre mutāto.

19. The best sauce.

Parvo cultu natūra contenta est. — Darēus in fuga cum aquam turbĭdam et cadaverĭbus inquinātam bibisset, negāvit umquam se bibisse jucundĭus; numquam scilĭcet sitĭens bi-25 bĕrat. Nec esurĭens Ptolemaeus edĕrat; cui cum peragranti Aegyptum comitĭbus non consecūtis cibarĭus in casa panis datus esset, nihil visum est illo pane jucundĭus. Socrătem ferunt, cum usque ad vespĕrum contentĭus ambulāret quaesitumque esset ex eo, qua re id facĕret, respondisse se quo 30 melĭus cenāret opsonāre ambulando famem. — Quid? victum Lacedaemonĭōrum in phicitĭis nonne vidēmus? Ubi cum

tyrannus cenavisset Dionysĭus, negāvit se jure illo nigro, quod
cenae caput erat, delectātum. Tum is qui illa coxĕrat: "Minĭme mirum; condimenta enim defuērunt". — "Quae tandem?"
inquit ille. — "Labor in venātu, sudor, cursus ad Eurōtam,
5 fames, sitis. His enim rebus Lacedaemoniōrum epŭlae con-
diuntur". — Atque hoc non ex homĭnum more solum, sed
etĭam ex bestĭis intellĕgi potest: quae, ut quidquid objectum
est quod modo a natūra non sit aliēnum, eo contentae non
quaerunt amplĭus. Civitātes quaedam universae, more doctae,
10 parsimonĭa delectantur, ut de Lacedaemonĭis paullo ante di-
xĭmus. Persārum a Xenophonte victus exponĭtur, quos negat
ad panem adhibēre quidquam praeter nasturtĭum.

20. Burial service at Athens.

Athēnis jam illo mos a Cecrōpe, ut ajunt, permansit cor-
15 pus terra humandi, quod cum proxĭmi fecērant obductāque
terra erat, frugĭbus obserebātur, ut sinus et gremĭum quasi
matris mortŭo tribuerētur, solum autem frugĭbus expiātum, ut
vivis redderētur. Sequebantur epŭlae quas inībant propinqui
coronāti, apud quos de mortŭi laude cum quidquid veri erat
20 praedicātum, — nam mentīri nefas habebātur, — justa confecta erant. Postĕa cum, ut scribit Phalēreũs, sumptuōsa
fĭeri funera et lamentabilĭa coepissent, Solōnis lege sublāta
sunt; de sepulcris autem nihil est apud Solōnem amplĭus quam
"ne quis ea delĕat neve aliēnum infĕrat", poenăque est "si
25 quis bustum, aut monumentum", inquit, "aut columnam violārit, dejecĕrit, fregĕrit". Sed post aliquanto propter has
amplitudĭnes sepulcrōrum, quas in Ceramīco vidēmus, lege
sanctum est "ne quis sepulcrum facĕret operosĭus quam quod
decem homĭnes effecērint tridŭo". Neque id opĕre tectorĭo
30 exornāri, nec Hermas hos, quos vocant licēbat impōni, nec de
mortŭi laude nisi in publĭcis sepultūris nec ab alĭo nisi qui
publĭce ad eam rem constitūtus esset dici licēbat. Sublāta

etĭam erat celebrĭtas virōrum ac muliĕrum, quo lamentatĭo minuerētur: auget enim luctum concursus homĭnum.

Sed ait rursus idem Demetrĭus increbruisse eam funĕrum sepulcrōrumque magnificentĭam, quae nunc fere Romae est. Quam consuetudĭnem lege minŭit ipse. Fuit enim hic vir, ut ₅ scitis, non solum eruditissĭmus, sed etĭam civis tuendae civitātis peritissĭmus. Iste igĭtur sumptum minŭit non solum poena, sed etĭam tempŏre: ante lucem enim jussit efferri. Sepulcris autem novis finīvit modum. Nam super terrae tumŭlum nolŭit quidquam statŭi nisi columellam tribus cubĭtis ₁₀ non altiōrem aut mensam aut labellum; et huic procuratiōni certum magistrātum praefecĕrat.

21. *Aratus of Sicyon.*

Arātus Sicyonĭus jure laudātur qui, cum ejus civĭtas quinquaginta annos a tyrannis tenerētur, profectus Argis Sicyōnem ₁₅ clandestīno introĭtu urbe est potītus, cumque tyrannum Nicŏclem improvīso oppressisset, sescentos exsŭles qui locupletissĭmi fuĕrant ejus civitātis restitŭit remque publĭcam adventu suo liberāvit. Sed cum magnam animadvertĕret in bonis et possessionĭbus difficultātem, quod et eos, quos ipse restituĕrat, ₂₀ quorum bona alĭi possedĕrant, egēre iniquissĭmum esse arbitrabātur, et quinquaginta annōrum possessiōnes movēri non nimis aequum putābat, proptereă quod tam longo spatĭo multa hereditatĭbus, multa emptionĭbus, multa dotĭbus tenebantur sine injurĭa: judicāvit neque illis adĭmi nec his non satis fiĕri ₂₅ quōrum illa fuĕrant oportēre. Cum igĭtur statuisset opus esse ad eam rem constituendam pecunĭa, Alexandrīam se proficisci velle dixit remque intēgram ad redĭtum suum jussit esse; isque celerĭter ad Ptolemaeum suum hospĭtem venit, qui tum regnābat alter post Alexandrīam condĭtam. Cui cum exposuisset ₃₀ patrĭam se liberāre velle causamque docuisset, a rege opulento vir summus facĭle impetrāvit, ut grandi pecunĭa adjuvarētur.

Quam cum Sicyōnem attulisset adhibŭit sibi in consilĭum quindĕcim princĭpes, cum quibus causas cognōvit et cōrum qui aliēna tenēbant, et cōrum qui sua amisĕrant; perfĕcitque aestimandis possessionĭbus ut persuadĕret alĭis ut pecunĭam 5 accipĕre mallent, possessionĭbus cedĕrent, alĭis ut commodĭus putārent numerāri sibi quod tanti esset quam suum recuperāre. Ita perfectum est, ut omnes concordĭa constitūta sine querēlla discedĕrent. O virum magnum dignumque, qui in re publĭca nostra natus esset!

10 ## 22. A remarkable dream.

Clarum admŏdum sommnĭum commemorātur. — Cum duo quidam Arcādes familiāres iter una facĕrent et Megăram venissent, altĕrum ad caupōnem devertisse, ad hospĭtem altĕrum. Qui ut cenāti quiescĕrent, concubĭa nocte visum esse in somnis 15 ei qui erat in hospitĭo illum altĕrum orāre ut subvenīret, quod sibi a caupōne interĭtus pararĕtur; cum primo perterrĭtum somnĭo surrexisse: dein cum se collegisset idque visum pro nihĭlo habendum esse duxisset, recubuisse; tum ei dormienti eumdem illum visum esse rogāre ut, quonĭam sibi vivo non 20 subvenisset mortem suam ne inultam esse paterĕtur, se interfectum in plaustrum a caupōne esse conjectum et supra stercus injectum; petĕre ut mane ad portam adesset, prius quam plaustrum ex oppĭdo exīret. Hoc vero cum somnĭo commōtum mane bubulco praesto ad portam fuisse, quaesisse ex eo quid 25 esset in plaustro: illum perterrĭtum fugisse, mortŭum erŭtum esse, caupōnem re patefacta poenas dedisse.

23. *The wolf and the lamb.*

Ad rívum*) eundem lúpus et agnus vénerant
Siti compulsi; súperior stabát lupus
Longéque inferior ágnus.　Tunc fauce improba　　　　5
Latro incitatus júrgii causam íntulit.
Cur, inquit, turbuléntam fecisti mihi
Aquám bibenti?　Lániger contrá timens:
Qui póssum, quaeso fácere, quod quererís, lupe?
A té decurrit ád meos haustús liquor.　　　　　　10
Repúlsus ille véritatis víribus:
Ante hós sex menses mále, ait, dixistí mihi.
Respóndit agnus: équidem natus nón eram.
Pater hércle tuus ibí, inquit, male dixit mihi.
Atque ita correptum lácerat injustá nece.　　　　15
　　Haec própter illos scrípta est homines fábula,
Qui fíctis causis ínnocentes ópprimunt.

24. *The frogs and their king.*

Athénae cum florérent aequis légibus,
Procáx libertas cívitatem míscuit　　　　　　　20
Frenúmque solvit prístinum licéntia.
Hic cónspiratis fáctionum pártibus
Arcém tyrannus óccupat Pisístratus.
Cum trístem servitútem flerent Attici,
(Non quía crudelis ílle, sed quoniám grave　　　25
Omne insuetis ónus) et coepissént queri,
Aesópus talem túm fabellam réttulit.
　　Ranáe vagantes líberis palúdibus
Clamóre magno régem petiere á Jove,

---

*) Syllables printed in *Italics* are suppressed by Elision. (**887.**)

Qui dissolutos móres vi compésceret.
Patér deorum risit atque illis dedit
Parvúm tigillum, míssum quod subitó vadi
Motú sonoque térruit pavidúm genus.

5 Hoc mérsum limo cúm jacēret diútius,
Forte úna tacite prófert e stagnó caput
Et éxplorato rége cunctas óvocat.
Illáe timore pósito certatim ádnatant
Lignúmque supra túrba petulans ínsilit.

10 Quod cum inquinassent ómni contumélia,
Aliúm rogantes régem misere ád Jovem,
Inútilis quoniam ésset qui fuerát datus.
Tum mísit illis hýdrum, qui dente áspero
Corrípere coepit síngulas. Frustrá necem

15 Fugitánt inertes, vócem praecludít metus.
Furtim igitur dant Mercúrio mandata ád Jovem,
Adflíctis ut succúrrat. Tunc contrá deus:
Quia nóluistis véstrum ferre, inquit, bonum,
Malúm perferte. — Vós quoque, o civés, ait,

20 Hoc sústinete, május ne veniát malum.

25. The wolf and the crane.

Qui prétium meriti ab ímprobis desíderat,
Bis péccat: primum quóniam indignos ádjuvat;
Impúne abire deinde quia jam nón potest.

25 Os dévoratum faúce cum haererét lupi,
Magnó dolore victus coepit síngulos
Illicere pretio, ut íllud extraherént malum.
Tandém persuasa est júre jurandó gruis,
Guláeque credens cólli longitúdinem,

30 Perículosam fécit medicínám lupo.
A quó cum pactum flágitaret práemium:
Ingráta es, inquit, óre quae e nostró caput
Incólume abstuleris ét mercedem póstules.

26. The ass and the lion in partnership.

Virtútis expers vérbis jactans glóriam
Ignótos fallit, nótis est derísui.

Venári asello cómite cum vellét leo,
Contéxit illum frútice et admonuít simul,   5
Ut insueta vóce terrerét feras,
Fugiéntes ipse excíperet.   Hic aurítulus
Clamórem subitó totis tollit víribus,
Novóque turbat béstias miráculo.
Quae dúm paventes éxitus notós petunt,   10
Leónis adíligúntur horrendo ímpetu.
Qui póstquam caede féssus est, asinum évocat
Jubétque vocem prémere.   Tunc ille insolens:
Qualís videtur ópera tibi vocís meae ?
Insígnis, inquit, síc ut, nisi nossém tuum   15
Animúm genusque, símili fugissém metu.

27. The fox and the crow.

Qui sé laudari gaúdet verbis súbdolis,
Será dat poenas túrpes poeniténtia.

Cum dé fenestra córvus raptum cáseum   20
Comésse vellet, célsa residens árbore,
Vulpés hunc vidit, deinde sic coepít loqui:
O quí tuarum, córve, pennarúm est nitor !
Quantúm decŏris córpore et vultú geris !
Si vócem haberes, núlla prior alés foret.   25
At ílle stultus, dúm vult vocem osténdere,
Emísit ore cáseum, quem celériter
Dolósa vulpes ávidis rapuit déntibus.
Tum démum ingemuit córvi deceptús stupor.

28. The aged lion.

    30

Quicúmque amisit dignitatem prístinam,
Ignávis etiam jócus est in casú gravi.

Deféctus annis ét desertus víribus
Leó cum jacēret spíritum extremúm trahens,

Apér fulmineis ád eum venit déntibus
Et víndicavit íctu veterem injúriam.
Inféstis taurus móx confodit córnibus
Hostíle corpus.   Asinus, ut vidít ferum
Impúne laedi, cálcibus frontem éxtudit.
At íllе exspirans: Fórtes indigné tuli
Mihí insultare: té, naturae dédecus,
Quod férre cogor, cérte bis videór mori.

29. The kite and the doves.

Qui sé committit hómini tutandum ímprobo,
Auxília dum requírit, exitium invenit.
Colúmbae saepe cúm fugissent miluum
Et céleritate pénnae vitassént necem,
Consílium raptor vértit ad falláciam
Et génus inerme táli decepít dolo:
Quaré sollicitum pótius aevum dúcitis,
Quam régem me creátis icto foédere,
Qui vós ab omni tútas praestem injúria?
Illác credentes trádunt sese míluo;
Qui régnum adeptus coépit vesci síngulas
Et éxercere impérium saevis únguibus.
Tunc dé relicuis úna: Merito pléctimur.

30. The two mules.

Muli gravati sárcinis ibánt duo:
Unús ferebat físcos cum pecúnia,
Altér tumentes múlto saccos hórdeo.
Ille ónere dives célsa cervice éminet
Clarúmque collo jáctat tintinnábulum,
Comés quieto séquitur et placidó gradu.
Subitó latrones éx insidiis ádvolant
Intérque caedem férro mulum sáuciant,
Dirípiunt nummos, néglegunt vile hórdeum.
Spoliátus igitur cásus cum flerét suos:

Equide*m*, ínquit alter, mé contemptum gáudeo,
Nam níl amisi néc sum laesus vúlnere.
Hoc árgumento túta est hominum ténuitas;
Magnác periclo súnt opes obnóxiae.

31. The dog and the wolf.

5

Quam dúlcis sit libértas, breviter próloquar.
Caní perpasto mácie confectús lupus
Forte óccucurrit.   Déin salu:atum ínvicem
Ut réstiterunt: Unde sic, quaesó, nites?
Aut quó cibo fecísti tantum córporis?   10
Ego, quí sum longe fórtior, pereó fame.
Canis simpliciter: éadem *est* condició tibi,
Praestáre domino si par offjciúm potes.
Quod? inquit ille.   Cústos ut sis líminis,
A fúribus tucáris et noctú domum.   15
Ego véro sum parátus: nunc patiór nives
Imbrésque in silvis ásperam vitám trahens:
Quantó *est* facilius míhi sub tecto vívere,
Et ótiosum lárgo satiarí cibo?
Veni érgo mecum.   Dúm procedunt, áspicit   20
Lupus á catena cóllum detritúm cani.
Unde hóc, amice? Nihil est. Dic, quaesó, tamen.
Quia vídeor acer, álligant me intérdiu,
Luce út quiescam et vígilem, nox cum vénerit:
Crepúsculo solútus, qua visúm est, vagor.   25
Adfértur ultro pánis; de mensá sua
Dat óssa dominus; frústa jactant fámilia
Et, quód fastidit quísque, pulmentárium.
Sic síne labore vénter impletúr meus.
Age, abíre siquo *est* ánimus, est licéntia?   30
Non pláne *est*, inquit. Frúere, quae laudás, canis:
Regnáre nolo, líber ut nou sim mihi.

32. The fox and the sour grapes.

Famé coacta vúlpes alta in vínea
Uvam áppetebat súmmis saliens víribus,
Quam tángere ut non pótuit, discedéns ait:
Nondúm matura est; nólo acerbam súmere.
Qui fácere quae non póssunt verbis élevant,
Adscríbere hoc debébunt exemplúm sibi.

33. The ungrateful snake.

Qui fért malis auxílium, post tempús dolet.
Gelú rigentem quídam colubram sústulit
Sinúque fovit, cóntra se ipse miséricors;
Namque út refecta est, nécuit hominem prótinus.
Hanc ália cum rogáret causam facínoris,
Respóndit: Nequis díscat prodesse ímprobis.

34. The discontented stag.

Laudátis utilióra, quae contémpseris,
Saepe inveniri haec ádscrit narrátio.
Ad fóntem cervus, cúm bibisset, réstitit
Et in liquore vídit effigiém suam.
Ibi dúm ramosa mírans laudat córnua
Crurúmque nimiam ténuitatem vitúperat,
Venántum subito vócibus contérritus
Per cámpum fugere coépit et cursú levi
Canés clusit. Silva tum excepit ferum,
In quá retentis impeditus córnibus
Lacerári coepit mórsibus saevís canum.
Tunc móriens vocem hanc édidisse dícitur:
O me ínfelicem! quí nunc demum intéllego,
Utília mihi quam fúerint, quae despéxeram,
Et, quáe laudaram, quántum luctus habúerint.

NOTES.

M. JUSTINIANUS JUSTINUS.

Justin, of whose personal history nothing is known, is supposed to have lived at Rome in the third century after Christ. He is the author of a work entitled: *Historiarum Philippicarum Libri XLIV*, founded on a lost work of *Trogus Pompejus*, a historian of the Augustan age. Justin seems to have compiled selections from it, and his history contains a great variety of information that would not otherwise have been preserved. His style is clear and sometimes elegant, and the greater part of his vocabulary may be found in Livy. He has some peculiarities in diction and construction which are not in accordance with those standards of prose, *Caesar* and *Cicero*, but they will hardly injure the Latinity of beginners.

1. The Assyrians.

Page

3 principio rerum, Abl. of time *when.* 672.*) — penes reges, *in the* 1. *hands of the kings.*

5 spectāta inter bonos moderatĭo, *moderation which had been tried among the good.*

6 nullis legĭbus, *by no laws,* Abl. of Means. 603. — pro legĭbus erant, *were instead of laws = supplied the place of laws.*

8 intra suam cuĭque patrĭam, *to each one within his own country;* quisque is generally placed after se, suus, qui; the Dative cuĭque depends on finiebantur; it is used instead of the genitive depending on patrĭam. — primus omnĭum; **Partitive Genitive.** 566. 6.

9 quasi avĭtum gentĭbus morem, *a custom as it were hereditary to the nations.*

10 imperĭi cupiditāte, *by his ambition for power;* **Instrumental** Abl. 603.

---

*) *These references are to paragraphs of* ADN-HENN's Latin Grammar.

Page
1.   11 rudes resistendi popŭlos, *nations inexperienced in making resistance;* adjectives denoting *knowledge* and their opposites take the **Genitive.** *567. 1; 843.*

12 usque, *as far as,* with the **Acc.** termĭnos, to denote the place *whither.* — quaesītae dominatiōnis, *of the dominion that he had sought for.*

13 continŭa possessiōne, **Instrumental Abl.** *605.* — domĭtis proxĭmis, *having subdued the nearest neighbors;* **Abl. Absol.** *837.*

14 accessiōne virĭum is **Instrumental Abl.** belonging to fortĭor. — proxĭma quaeque victorĭa, *every last victory.*

16 illi fuit, *he had;* **Dative** denoting the *possessor.* *594.*

17 qui dicītur, *who is said;* **Nom. w. Inf.** *891.*

19 hoc occīso, **Abl. Absol.** *836.* — relicto filĭo Ninўa et uxōre Semiramīde; **Abl. Absol.**; the Participle relicto agrees with Ninўa, and is understood to Semiramīde. *836.*

21 murumque urbi cocto latĕre circumdĕdit, *she put round the city a wall of baked brick;* circumdăre takes a dative with an accusative, or an accusative with an ablative. *593.* — cocto latĕre, **Abl.** of **Quality,** *616.*

22 harēnae vice, *instead of sand.* — bitumĭne interstrŭto, **Abl. Absol.** *836.*

24 praeclāra, *illustrious deeds;* the neuter of the adjective used as a substantive. *702.*

25 imperĭo adjēcit; verbs compounded with ad take the **Dative.** *592.*

26 quos..nemo intrāvit, *into whose country..no one penetrated.*

2.   1 duo et XXX annos; time *how long* is in the **Acc.** *674.* — regno potīta, *having held possession of the kingdom;* potīri takes the **Abl.** *626.*

2 contentus takes the **Abl.** *625.* — elaborāto a parentĭbus imperĭo, *with the dominion acquired by the labors of his parents.*

3 velŭti mutasset, *as if he had changed;* velŭti, conjunction of comparison, takes the **Subjunctive.** *779.*

6 mille trecentos annos, time *how long* is in the **Acc.** *674.*

8 mulĭĕre corruptĭor, *more corrupt than a woman;* **Abl.** of **Comparison.** *609.*

9 ad hunc videndum, *to see him;* the Acc. of the Gerund is fre- 2.
quently used after ad to denote *purpose.* *845.*

10 praefectus ipsīus Medis praepositus, *his own prefect whom he
had placed over the Medians.*—nomine Arbactus, Abl. of Limitation. *608.*

11 invēnit eum nentem et partientem, *he found him spinning and
distributing;* verbs of *perceiving* take the Acc. with the Present
Participle when the object is to be represented as *actually* seen. *833.*

12 colo nentem, *spinning with a distaff;* colo, Abl. of Means. —
muliēbri habītu, *in a woman's dress;* Abl. of Manner. *613.*

13 quibus visis indignātus, *being indignant at what he had seen;*
the relative used instead of the demonstrative, and the Abl. of Cause
depending on indignātus. *604.*

14 tot viros..parēre, Acc. w. Inf. after indignāri, a verb of
emotion. *815.*

15 quid vidĕrit refert, *he reports what he has seen;* the Subjunctive vidĕrit in an Indirect Question. *801;* refert, Historical Present. *739.*
— negat se parēre posse, *he says he cannot obey;* instead of dicĕre
with a *negative* clause the Latins generally use negāre with an
affirmative clause.

16 qui se femĭnam malit esse quam virum, *who likes better to
be a woman than a man;* Acc. w. Inf. after a verb of *wishing.* *814.*
— malit is in the Subjunctive depending on the Accus. with Inf. se
parēre posse. *826.*

17 quo audīto, *having heard this;* Abl. Absol.

18 regnum defensūrus, *in defense of his kingdom;* the Future
Participle denotes either *intention* or *being on the point of.* *741.* —
metu mortis, *from fear of death.* *604.*

21 exstructa incensāque pyra, *having erected and set on fire a
funeral pile;* Abl. Absol. *837.*

22 hoc solo, *hereby alone;* Abl. of Means. *603.*

2. Astyages and Cyrus.

26 per ordĭnem successiōnis, *in regular succession;* per denoting
the *manner* in which a thing is done. *645.*

27 per somnum, *during = in his sleep.* — ex fīlia quam unĭcam
habēbat, *from the only daughter he had;* the adjective unĭcam in
the relative clause properly belongs to the antecedent fīlia. *554.*

Page

2.   28 vitem enātam, supply esse; **Acc. w. Inf.** depending on vidit. *812.*

20 obumbrarētur, *would be overshadowed;* the Subjunctive in a clause depending upon the **Acc. w. Inf.** *826.* — consulti hariŏli, *the soothsayers who had been consulted;* Participle equivalent to a relative sentence. *833.* — nepôtem futūrum (esse), **Acc. w. Inf.** depending on respondērunt.

30 praenuntiĕtur; the Subjunctive in a clause depending on an **Acc. w. Inf.** *833.* — regni amissiōnem portendi; **Acc. w. Inf.** depending on respondērunt, which is the predicate to hariŏli consulti.

31 hoc responso, **Abl. of Means.**

32 ne, *lest, that not,* takes the Subjunctive extollēret. *756.* I.

3.   1 nepŏti anĭmos, *to the grandson his mind,* i. e. *the grandson's mind;* the **Dative** depends on extollēret. — tum tempŏris, *at that time.*

3 somnĭi metu deposĭto, *having given up the fear of the dream;* **Abl. Absol.** *837.*

4 sub avi ocŭlis, *in the sight of his grandfather.*

5 datur occidendus, *is delivered to be killed;* the **Gerundive** is joined with the verbs do, curo, mitto, &c., to express the *purpose* or *end* for which anything is given; the Gerundive agrees with the object of the active form, and with the subject of the passive. *841.*

6 verĭtus, ne .. exigĕret, *fearing that she would exact;* after verĕor, timĕo, &c., ne must be rendered by *that.* *761.* — mortŭo rege, *after the king's death;* **Abl. Absol.**

7 necāti infantis ultiōnem, *revenge for the murdered child.*

11 audīta regis infantis expositiōne, *having heard of the exposing of the king's child;* **Abl. Absol.**, to supply the want of the perfect act. participle. *837.* — summis precĭbus, *with every entreaty.* **Abl. of Means.** *603.*

12 ut sibi puer ostenderētur, *that the boy might be shown to her* = *to show her the boy;* the regular construction with verbs of *urging* and *demanding* is ut or ne with the **Subjunctive.** *758.* — sibi, i. e. uxōri; for all references to the subject of the leading sentence, the Reflexive sui must be used. *828.* — cujus precĭbus fatigătus, *wearied by her entreaties;* the Relative for the Demonstrative at the beginning of the sentence. *556.* — precĭbus is **Causal Abl.** *604.*

13 canem femĭnam, *a she-dog;* with names of animals, the sexes are distinguished by mās, *male,* and femĭna, *female.* *47.*

14 praebentem et defendentem; the participles depend on in- 3.
vēnit, a verb of *perceiving*, to represent the object as *actually*
seen. *835.*

15 motus misericordĭa, *moved by compassion;* the moving cause
is often expressed by a participle with the Ablative, such as motus,
adductus, &c.

16 eādem cane anxĭe prosequente, **Abl. Absol.**

17 quem ubi; the Relative instead of the Demonstrative; ubi, *as
soon as*, takes the **Perf. Indic.** *737.* II.

18 tantus ut..; a clause of *result* introduced by ut, *so that*, is used
after tam, tantus, &c. *759.*

20 permittĕret, *he might permit her*, depends on rogāret, a verb
of *asking* or *demanding;* the regular construction is ut. *758;* but
when the idea of wishing, &c. is *emphatic*, the simple Subjunctive
without ut may be employed. — permutāta sorte, **Abl. Absol.**

22 nomen Spaco fuit; the name is either in the Dative or in the
Nominative. *594.*

25 rex inter ludentes sorte delectus, *having been chosen by lot
king among the boys when playing.* — per lascivĭam, *from wantonness;* per often denotes the *manner* in which a thing is done. *645.*

27 querella regi delāta, *a complaint being brought before the
king;* **Abl. Absol.** — indignantĭbus belongs to parentĭbus and is best
rendered by a relative sentence: *by the parents who were indignant
at.* — indignāri, a verb of *emotion*, may be considered as a verb of
thinking, and as such takes an **Acc. w. Inf.** *815.* — adfectos, scil. esse.
Cyrus is the subject of the subordinate clause beginning with mox;
the principal clause begins with ille, i. e., Astyāges.

28 arcessīto puĕro et interrogāto, **Abl. Absol.**

29 nihil mutāto vultu, **Abl. Absol.**; nihil is here an Adverb, *not at
all.* — fecisse se ut regem, *that he had acted like a king;* **Acc. w. Inf.**
depending on respondisset; this verb is in the Subjunctive depending
on *historical* cum.

33 quonĭam sibi viderētur, *since he seemed to him;* as a rule, quonĭam takes the **Indicative;** here the **Subjunctive** is used to express the
opinion of Astyages. — agitāto inter pastores regno, *having spent
his reign among the shepherds.*

4.　2 infestus, takes the **Dative.** *598.* — in ultiōnem servāti nepōtis, *to revenge himself for the rescue of his grandson.*

3 epulandum tradĭdit, see Note on p. 3. 5.

4 dissimulāto dolōre, **Abl. Absol.** — odĭum regis, **Objective Genitive.** *566.* 2. — in vindictae occasiōnem, *to a favorable time for his vengeance.*

6 dolōre orbitātis, *by grief for his bereavement.*

7 ut ablegātus fuĕrit, *how he had been sent away;* **Indirect Question** after scribit, with the verb in the Subjunctive; ut is the comparative particle which would have required the Indicative if not used in indirect question.

10 hortātur, exercĭtum paret, *he exhorts him to get ready an army;* the regular construction with verbs of *exhorting* is ut; but the simple **Subjunctive** without ut may also be employed when the wish is *emphatic;* see Note on p. 3. 20.

13 exinterāto lepŏri inserĭtur, *is put into an eviscerated hare;* inserĕre being compounded with in takes the **Dative.** *592.* — in Persas, *to Persia;* Persae, *the Persians,* the people for the territory.

14 addĭta, sc. sunt.

16 eādem adgrĕdi jussus est; **Nom. w. Inf.** after jubēre. *822.*

17 praemonĭtus, ut..adsumĕret; with verbs of warning, *purpose* is expressed by ut with the **Subjunctive.** — quem primum obvĭum habuisset, *whom he should meet first;* the Subjunctive is used to express the indirect statement of the dream. — quem is for eum quem.

18 adsumĕret, like verbs of *naming,* takes a second Accusative denoting the *character.* *578.* — coeptis, **Dat. of Advantage.** *587.* — ruri, *in the country;* rus is used like a name of a town. *686.*

20 nomĭne, *by the name,* **Abl. of Limitation.** *608.* — hujus requisīta origĭne, the **Abl. Absol.** may be rendered: *having inquired after his descent.* — ut, *as soon as, when,* takes the **Perf. Ind.** *737.* II. — in Persis, *among the Persians,* or *in Persia;* the people for the territory.

21 genĭtum, sc. esse.

22 Persepŏlim, *to Persepolis;* in answer to the question *whither?* names of towns are put in the **Acc.** *683.* Persepŏlis being a Greek noun has im in the **Acc.** *143.* 1. — jubet takes the **Acc. w. Inf.** *814.*

Page

23 silvam viae circumdătam, lit. *a wood put around the way* = *a* 4.
wood surrounding the way; circumdăre has a twofold construction. *593.*

24 quod, at the beginning of a sentence instead of id. — appa-
rătis epŭlis invītat, *he invites them to a feast he had prepared for
them;* the Participle is here best rendered by a relative clause. *833.*

25 factos, sc. esse, Acc. w. Inf. after vidēret.

26 si ponătur, the Subjunctive of the Present, because the condition is represented as *possible.* *788.* II.—legant, *they would choose,*
the Subjunctive in Indirect Question. *801.*

27 ut adclamavēre omnes, *when all cried out;* the Perfect after ut
when. *737.* II. — adclamavēre for adclamavērunt. *334.*

28 ait hesterno simĭlem labōri omnem vitam actūros (esse), *he
says they would spend a whole life in work similar to yesterday's;*
similĭs governs the Dative. *598.*

29 quoad parčant; the Subjunctive in a clause dependent upon an
Acc. w. Inf. — se secūtos; this Participle is equivalent to a conditional
clause: *if they would follow him.* To hodiernis epŭlis we must
supply simĭlem omnem vitam, *a whole life in feasting such as to-day.*

30 laetis omnĭbus, Abl. Absol.; an Adjective may take the place of
the Participle. *836.*

31 merĭti sui in Harpăgo oblītus, *having forgotten his desert,* i. e.
what he had deserved of Harpagus; verbs of *forgetting* take the
Genitive. *568.*

33 perfidĭa defectiōnis, Abl. of Means or Instrument. *605.*

3 pugnantĭbus suis partem exercĭtus de tergo ponit, *to his fight-* 5.
ing men he posts a part of his army in the rear, i. e. *he posts a
part of his army in the rear of the fighting men;* the Dative pugnantĭbus, depending on the verb ponit, is used instead of the Genitive
pugnantĭum depending on tergo.

4 ferro agi jubet, Acc. w. Inf., depending on jubet. — sui, *his men.*

5 inventūros (esse), Acc. w. Inf., depending on denuntĭat.

6 proinde vidĕant, *accordingly they should see;* proinde is used
in exhortations only; vidĕant is the Hortatory Subjunctive. *752.* —
fugientĭbus haec an illa pugnantĭbus acĭes rumpenda sit; this is
an indirect disjunctive question; the interrogative particle is omitted
in the first member, and, therefore, ne stands in the second. *803.*

5. The participles fugientĭbus and pugnantĭbus depend on rumpenda sit; they are in the **Dative** to denote the person *by whom* the line is to be broken and may be rendered *when fighting, when fleeing.*

7 ingens pugnandi anĭmus, *eager desire to fight.*

8 exercitŭi accessit, *was added to the army* = *seized the army.*

10 orant revertantur; the **Subjunctive** without ut is used after verbs of *beseeching,* for the sake of emphasis; see Note on p. 4. 10.

11 quos fugiēbant, fugĕre conpĕllunt, *and compelled those to flee from whom they had fled;* the pronoun **ĭs** is often omitted, especially when it would stand in the same case as the Relative. **553**

12 cui Cyrus abstŭlit; the verb auferre, *to take away,* takes the indirect object in the **Dative,** to be translated *from.* **588.**

13 nepōtem agĕre, *to act as his grandson.*

14 genti praeposŭit, *he set him over the nation;* praeponĕre, being compounded with prae, governs the **Dative.** **592.**

15 in Medos, *to the Medes* = *to Media;* the people for the territory.

16 annis CCCL; *duration* of time is commonly expressed by the **Accusative,** but occasionally, as here, by the **Ablative.**

3. The Athenians. Battle of Marathon.

19 quem biformem tradidēre, *whom they represented as being two-shaped;* tradĕre like a verb of *naming* takes two **Accusatives.** **578.** — ut omnis antiquĭtas fabulōsa est; ut is here comparative, *as;* else it would have required the Subjunctive.

24 superfuērunt, *some survived.* — quos refugĭa montĭum recepērunt, *whom the refuges of the mountains took in* = *who took refuge in the mountains.*

25 aut..evecti sunt, supply qui, after aut.—ratĭbus, Abl. **of Manner,** like navĭbus, &c. **614.**

26 a quo genus homĭnum condĭtum (esse) dicĭtur; **Nom. w. Inf. 821.**

28 Eleusīne, Abl. of Eleusin, *at Eleusis;* in answer to the question *where?* **683.**

29 in cujus munĕris honōrem, *and in honor of this gift.* — noctes initiōrum, *the nights of the mysteries.* — sacrātae, sc. sunt.

6. 2 vindicatūri bello, *being about to take revenge in war.*

3 responsum (sc. est) superiōres fore; *an answer was given that* 6. *they would have the advantage.* — ni occidissent, *if they had not killed;* the Pluperfect Subjunctive occidissent after the Historical Perfect responsum est in the principal sentence.

4 cum ventum esset, *when they had come;* **Impersonal Passive.** *423.*

6 et responso dei et praeceptis hostīum cognĭtis, **Abl. Absol.** to supply the want of the perfect active participle: *having learned both the answer of the god and the orders of the enemy.*

8 sarmenta collo gerens, *carrying fagots on his shoulders;* the Participle is in apposition to Codrus; collo is **Instrumental Abl.** *605.*

9 falce, *with his sickle,* **Abl of Means.** *605.* — astu, **Abl. of Manner,** *craftily, cunningly.*

10 cognĭto regis corpŏre, **Abl. Absol.** to supply the want of the perfect active participle, *having recognized the king's body.*

11 ducis se offerentis, *of their leader who offered himself;* the participle is here best rendered by a relative sentence. *833.*

12 bello liberantur, *are delivered from war;* verbs signifying *to set free,* take the **Ablative.** *620.* Observe the liveliness of the multiplied *historical* Presents.

15 permissa, sc. est.

17 vir justitĭae insignis, *a man of distinguished uprightness,* **Genitive of Quality.** *566.* 5. — qui veˍut novam civitātem legĭbus condĕret, *who should found the state anew, as it were, by the establishment of laws;* condĕret is here in · the Subjunctive, because it denotes a *purpose,* the relative clause being equivalent in fact to a clause with ut. *792.*

18 qui = et is, *and he.*—tanto temperamento, *with so great moderation;* **Abl. of Manner.** *613.*

19 cum si quid pro altĕro ordĭne tulisset, altĕri displicitūrum vi derētur, *since if he had proposed anything in favor of one order, this would seem to displease the other;* the condition is represented as contrary to fact; accordingly the **Subjunctive** of the **Imperfect** or **Pluperfect** is used. *788;* after si, nisi, &c. the prefix ali- in alĭquis is dropped. *762.*

20 ut...trahĕret, *that he drew;* clause of *result* after tanto temperamento. *759.*

21 inter multa egregĭa, *among many noble deeds;* egregĭum, the adjective used as noun. — illud, *the following.*

6. 23 armis dimicătum fuĕrat, *fighting had been going on;* the passive used *impersonally.*

24 capităle esse coepit, *it began to be a capital crime = it was pronounced a capital crime.* — si quis legem de vindicanda insŭla tulisset, *if anybody should make a motion to claim the island;* quis for alĭquis. *762.*

25 legem ferre, *to introduce a bill, to make a motion.* — de vindicanda insŭla, *on the claiming of the island = to claim the island;* de is one of the few prepositions commonly used with the **Gerund or Gerundive.** — tulisset; the pluperfect subjunctive is used after the historical perfect coepit in the leading clause. *743.* III. — sollicĭtus, *anxious,* is construed like a verb of *fearing;* accordingly ne must be rendered by *that. 761.*

26 tacendo…censendo, *by being silent, by speaking his mind;* the Ablative of the Gerund used as **Abl. of Means.** *846.*

27 cujus venĭa, *on which pretext.* — non dictūrus modo, sed et factūrus erat, *he intended not only to say but also to do;* the active periphrastic conjugation denotes *intention. 741.*

28 prohibĭta, *forbidden things.* — deformis habĭtu, *disfigured by his dress.*

29 more vaccordĭum, *after the manner of madmen.*

30 quo magis consilĭum dissimulăret; quo is usual final conjunction with comparatives. *763.* — insolĭtis sibi versĭbus, *in verses to which he was not accustomed.*

32 ut bellum decernerĕtur; the subjunctive clause denoting the *result. 739.*

33 devictis hostĭbus, *the enemy being defeated.* — Atheniensĭum fiĕret, *came under the dominion of the Athenians. 571.*

7. 1 memŏres inlāti Atheniensĭbus belli, *mindful of the war they had made on the Athenians;* memor takes the **Genitive.** *567. 1.* Atheniensĭbus depends on inlāti.

2 verĭti; the perfect participle is often used where we should employ the present; ne, *that,* after verbs of *fearing. 761.*

3 oppressūri, *intending to surprise. 741.*

4 qua re cognĭta, may be translated by the perfect active participle with Pisistratus as subject: *Pisistratus having learned this circumstance. 837.*

5 in insidĭis locat; verbs of *placing* take in with the **Abl.** *689.* — 7. jussis matrōnis..sacra celebrāre, *the ladies having been ordered to celebrate the mysteries;* after jubĕo the **Infinitive** can be used without a subject — solīto clamōre ac strepĭtu, *with the usual clamor and noise;* Abl. of **Manner.** *613.*

6 ne intellectos se sentĭant, *that they should not become aware of their being observed;* ne with the Subjunctive to denote the *purpose.* *756.* I. — intellectos se (esse) is **Acc. w. Inf.** depending on sentĭant.

7 egressosque navĭbus Megarenses, *and the Megarenses when they had landed.*

8 classe captīva, **Abl. of Means.** *605.* — intermixtis mulierĭbus, *women being among them.*

9 ut, with the Subjunctive, to denote the *purpose.* *756.* I. — Megăra contendit, *he made for Megara;* in answer to the question *whither?* names of towns are in the **Accusative.** *683.*

10 illi, *the latter* = *the Megarenses.* — petītam praedam, *the expected booty.*

11 quibus caesis, **Abl. Absol.**

12 paulum a capienda urbe afŭit, *he was not far from taking the city.* — suis dolis, **Abl. of Means.** *605.*

14 quasi..vicisset; quasi takes the **Subjunctive.** *772.*

15 per dolum, *deceitfully;* per denoting the *manner.* *643.* — voluntarĭis verberĭbus adfectus; *having been affected with voluntary flogging;* i. e. *having flogged himself;* the verb adficĕre is often to be translated by a verb corresponding to its Ablative; verberĭbus adficĕre, *to flog;* verberĭbus voluntarĭis adfici, *to flog one's self.*

16 lacerāto corpŏre, **Abl. Absol.**

18 e quibus haec se passum (esse) simŭlat, *from whom he pretends to have suffered this.*

19 vocĭbus, *remarks.* — invidiōsa oratiōne, **Abl. of Means.** *605.*

20 amōre plebis, *in consequence of the people's affection for him*

21 per quos occupāta tyrannĭde, *having obtained absolute power through them.*

22 per annos XXXIII; the preposition per is used to denote *from beginning to end.* *674.*

24 alter ex filĭis, *one of his two sons;* e, ex is more common than the Partitive Genitive after numerals and the like. *660.*

Page

7. 24 Hippĭas nomĭne, *by the name of Hippias*, Abl. of Limitation. *608.*

25 qui = et is.

27 quibus interfectis, *and these having been killed;* Abl. Absol. — quaerenti tyranno...ait, *to the tyrant when asking...he said.* — an adhuc alĭqui conscĭi essent, *whether there were any more accomplices;* the Subjunctive in Indirect Question. *801.*

28 nemĭnem superesse, quem amplĭus mori gestĭat, *that no one else was left whom he wished to die;* gestĭat is in the Subjunctive, being dependent upon the Acc. w. Inf. *826.*

31 libertātis, the Genitive after a verb of *reminding. 568.* — regno pulsus, *driven from the state;* Abl. after a verb of *removing. 620.*

32 in Persas; the people for the territory. — Darēo inferenti Atheniensĭbus bellum, *to Dareus when making war on the Athenians;* clauses introduced by particles of *time (as, when, since, &c.)* may be expressed in Latin by a participle without such particle. *833.*

33 adversus patrĭam belongs to ducem.

8. 1 auxilĭum a Lacedaemonĭis petivērunt, *they entreated aid from the Lacedaemonians;* we always say: petĕre alĭquid ab alĭquo. *580.*

2 quos ubi vidērunt, *and when they saw that they;* in historical narrative ubi, simŭlac &c., take the Historical Perfect Indicative. *737.* II.

3 non expectāto, *without waiting;* especially to be noted is the Ablative of a participle without a Substantive; the participle with non is often best rendered by *without. 834.* — instructis decem milĭbus, *having drawn up ten thousand in battle array.*

6 auctor non exspectandi auxilĭi, *the source of unexpected assistance.*

7 ut...ducĕret, *that he deemed;* clause of *result* after tanta fiducĭa. *759.* — plus praesidĭi, *more protection;* Partitive Gen. after plus. *566. 5.*

8 magna in pugnam euntĭbus animōrum alacrĭtas fuit, *when going to battle they were in high spirits,* lit. *to those going into battle were high spirits;* the Dative with esse, to denote *possession. 594.*

9 adĕo ut, *to such a degree that,* introducing a clause of *result* with the Subjunctive.

10 citāto cursu, *at full speed.*

12 tanta virtūte, Abl. of Manner. *613.* — ut..putāres, *that you should suppose.*

15 ut viderētur, is a clause of *result;* cujus laus prima esset, an 8. indirect question depending on difficile judicīum.

20 post proelīi innumĕras caedes, *having slain enemies without number in battle,* lit. *after numberless slaughters of the battle.*

22 dextra manu, *with his right hand;* Instrumental Abl. *605.* — priusquam amittĕret; priusquam has, in narrative, the same construction as *historical* cum. *779.*

24 morsu, *with the teeth;* Instrumental Abl. *605.*

25 tantam in eo virtūtem fuisse, supply dicunt. — tot caedĭbus fatigātus, *wearied with such a carnage.*

26 non duăbus manĭbus amissis victus, *not overcome by the loss of both his hands.*

28 seu proelĭo sive naufragĭo, *either in battle or by shipwreck.*

29 dis patrĭae ultorĭbus poenas repetentĭbus; the Ablative Absolute, expressing the *cause: because the gods, the avengers of the country, demanded satisfaction.*

4. Xerxes. Third invasion of Greece.

3 relictis multis filĭis, *having left behind many sons.* 9.

4 susceptis, *who were born;* suscipĕre means *to take up a newborn child;* hence in the Pass. *to be born.* — maxĭmus natu, *the oldest;* natu, Abl. of Limitation. *608.* — aetātis privilegĭo, *by the privilege of age;* Causal Abl. *604.*

5 quod jus, *a right which,* is in the Accusative governed by dedit; ordo nascendi and natūra are taken conjointly as a single idea and have the singular verb dedit. *542.* — non de ordīne sed de nascendi felicitāte, *not from priority, but from the lucky circumstance of birth.*

7 The whole passage from nam Ariaemĕnem down to avīto vincēre (line 18) is in the oratĭo oblīqua, depending on referēbat which implies dicens. It will be useful to the pupil to become accustomed to arrange the sentences in the form which they would have in the oratĭo recta or *direct narrative;* here it is as follows: "nam Ariaemēnes primus quidem Darēo, sed privāto provēnit: ego regi primus natus. Ităque fratres mei, qui ante genĭti sunt, privātum patrimonĭum, quod eo tempŏre Darēus habŭit, non regnum, sibi vindicāre possunt, ego sum quem primum in regno jam rex pater sustŭlit. Huc accēdit, quod Ariaemēnes non patre tantum sed et matre privātae adhuc fortūnae, avo quoque materno privāto procreātus est;

9. ego vero et matre regīna natus et patrem nonnīsi regem vidi; avum quoque maternum Cyrum ego regem habŭi, non herēdem, sed conditōrem tanti regni; et si in aequo jure utrumque fratrem reliquĕrit, materno tamen ego jure et avīto vinco." The English word to introduce the indirect discourse is THAT; sometimes it is well to omit *that* in translation and to change the form to direct discourse, inserting the verb of *saying* by way of parenthesis.

8 privāto, *when a private citizen.* — provenisse and

9 natum (esse), **Acc. w. Inf.** of the **Indirect Discourse.** When a speech is transferred to the oratīo oblīqua the following changes of mood take place:

I. The **Indicative** in direct statements is changed into the **Infinitive**, becoming dependent on some such form as dixit, *he said*, expressed or implied, and the **Nominative** will then be changed to an **Accusative**;

II. The **Indicative** in dependent relative sentences is changed into the **Subjunctive**;

III. The **Indicative** in questions becomes the **Subjunctive**, being dependent on rogāvit, expressed or implied;

IV. The **Imperative** becomes the **Subjunctive**;

V. Verbs used by the speaker in the **Subjunctive** remain in the same mood.

9 genīti essent, **Subjunctive** according to Rule II.

10 habuisset, **Subjunctive** according to Rule II.

11 vindicāre posse, **Infinitive** according to Rule I. — se esse, **Acc. w. Inf.** according to Rule I.

12 quem sustulĕrit, **Subjunctive** according to Rule II. — tollĕre has the same meaning as suscipĕre, above, *to take up a child, to bring up.* — accedĕre, **Infinitive** according to Rule I.

13 non patre tantum &c.; the Ablatives patre, matre, avo, are governed by procreātus sit, a verb expressing *origin.* **604.**

15 patrem nonnīsi regem vidisse; regem, *as a king,* is in *apposition* to patrem.

17 si..reliquisset; the condition is represented as *contrary to fact,* hence the **Pluperfect Subj.,** both in direct and indirect discourse. **788.** III.

18 materno tamen se jure et avīto vincĕre, *that he by his mother's and grandfather's right should gain the cause;* **Acc. w. Inf.** according to Rule I.

19 concordi anĭmo, *of one mind, unanimously.*

21 cognĭta causa, *having investigated the case.* — adeōque fraterna contentĭo fuit, ut..insultārct..dolēret..mittĕrent, &c.; Subjunctives of Consequence after adĕo ut. *759.*

22 victor..victus, *the winner..the loser.*

25 tanto moderatĭus, *so much more moderately;* the Ablative tanto is used to denote the *degree of difference.* *612.*

28 quinquennĭum, *for 5 years;* time *how long* is in the Acc. *674*

29 quod; the Relative for the Demonstrative. *556.* — ubi primum *as soon as,* takes the Perfect Ind. *737.* II.

30 apud Xerxen, *at the court of Xerxes;* apud designates *nearness* in respect of persons. *630.* — amicĭor patrĭac; the Dative governed by amĭcus. *598.*

33 cera delĭta, *with wax which he had smeared over it;* Abl. of Means. *603;* the participle rendered by a relative clause. *833.*—ne, introducing a clause of *purpose.* *756.* The ancients wrote with a style on waxen tablets; the writing on wax was rubbed out with the broad end of the style. To avoid discovery Demaratus wrote on wooden tablets and then smeared them over with wax, so that it might seem they had not been used at all.

1 recens cera, *the freshly-written tablet.* **10.**

2 perferendas tradit; the Gerundive is joined with the verb tradĕre to express the *purpose.* *841.* — jusso refers to servo, and may be translated by a relative sentence, *who had been ordered.*

3 quibus perlātis; the Abl. Absol. may be translated by a clause with *when.* — Lacedaemŏne, *at Lacedaemon.* — quaestiŏni res diu fuit, *the affair was doubtful for a long time;* the Dative of the object *for which* is used after esse. *595.*

4 quod neque scriptum alĭquid vidērent nec frustra missas suspicarentur, *because on the one hand they did not see anything written, and on the other they supposed that they were not sent to no purpose;* quod usually takes the Indicative; but the Subjunctives vidērent and suspicarentur are used to express the thought and belief of the Lacedaemonians. *782.* — nec is to be resolved into et non, and the negative belongs to frustra; in this way arises the corresponsive conjunction neque..et, *on the one hand not...and on the other.* *857.* — missas, sc. esse, Acc. w. Inf. after suspicarentur.

5 tantōque rem majōrem, quanto esset occultĭor, putābant, *and*

Page

10. *they considered the affair to be the more important, the more mysterious it was;* the words quanto..tanto, signifying *by how much..by so much,* are usually to be translated by the emphatic *the;* esset is in the Subjunctive depending on the Acc. w. Inf. tanto rem majōrem esse. *820.*

6 haerentĭbus in conjectūra viris, *while the men were hesitating in the conjecture;* Abl. Absol.

7 erāsa cera, *having erased the tablet;* Abl. Absol. *837.*

10 ut prodītum sit, *that there is a tradition;* Subjunctive of result; in clauses of *result* the verb of the dependent clause has the same tense as it would have if the clause were a principal one. *746.*

11 siccăta, sc. esse, Acc. w. Inf.

13 numĕro, in answer to the question, *in respect of what?* Abl. of Limitation. *608.*

14 si regem spectes, laudes; the condition is represented as *possible* or *likely to be realized.* *788. II.*

15 cum, *though;* Concessive Conjunction with the Subjunctive. *767.*

16 opes tamen regīae superessent, *the king's riches, however, were more than sufficient.*

18 timĭdus, supply erat. — sicŭbi metus abesset, *wherever there was no cause of fear;* the Subjunctive is used to express the thought of Xerxes.

19 fiducīa virīum, *from confidence in his power;* Causal Abl. *604.*

20 convexa vallīum, *the hollows between hills.*

21 quaedam marīa pontĭbus sternĕbat, *some seas he made passable by bridges.* — ad navigatiōnis commŏdum, *for the promotion of navigation.*

23 cujus; the Relative for the Demonstrative; begin with quam terribĭlis, *as terrible as..;* quam..tam, *as..so.*

26 contemptu paucitātis, *from contempt of their small number;* Causal Abl. *604.*

27 Marathonīa pugna, *in the battle of Marathon;* in is omitted with an Adjective. *673.*

28 qui = et hi. — suos, *their relatives.* — succedente inutĭli turba, *when a useless crowd followed;* Abl. Absol.

20 triduo; *duration* of time is commonly expressed by the Accusa- 10.
tive, but occasionally, as here, by the Ablative. — cum dolōre et
indignatiōnc Persārum, *with = to the grief and indignation of the
Persians.*

30 dimicātum, sc. est, **Impersonal Pass.** *423.* triduo dimicātum est,
the fight lasted three days. — quarta die; this is the proper usage of
the **Ablative** in relations of time to express *when* an action is done
or completed. *672.*

31 summum cacūmen, *the top of the mountain.*

32 hortātur, recēdant et se reservent, *he exhorts them to retire
and save themselves;* the regular construction with verbs of *exhorting* would be ut; but the simple **Subjunctive** may also be employed
(see Note on 3. 20; 4. 10.).

33 sibi cum Spartānis..servandos; this sentence is in the
oratio oblīqua, depending on hortātur, which implies dicens.

1 experiendam (esse); the Passive Periphrastic conjugation ex- 11.
presses *necessity;* the person *by whom* is in the **Dative.** *741.*

2 servandos, sc. esse.

3 audīto regis imperio, *having heard the order of the king.*

4 sciscitantĭbus Delphis oracŭla responsum fuĕrat, *to them when
inquiring for oracles at Delphi the answer had been given.*

5 aut regi aut urbi cadendum, sc. esse, *that either the king or the
city ought to fall.* *741.*

7 parāto ad moriendum anĭmo, *with a mind ready to die;* parā-
tus, *ready,* takes ad with the Gerund *844.*

10 dimissis sociis, may be translated by the perfect active participle with Lycurgus as subject, *Lycurgus having dismissed his
allies.* — hortātur, takes the **Hortatory Subjunctive** (meminĕrint, cavērent), as above.

11 qualitercunque prociātis cadendum esse, *that in whatever
way they might fight they had to die;* cavērent, ne fortīus mansisse
quam dimicasse viderentur, *they should take care lest it might seem
they had shown greater courage in remaining than in fighting.*

12 nec exspectandum (esse); this sentence is in the oratio oblīqua,
depending on hortātur, which implies dicens, *they ought not to wait
(he says).*

13 dum nox occasiōnem daret, *while the night offered an opportunity.*

11.   14 secūris et lactis superveniendum (esse), *they ought to fall suddenly upon the careless and exulting enemy.*

15 peritūros, sc. esse, *would die.*

16 nihil erat difficĭle persuadēre persuāsis mori, *it was not at all difficult to persuade those who had persuaded themselves to die,* i. e., *were resolved to die;* persuadēre governs the **Dative.** *589.*

19 si ipsi oppressi essent, *if they should have been oppressed themselves.* — moritūri, *ready to die.* *741.*

20 totis castris; with nouns qualified by totus, the **Ablative** without a preposition is used to denote the place *where?* *687.*— postquam invenĭunt; postquam here takes the **Historical Present.**

22 ut qui sciunt, *like men who know.* — spe victorĭae, *with the hope of victory.*

23 in mortis ultiōnem, *to take vengeance for their death.*

24 tractum, sc. est. — vincendo fatigāti, *wearied of conquering.*

26 duōbus vulnerĭbus acceptis, *having received two wounds.*— terrestri proelĭo, *in the battle by land;* Abl. **of Time.** *673.*

29 bellum Persārum, *the war with the Persians;* Objective **Genitive.** *566. 2.* — in auxilĭum regis classe venisse, *had come with a fleet to the king's assistance;* **Acc. w. Inf.** depending on animadvertisset.

30 sollicitāre in partes suas, *to draw over to his side.*

31 colloquendi copĭam, *opportunity of a conference;* the **Gerund** is frequently used with substantives as a complement. *843.*— symbŏlos propōni et saxis proscrībi curat, *he had a proclamation issued and written upon the rocks;* curāre takes the **Acc. w. Inf.** — symbŏli, *symbols, significant letters;* a *proclamation* is meant.

12.   2 quid si non haec Darēo prius et nunc Xerxi belli causa nobiscum foret, quod vos rebellantes non destituĭmus? *What cause of war would there have been formerly with Dareus and now with Xerxes, if not the fact that we did not forsake you when revolting?*

4 quiu, *why not?*

6 commisso proelĭo, *the battle having begun.* — inhibēre remis, *to row a ship backwards.*

9 ad templum Apollĭnis diripiendum, *to destroy the temple of Apollo;* ad with Gerund or Gerundive denotes *purpose.* *845.*

10 quasi, *as if,* takes the Subjunctive. *772.*

11 imbrĭbus et fulminĭbus, Abl. **of Means.** *605.*

Page

12 ut intellegĕret; ut with the Subjunctive to express the *purpose.* 12. 756. I. — quam nullae essent, *how insignificant are;* the Subjunctive in Indirect Question. 801.

14 vacŭas hominĭbus, *empty of men,* i. e. *deserted.*

16 praemonente Themistŏcle, *Themistocles forewarning them =* *forewarned by Themistocles.*

18 adventante Xerxe, *upon the arrival of Xerxes.*

19 consulentĭbus Delphis oracŭlum responsum fuĕrat, *to them consulting the oracle at Delphi the answer had been given* (see Note on 11. 4.). — salûtem muris lignĕis tuerentur, *they should secure their safety behind wooden walls.*

20 demonstrātum, sc. esse.

22 non in aedificiĭs, sed in civĭbus posĭtam, sc. esse, *consisted not in its buildings, but in its citizens.*

23 commissûros, sc. esse. — All these Acc. w. Inf. constructions depend on persuādet.

25 probāto consilĭo, *having approved the plan.*

26 abdĭtis insŭlis demandant, *they send them to sequestered islands for safety.* — relicta urbe, *having left the city.*

28 imitātae, sc. sunt.

29 ne circumvenīri posset, Subjunctive of *purpose.* 756. 1.

31 deserto bello, may be rendered by the **perfect active** participle with qui as subject, *these having given up war.* — ad sua tuenda, *to protect their own property;* ad, with the Gerundive, expressing *purpose.* 845.

32 timens ne, *fearing that;* after timĕo, ne must be rendered by *that.* 761.

33 per servum fidum, *by means of a faithful slave;* the person considered as means or instrument is expressed by per with the Acc. — uno in loco contractam Graeciam, *Greece concentrated at one place.*

1 quod si; in order to indicate the connection with a preceding 13. proposition the relative pronoun quod (which, however, loses its signification as a pronoun) is frequently put before si, so that quodsi may be regarded as one word.

2 vellent, dissiparentur, Subjunctives in indirect discourse.

3 ei singŭlas consectandas esse, *he had to pursue them singly;* Acc. w. Inf. depending on nuntĭat. — hoc dolo, Abl. of Means. 605.

13.   4 adventu hostĭum occupāti, *surprised by the approach of the enemy.*

5 collātis virĭbus; the **Ablative Absol.** may be translated *with united forces.*

9 ut..ita cernĕres; transpose: ita ut cernĕres, *so that you could see.*

10 juxta praecceptum Themistŏclis, *according to the order of Themistocles.*

13 circumspicientes fugam, *looking out for flight.*

15 mersae, sc. sunt.

17 dubĭum consilĭi, *wavering in resolution.*

18 ne quid seditiōnis; seditiōnis governed by quid which after ne is used instead of alĭquid; the **Partitive Genitive** is often found after the neuters of adjectives and pronouns. *566. 6.*

19 fama adversi belli et in majus omnĭa, sicŭti mos est, extollens, *the rumor of the defeat exaggerating every thing, as is customary;* this is the Subject of the final sentence introduced by ne.

20 sibi relinquat, **Hortatory Subjunctive** depending on hortātur.

21 aut perdomitūrum se Graecĭam aut cessūrum (esse); this **Acc. w. Inf.** is in oratĭo oblĭqua, and depends upon a verb of *saying* implied in hortātur.

23 probāto consilĭo, *the plan being approved.*

25 audĭta regis fuga, *having heard of the flight of the king.*

27 interclūsus redĭtu, *cut off from his retreat;* intercludĕre, being a verb of *separation,* takes the **Ablative.** *620.* — desperatiōne rerum, *by the hopelessness of the undertaking.*

29 timens ne, *fearing that. 761.* — interclŭsi hostes, *the enemy when cut off;* the Participle represents a *condition. 833.*

30 quod alĭter non patĕret, *which otherwise could not be open;* quod = cum id; with the Subjunct. *792. II.*

32 retinendo, *by keeping them back,* Abl. of Gerund as Abl. of **Means.** *846.*

33 cum vincĕre consilĭo cetĕros non posset, *as he could not win over the rest by his opinion.*

14.   1 certiōrem consilĭi facit, *he informs him of the plan.* — maturāta fuga, *by accelerating his flight.*

2 perculsus nuntĭo, *panic-stricken by the news.* — tradit milĭtes 14. perducendos; the **Gerundive** is joined with the verb tradĕre, to express the *purpose* for which anything is delivered. *841.*

4 solūtum pontem hibernis tempestatĭbus, *the bridge destroyed by winter storms.* — offendisset, *had hit upon.*

5 res spectacŭlo digna et aestimatĭōne, *an event worth seeing and estimating;* dignus, *worth,* takes the Abl. *625.*

6 rerum varietāte miranda, *by the wonderful fickleness of human affairs;* the Ablative depends on aestimatĭōne.

7 vix capiēbat, *was hardly able to hold him.*

8 carentem omni etĭam servōrum ministerĭo, *wanting all service of slaves,* i. e., *without even a slave to wait upon him.*

9 terris graves, *oppressive to the countries;* **Dative of Advantage** or **Disadvantage.** *387.*

10 felicĭus iter fuit, *had a luckier march;* esse with the **Dative** denotes *possession.* *594.*

11 neque enim, *for.*

12 multōrum diĕrum inopĭa, *want of necessaries for many days.*

13 ut viae cadaverĭbus implerentur, Subjunctive of *result* after tantus. *759.* — cadaverĭbus, Abl. after a verb of *filling.* *622.*

14 escae inlecĕbris sollicitātae, refers to alĭtes et bestĭae, *allured by the bait of food.*

18 etĭam iu majus restitutiōnem, *rebuilding even on a larger scale.*

19 nullo pretĭo, *at no price;* Abl. **of Price** after venālis. *617.* — videt, **Historical Present** after postquam.

20 incensis (supply iis) quae aedificāre coepĕrant, *having set on fire what they had begun to build.*

22 commissum, sc. est.

24 referta regŭlis opulentĭae, *filled to overflowing with kingly wealth;* as a rule, refertus takes the **Genitive.** *567.* I.; but it also takes the **Ablative** following the analogy of verbs of *filling.* *623.*

25 unde primum Graecos dīvitiārum luxurĭa cepit, *since that time the luxury of riches first took possession of the Greeks.*—dīvīso inter se auro Persĭco, *when they had divided among them the Persian gold.*

28 navāli proelĭo dimicātum est, *a sea-fight took place.*

14. ₃₀ vicisse **Graecos** et Mardonii copias occidiōnc occidisse, *that the Greeks had won and completely cut down the troops of Mardonius;* **Graecos** is **Subject-**Accusative and copias **Object-**Accusative in the **Acc. w. Inf.** construction. — tantam famae velocitātcm fuisse (supply dicunt), *the velocity of the report was so great, they say.*

₃₂ matutīno tempŏrc, *in the morning.* — meridiānis horis, *at noon;* time *when* is in the Abl. *672.*

15. ₁ tantum spatii; the **Gen.** after a neuter pronoun. *566. 6.* — tam brevi horārum momento, *in the short space of a few hours.* — de victoria nuntiātum est, *word was brought about the victory.*

₂ confecto bello, *the war being terminated.*

₃ omnium judicio, *in the opinion of all.* — praclāta, sc. est.

₄ princeps civitātum testimonio judicātus, *being declared the chief according to the testimonial of the states.*

5. Sparta and Lycurgus.

₇ ducĭbus Laccdaemoniis et Athcniensĭbus, *under the leadership of the Lacedaemonians and Athenians;* **Abl. Absol.** *830.*

₁₂ trahĕrc, **Historical Inf.** *809.*

₁₃ gestis rcbus inlustres, *famous by their exploits.* — propriis virĭbus, **Abl.** depending on confidēbant. *628.*

₁₄ institūtis Solōnis ct legĭbus Lycurgi, **Abl. of Means.** *605.*

₁₅ cx aemulatiōne virĭum, *from jealousy of their power.*

₁₆ cum successisset...vindicāre potuisset, *though he succeeded and could claim;* cum, Concessive Conjunction with the **Subj.** *767.*

₁₉ summa fide, **Abl. of Manner** without cum. *613.*

₂₀ quanto plus pietātis jura valērent, *how much more influence the rights of piety had;* **Abl.** to denote the *degree of difference. 612;* the Subjunctive in **Indirect Question.** *801.*

₂₁ medio tempŏre, *in the mean time;* time *when* in the Abl. *672.*

₂₂ non habentĭbus Spartānis leges institŭit, *he enacted laws, the Spartans not having any;* leges belongs to institŭit and is to be understood to habentĭbus.

₂₃ magis..clarĭor; magis is sometimes used with Comparatives adding to their force.

₂₅ documentum daret, *would give an example;* the Subjunctive to express the opinion of Lycurgus.

28 emi singŭla jussit, *he ordered every thing to be bought.*

29 compensatiōne mercĭum, *by bartering.*

1 sublegendi senātum vel creandi quos vellet magistrātus po- 16. testātem, *the power of electing to the senate or to appoint those whom they wished to be their magistrates;* the **Genitive** of the **Gerund** after potestas; vellent in the Subjunctive to express the opinion of the Lacedaemonians.

3 aequāta patrimonĭa, *the properties being made equal = the equality of property;* a common translation of a participle is an abstract noun.

4 potentiōrem altĕro, *more powerful than the other;* **Abl. of Comparison.** *609.* — reddĕrent takes two **Accusatives.** *578.*

5 ne cujus; cujus, instead of alicŭjus after ne. *762.*

6 non amplĭus una veste uti, *to use no more than one dress;* uti takes the **Abl.** *626;* quam is omitted after amplĭus without influence on the construction. *610.* — toto anno, *all the year round; duration* of time is commonly expressed by the **Accusative,** but occasionally, as here, by the **Ablative.** — permissum, sc. est.

8 ne..verterētur; the Subjunctive after ne to denote the *purpose.* *758.*

9 ut..agĕrent, *to pass;* Subjunctive of *purpose.* *756.*

11 nihil eos substernĕre, degĕre, &c.; **Acc. w. Inf.** depending on statŭit.

12 priusquam viri facti essent; the Subjunctive depending on the **Acc. w. Inf.** *826.*

14 ut eligerentur..coercĕrent; ut with the Subjunctive to denote *purpose.* *756.* — matrimonĭa sua, *their wives.*

16 nullis frenis, **Abl. of Means.**

17 non divĭtum et potentĭum esse, *should not belong to the rich and powerful;* **Genitive** with esse to denote the *predicate.* *571.*

18 nec usquam terrārum, *nowhere in the world;* **Partitive Genitive** with Adverbs. *566.* c.

19 solūtis antĕa morĭbus, *their manners having been formerly loose.*

20 et inde se detulisse; **Acc. w. Inf.** depending on fingit.

21 consuescendi taedĭum, *the trouble of getting accustomed.*

Page
16. 22 vincat; in this sentence the Present Subjunctive is used after
the historical Present in the leading clause according to the general
rule. *743.*

23 obligat takes the **Acc. w. Inf.**, nihil eos mutaturos (esse).

24 priusquam reverteretur; the **Subjunctive** after priusquam implies
intention: *before he should return.*

25 consulturum, referring to se (Lycurgum), denotes *purpose: to
consult the oracle.* — quid addendum mutandumque legibus videre-
tur, *what seemed worth changing or adding to his laws;* the Subjunctive in **Indirect Question.** *801.*

27 moriens, *when dying. 833.*

28 ne arbitrarentur, *lest they should consider.* — relatis Lacedae-
monem; supply ossibus, *when they were brought back to Lacedaemon.*
833. — solutos se religione, *that they were freed from their obligation;* verbs of *separation* take the **Abl.** *620.*

29 in dissolvendis legibus, *in abolishing the laws.*

6. Sicily. Invasion of the Athenians.

31 Italiae adhaesisse, *was united with Italy;* adhaerere being
compounded with ad takes the **Dative.** *592.*

32 diremptamque, sc. esse. — a corpore; **Abl. of Separation** with
preposition after dirimere. *620.* — majore impetu, **Instrumental Abl.**, *by
the greater violence.*

17. 1 toto undarum onere, *with the whole burden of its waves.*

3 ut pateat, Subjunctive of *result* after ita. — tota ferme, *nearly
the whole of it.* — nec non, sc. est, *and there is besides;* nec non is
emphatically affirmative.

4 ignibus generandis nutriendisque; the **Dative** of the **Gerundive**
denoting purpose: *for producing fire and feeding it.* — soli ipsius
naturalis materia, *natural material of the soil itself;* this is the
Subject of the sentence.

5 quippe intrinsecus stratum sulphure et bitumine traditur, *for
indeed they say it (the soil) is covered on the inside with sulphur
and pitch;* **Acc. w. Inf.** depending on traditur.

6 ut..eructet, Subjunctive of *purpose. 758.* — spiritu cum igne
in materia luctante, *while the air is fighting with fire in the material.*

7 complurĭbus locis; the Ablative is used without a preposition 17. to denote the place *where* in the case of loco, locis, when qualified by Adjectives. *687.*

11 nomĭne, *by this word;* Abl. of Means.

12 mirum, supply est. — in quem res tot coiēre mirae, *where so many wonderful things (concur) are to be found.*

13 quod nusquam latĭus torrens fretum, *because the straits are nowhere rolling in a wide stream;* torrens is a Participle, and latĭus an Adverb qualifying the same.

14 nec solum citāto impĕtu sed etĭam saevo, *not only with rapid motion but even a raging one;* Descriptive Abl. *616.*

15 experientĭbus, *for those who experience it.* — procul visentĭbus, *for those who see it from afar.*

16 ut vidĕas..exaudĭas, *that you may see, hear;* Subjunctive of *result* after tanta.

21 velŭti, *as if,* takes the Subj. *772.*

22 in tam angustis termĭnis, *within so narrow limits.* — aliter durāre potuisset, *could have lasted otherwise.* — tot saecŭlis, *for so many centuries;* time *how long* is here expressed by the Abl.

23 nisi..alerētur; the condition is represented as *contrary to fact.* *788.* III. — nutrimentis, Abl. of Means. *605.*

25 hinc latrātus audītus, sc. est, *from this source comes the barking which is heard.* — hinc monstri credĭta simulācra, sc. sunt, *hence the phantoms of the monster are believed (to come).* — navigantes is Subject to putant, *the sailors believe.*

26 magnis verticĭbus pelăgi desidentis exterrĭti, belongs to navigantes: *being terrified by the great whirlpools of the tumbling sea.* — latrāre undas, Acc. w. Inf. depending on putant.

29 raptum secum spirĭtum in imum fundum trahit, *carries the air with it AND draws it to the lowest bottom.* It is sometimes convenient to translate a participle by a co-ordinate sentence.

30 donec..incendat, *until it sets on fire;* donec, *until,* implying *purpose* takes the Subjunctive. *778.*

33 ut..dedĕrit; Subjunctive of *result* after ita. *759.* — quantum admirationis; the Genitive after a neuter pronoun. *566. 6.*

1 dedĕrit; the Perfect Subjunctive in the dependent clause after 18. the Present in the principal clause. — credentĭbus, sc. antĭquis, *who*

18. *believed.* — coëuntĭbus in se promuntoriis ac rursum discedentĭbus, *when the promontories dash against each other and separate again.*

2 solĭda intercĭpi absumĭque navigĭa; **Acc. w. Inf.** depending on credentĭbus.

3 in dulcedĭnem fabŭlae conposĭtum, *gotten up for the charm of the story.*

4 ea est natūra loci, ut putes, arbitrēris, *such is the natural position of the site, that you may take it..believe.* — procul inspicientĭbus, *to those looking at it from afar.*

6 quo cum accessĕris, for cum eo accessĕris.

7 arbitrēre for arbitrēris, depending on ut.

9 quibus exstinctis, *when they were undone.*

10 post quem = post eum.

13 justitĭa, **Abl. of Means.** — cujus moderatiōnis, *a moderation of which.*

14 haud mediŏcris, *not common.* — decēdens, *dying* = at his death.

15 spectātae fĭdĕi servo, *to a slave of tried honesty;* **Genitive of Quality.** *566. 5.*

17 ut .. mallent ... paterentur; Subjunctives of *result* after tantus. *759.*

18 oblīti dignitātis suae, **Genitive** with verbs of *forgetting. 568.*

20 varĭa victorĭa, *with varying victory;* **Abl. of Manner.** *613.*

21 dimicātum, sc. est. — amisso Hamilcăre imperatōre cum exercĭtu; **Abl. Absol.**, but it may be rendered in English: *after the loss of their general Hamilcar with his army.*

23 discordĭa laborārent, *were suffering from discord;* discordĭa, **Causal Abl.** *604.*

25 ab Himĕra, *from Himera;* with names of towns the prepositions a, ab, and e, ex are sometimes used for the sake of greater exactness. — in auxilĭum vocāti, is best rendered by a relative clause.— pulsis civitāte contra quos implorāti fuĕrant, et mox caesis quibus tulĕrant auxilĭum; the **Abl. Absol.** to supply the want of the perfect active participle, *having driven from the state those against whom they had been called upon for aid, and having slain those to whom they had brought relief.*

28 ausi facĭnus, *during a crime;* the perfect participle is often **18.** used where we should employ a Present. — nulli tyranno comparandum, *not to be compared to any tyrant,* i. e. *to that of any tyrant.* — ut melĭus fuĕrit, *that it had been better;* clause of *result* introduced by ut.

29 captivitātis jure, *by the right of captivity.*

30 servissent, necesse fuisset, reliquissent, are verbs of an incomplete conditional sentence, the protāsis to be supplied from the context would be: *"if they had been defeated";* the condition being *contrary to fact,* the **Pluperfect Subjunctive** is the proper tense. *788.* III. — amissa patrĭa, *with the loss of their country.*

31 inter aras et patrĭos lares trucidāti, *having been butchered among the altars and household gods.*

32 patrĭam praedam reliquissent; relinquĕre besides its proper Accusative (patrĭam) takes another Accusative (praedam) as a secondary Object. *578.*

1 cum graves paterentur, *since they were indignant at;* the **19.** Adjective graves is used instead of the Adverb gravĭter. *550.*

2 diffīsi virĭbus, *distrusting their own strength;* diffĭdĕre takes the **Dative.** *589.* — petivĕre = petivērunt; petĕre alĭquid ab alĭquo. *580.*

3 qui, *and the latter.* — studĭo majōris imperĭi, *with a view to enlarge their dominion;* **Objective Genitive.** *566.* 2.

4 metu factae pridem a Syracusānis classis, *from fear of the fleet which the Syracusans had built long since.*

5 ne, after expressions of fear is *that.* — Lacedaemonĭis accedĕrent, *might be added to the Lacedaemonians.*

6 sub specĭe ferendi Catiniensĭbus auxilĭi, *under the pretext of coming to the aid of the Catinienses;* the **Genitive** of the **Gerundive** is used with nouns. *843.*

8 frequenter caesis hostĭbus, *the enemy having been frequently defeated* or *by frequent defeats of the enemy.*

9 Lachĕte et Chariāde ducĭtus, Abl. Absol.

10 sive metu sive taedĭo belli, *either from fear or from disgust with the war;* **Causal Abl.** *604.*

11 remissis Atheniensĭum copĭis, may be taken with Catinienses as subject to supply the want of the perfect active participle, *the Catinienses having sent back the forces of the Athenians.*

19. 13 interjecto tempŏre, *some time having intervened.*

14 sordīda veste, capillo barbāque promissis, are **Ablatives of Means** governed by deformes, *disfigured by their dirty dress,* &c., &c.

15 omni squalōris habītu ad misericordīam commovendam adquisīto, *having assumed every appearance of squalor to excite compassion;* ad with the **Gerundive** to express *purpose.* *845.*

20 Sicilīa repetītur, *Sicily is sought again,* i. e., *they return to Sicily.*

21 ut ipsis terrōri essent, *that they were a terror even to those;* both ipsis and terrōri are governed by essent; with the verbs esse, dare, &c., besides the **Dative** of the *person,* another is used to express the *purpose, intention,* or *destination.* *595.*

22 brevi post tempŏre, *after a short time;* distance of time *how long after* is expressed by the **Abl.** with post following. *675.* — revocāto Alcibiāde, **Abl. Absol.**

24 munitionībus circumdātis, *having put around fortifications;* **Abl. Absol.** to supply the want of the perf. active participle. — hostes to be joined with in urbe clausos.

27 sed qui, *but he.*

28 instar omnīum auxiliōrum, *as good as all the auxiliary troops.* — audīto genĕre belli jam inclināto statu, *having heard of the kind of war, the situation being already on the decline;* **Abl. Absol.**

29 auxilīis contractis opportūna bello loca occŭpat, *he concentrates troops AND occupies places suitable for war purposes.*

31 congressus tertĭo, sc. proelĭo, *engaged in a third.*

20. 1 quo cognīto, *this circumstance having become known;* **Abl. Absol.**

4 commūni civitatīum decrēto, *by a joint decree of the states,* or *according to,* &c.

5 quasi, *as if,* governs the **Subjunctive.** *772.*

6 ex utrāque parte, *from both sides.* — summis virībus, *with might and main.* — dimicabātur, **Impers. Pass.,** *the fight was continued.*

10 censēre coepit, ut abīrent Sicilīa, *began to believe they should leave Sicily;* censēre, *to believe,* is here used as a verb of *willing* or *demanding,* and as such it must take ut with the **Subjunctive.** *758.*

11 dum res quamvis adflictae nondum tamen perdītae forent, *as long as their affairs, though in a bad state, were not yet utterly lost.*

12 neque in bello perseverandum (esse), *they ought not to persist* 20.
in war, he said; this is the **Acc. w. Inf.** of the oratĭo oblīqua, depending on censet.

13 esse domi gravĭōra bella, **Acc. w. Inf.** — in quae servāre oportēret, *for which it would be proper to save;* the Subjunctive in the
oratĭo oblīqua.

14 pudōre male actae rei, *from shame of his failure;* **Causal Abl.**
— metu destitūtae spei civĭum, *from fear of the disappointed hope
of the citizens.* — impellente fato, *because fate impelled him;* the **Abl.
Absol.**, expressing the *cause. 833.*

17 inscitĭa ducum, **Causal Abl.**

18 inter angustĭas maris tuentes se Syracusānos adgressi, *having
attacked the Syracusans who defended themselves within the narrow passage of the sea;* tuentes is best rendered by a relative
clause.

22 tutiōrem fugam rati itinĕre terrestri, supply esse, *supposing
the flight would be safer by land;* the way *by which* is in the **Abl.**
638. — ab his relictas naves, *the ships deserted by them.*

25 a captivitāte se vindĭcat, *he saves himself from captivity;* **Abl.
of Separation.** *620.*

26 ne Demosthĕnis quidem exemplo ut sibi consulĕret admonĭtus,
*not reminded even by the example of Demosthenes to take care of
himself;* ut sibi consulĕret, clause of *purpose* after admonĭtus.

27 cladem suōrum, *the defeat of his countrymen.* — dedecŏre,
Abl. of Means. *605.*

7. Character of Philip and Alexander.

29 XL et septem annōrum, *at the age of 47 years;* **Gen. of Quality.**
566. 5. — annis XXV, *for 25 years; duration* of time is occasionally
expressed by the Ablative.

30 apparatĭbus studiosĭor, *more fond of preparations;* studiōsus
here governs the **Dative;** this is exceptional, the regular construction
is the **Gen.** *567.*

31 maxĭme opus erant, *were of the utmost necessity;* opus est
takes the **Dative** of the person; the thing wanted may be the Subject,
as here. *624.*

32 divitĭārum quaestus quam custodĭa sollertĭor, *his acquiring
riches was more skilful than his keeping,* i. e. *he was more skilful*

Page

20. *in acquiring riches than in keeping them.* — inter cotidiānas rapīnas, *in the midst of his daily plunders.*

21. 1 in eo, *by him.*

2 pari jure, *with equal right, equally.* — dilectae, sc. erant. — ratĭo vincendi, *way to gain victory;* the **Gen.** of the **Gerund** after a Substantive.

3 alloquĭo qui plura promittĕret quam praestāret; the Subjunctive here denoting the *result;* qui for ut is. *791.* III.

4 in serĭa et jocos artĭfex, *a master in serious matters and joking;* in, denoting the *object* or *purpose.*

5 utilitāte non fide, *on account of utility and not from conscien-tiousness;* **Causal Abl.** *604.*

6 apud utrumque, *with both parties.*

7 inter haec, *withal;* inter, means *during,* and hence, *under the circumstances described;* supply the copula after inter haec.

8 acumĭnis et sollertĭae plena; the **Gen.** governed by plenus. *567. 1.* — ut nec ornatŭi facilĭtas nec facilĭtāti inventiōnum deesset ornātus; *so that facility of expression was not wanting to beauty, nor beauty to readiness of invention,* i. e., *so that facility of ex-pression was not without beauty of style, or beauty of style without readiness of invention.*

10 et virtūte et vitĭis, *both in virtue and vice;* **Abl. of Limitation.** *608.* — patre major, **Abl. of Comparison.** *609.*

11 utrīque diversa, sc. erat; the **Dat.** with esse to denote *posses-sion. 594.* — hic, *this one, the last mentioned;* ille, *the former.*

12 deceptis gaudēre hostĭbus, **Historical Inf.** *809;* gaudēre takes the **Causal Abl.** *604.*

13 prudentĭor ille consilĭo, hic anĭmo magnificentĭor, *the former more prudent in counsel, the latter more elevated in mind;* con-silĭo, anĭmo, **Abl. of Limitation.** *608.*

14 dissimulāre..vincĕre, **Hist. Inf.** *809.*

15 vini nimis avĭdus, *too fond of the cup;* avĭdus takes the **Gen.** *567. 1.*

16 ebrietātis vitĭa, *the injurious effects of drunkenness.*

17 de convivĭo, *from* or *directly after the banquet.*

20 convivĭo excessit, *departed from a banquet;* verbs of *sepa-ration* take the **Abl.** *620.*

66666666666336666666666363666666666666636663636666666668

Page

22 malle, **Hist. Inf.** for malĕbat. — littĕrārum cultus utrīque simīlis, **2** supply erat: *the cultivation of science was alike in father and son.*

23 sollertĭae pater majōris, hic fĭdĕi (supply majōris), *the father was a man of greater skill, the son of greater uprightness;* the **Genitive of Quality** used *predicatively.* **566. 5.** — verbis atque oratiōne Philippus, hic rebus moderatĭor, *in his words and speech Philip was more moderate, the other more so in his deeds.*

24 parcendi victis anĭmus, *the inclination to spare the conquered;* since parcĕre governs the Dative, the Gerundive could not be used instead of the Gerund. **842.**

26 dedītus, *given,* takes the **Dat. 598.** — quibus artĭbus, for iis artĭbus quibus.

8. The death of Alexander.

31 defunctos (esse), **Acc. w. Inf.** depending on ait. — tumultuantes milītes et.. suspicantes, *the soldiers being in confusion and suspecting.* — regem insidĭis perīre, **Acc. w. Inf.** depending on suspicantes.

2 osculandam dextram flentĭbus porrexit, *reached to the weeping his hand to kiss;* the **Gerundive** is joined with porrigĕre to denote the *purpose.* **841.**

4 sine ullo tristiōris mentis argumento, *without any sign of deeper affliction.*

6 ut consolarētur, Subjunctive of Result after ut, *so that.*

6 in hostem, in mortem, *against the enemy, against death,* i. e., *in face of the enemy, in face of death.*

7 dimissis militĭbus, **Abl. Absol.**

8 videanturne simĭlem sibi repertūri regem, *whether it seemed to them that they would find another king like him;* the **Subjunct.** videantur, in the Indirect Question. **801;** repertūri (esse) is **Nom. w. Inf.** after vidēri. **822.**

9 tacentĭbus cunctis, **Abl. Absol.,** *while all were silent.* — se hoc ...ocŭlis vidēre; **Acc. w. Inf.** depending on dixit.

11 quantum sanguĭnis sit fusūra Macedonĭa, quantis caedĭbus parentatūra sit, are Indirect Questions depending on ocŭlis vidēre; quantum sanguĭnis, **Part. Gen.** after quantum. **566. c.**

12 quantis caedĭbus, quo cruōre, *what slaughter and gore.* — mortŭo sibi parentatūra (sit), *it (Macedonia) would offer as a sacrifice for him when dead.*

Page

22. 13 corpus suum condi jubet, *he ordered his body to be interred,* Nom. w. Inf. *821.*

15 tanta illi anĭmi magnitūdo fuit, *he had such greatness of mind.* — ut... nuncupăret, Subjunctive of *result,* after ut.

16 cum relinquĕret, *though he left;* cum, concessive conjunction with Subjunct. *767.*

18 quasi...esset; quasi, *as if,* takes the Subjunctive. — nefas est takes the Acc. w. Inf.

20 velŭti..cecinisset; velŭti, *as if,* takes the Subjunctive. — ambitiōne vulgi, *by paying court to the masses;* Instrumental Abl. *605.*

23 praeclūsa voce, *his voice failing;* Abl. Absol.

24 exemptum digĭto anŭlum tradĭdit, *he took the ring from his finger AND gave it.* — quae res, *and this circumstance.*

25 non voce, tamen judicĭo, *not by word of mouth, yet by these proceedings,* i. e., *by his last will.*

28 supra humānam potentĭam, *above human capacity.* — magnitudĭne anĭmi, Abl. governed by praedĭtus. *643.*

29 ipso ortu, *at his very birth;* Abl. denoting *time. 673.*

30 tota die, *all day long; duration* of time is occasionally expressed by the Ablative.

23. 3 puer, *when a boy.* — acerrĭmis litterārum studĭis erudĭtus, Abl. of Means with erudĭtus. *607; instructed in the most acute studies.*

4 exacta puerĭtĭa, *having spent his boyhood.*

5 accepto imperĭo, Abl. Abs., *having received the crown.*

6 se appellāri jussit, Acc. w. Inf.; appellāri takes two Nominatives, but in the Acc. w. Inf. they become Accusatives.

7 fiducĭam sui, *confidence in him;* Objective Gen. *566. 3.* — ut..timērent, Subjunctive of *result* after tantam fiducĭam..ut. *759.* — illo presente, Abl. Abs., *in his presence.*

8 cum nullo hostĭum, Part. Gen. after nullus. *566. 6.*

9 quem non vicĕrit; qui after a general negative as: nemo, nullus, takes the Subjunctive. *793. b.*

13 exstincto Alexandro Magno, *Alexander the Great having expired.*

14 tota Babylōne, *in the whole of Babylon;* the Abl. in answer to the question *where? 683.*

15 quod, *because*, takes the Indicative (credidĕrant).— ut..sic, 23.
as..so.

17 quotĭens ereptus esset, quam saepe se obtulisset; Indirect
Questions with the verb in the **Subjunct.** after recordantes. — praesenti morte ereptus esset, *had been delivered from imminent death;*
the usual construction is alĭquem a morte cripĕre; but here the **Abl.**
is used without a preposition. *620.* — pro amisso, *instead of being
lost.*

19 ut mortis ejus fides adfŭit, *when the news of his death proved
to be true.*

21 quam indulgentĭa victōris vitae non poenituĕrat, *who through
the generosity of the conqueror did not regret that she had been
spared;* paenĭtet takes the *person* in the **Acc.** and the *exciting
cause* in the **Gen.** *584.* — indulgentĭa victōris is **Causal Abl.** *604.* —
amisso filĭo a fastigĭo tantae majestātis in captivitātem redacta,
*having lost her son, and being reduced from the summit of such
grandeur to captivity;* this is in apposition to mater; to facilitate
the translation arrange the sentence as follows: mater quoque Darēi
regis amisso filĭo a fastigĭo tantae majestātis in captivitātem redacta,
quam indulgentĭa, &c.

24 non quod, *not as if*, takes the **Subjunct.** *785.*

26 versa vice, *reversedly.* — non ut civem et regem, verum ut
hostem amissum gaudēbant; in the first part of the clause we must
supply lugēbant; *they did not mourn for the loss of their citizen
and king, but rejoiced as if they had lost an enemy*; hostis amissus
is *the lost enemy* or *the loss of an enemy;* but here it is equivalent
to a comparative clause with *as if.*

27 gaudēbant is here *transitive.* *575.*

28 exsecrantes, in apposition to Macedōnes.

9. *The earliest history of Carthage.*

30 ventum est, **Impers. Pass.**

31 pauca dicenda sunt, *a few remarks ought to be made;* the **Pass.**
Periphrastic Conjugation expresses *necessity.* *741.* — repetītis Tyriōrum paulo altĭus rebus, **Abl. Abs.**, *by beginning a little farther back
with the history of the Tyrians.*

32 dolendi, *deplorable.*

1 condĭta est, *was founded*, i. e., *derived its origin.* — terrae 24.
motu vexāti, *being harassed by an earthquake.*

24.   2 mari proxĭmum litus, the **Dat.** depending on proxĭmus. *598.*

4 vocant takes **two Acc.** *578.*

5 expugnāti, *having been subdued.*

6 navĭbus appulsi, *having landed.* — ante annum Trojānae cladis, *a year before the fall of Troy;* time *how long before* is expressed by the **Abl.** or **Acc.** *675.*

7 Persārum bellis, *at the time of the Persian wars.* *673.*

8 attrītis virĭbus, *their forces being impaired.* **Abl. Abs.** — a servis suis multitudīue abundantĭbus, *at the hands of their slaves who were very numerous.*

9 conspiratiōne facta, **Abl. Abs.**, *having formed a conspiracy.*

10 libĕrum popŭlum, *the free population.*

11 potīti; the perfect participle of a deponent verb may be used exactly as our perfect active participle.

14 unus ex tot milĭbus servōrum; e, ex is often used for the **Partitive Gen.** — miti ingenĭo, fortūna, **Causal Abl.** *604.*

15 movcrētur, respicĕret; **Subjunctives** after unus qui. *793. a.*

16 truci ferocitāte, pia..humanitāte; **Abl. of Manner.** *613.*

17 itāque cum velut occīsos alienasset, *therefore when he had removed them as if they had been killed.* — servisque de statu reipublicae deliberantĭbus placuisset, *and the slaves after deliberating on the state of affairs had resolved;* mihi placet, *I am of opinion, I resolve.*

18 regem creāri, eumque potissĭmum; **Acc. w. Inf.** depending on placuisset, *that a king should be appointed and in preference to all others he, &c.*

19 acceptissĭmum dis; **Dat.** after acceptus. *598.* — qui solem orientem primus vidisset, *who should first have seen the rising sun;* the **Subjunct.** in a clause depending upon the **Acc. w. Inf.**

22 medĭo noctis, *at midnight.*

24 vidēri, **Historical Inf.**

25 editissĭmisque culminĭbus, *on the highest roofs.*

26 oriens, sc. sol. — ut ipsum solem aspicĕrent, *to see the sun himself;* **Subjunctive** in a clause of *purpose* after ut.

29 visa, sc. est. — requirentĭbus..confitētur, *to those inquiring after..he confesses.*

30 intellectum est, *they saw clearly;* **Impers. Pass.** — quantum in- 24.
genŭa servilĭbus ingenĭa praestārent, *how much freeborn minds
excel those of slaves;* the Subjunctive is used in Indirect Question. *801.*

33 reservātos (sc. esse), **Acc. w. Inf.** depending on arbitrantes. —
creāre takes **two Acc.** *573.*

2 toto orbe terrārum; **Abl.** without the preposition to denote the 25.
place *where* when a noun is qualified by totus. *687.*

6 crucĭbus adfixit, *nailed them to the cross = crucified them;*
adfigĕre being compounded with ad takes the **Dat.** *592.*

8 ingenŭis et innoxĭis incŏlis insŭlae attribūtis, *having assigned
the freeborn and innocent inhabitants to the island;* **Abl. Abs.** — exstirpāto servīli germĭne, **Abl. Abs.**, *the breed of the slaves being ex-
tirpated.* — genus urbis, *the stock of the city.*

10 hoc modo, **Abl. of Manner.** *613.* — Tyrĭi Alexandri auspicĭis con-
dīti, *the Tyrians being established under the auspices of Alexander.*

11 parsimonĭa et labōre quaerendi, *by economy and acquisitive
disposition,* **Abl. of Means.**

12 missa in Afrĭcam juventūte, **Abl. Abs.**

13 cum intĕrim Mutto decĕdit, *while in the meantime Mutto died;*
this is *temporal* cum; accordingly it takes the **Indic.** *774.*

14 Pygmaliōne et Elissa heredĭbus institūtis, *having appointed
Pygmalion and Elissa his heirs;* **Abl. Abs.** — insignis formae virgĭne,
a virgin of great beauty; **Gen. of Quality.** *566. 5.*

17 qui honos, *a dignity which.* — nubit, *marries,* takes the
Dat. *589.*

18 huic magnae opes erant, *he owned great riches;* esse with the
Dat. of the *possessor.* *594.* — metu regis, *from fear of the king;*
Causal Abl. *604.*

21 qua, sc. re. — oblītus juris humāni, *forgetful of human law;*
verbs of *forgetting* take the **Gen.** *568.*

22 eundemque genĕrum, *and at the same time his brother-in-law;*
idem is often equivalent to an *adverbial* phrase. *717.*

23 aversāta, *having avoided;* the perfect participle of a deponent
verb may be used exactly as our perfect active participle. — dissimulāto odĭo mitigātōque vultu, **Abl. Abs.**; translate the participle
actively.

Page
25.   25 adsumptis quibusdam principĭbus in societătem, *having ad-
mitted a few chiefs into her company.* — quibus par odĭum in regem
esse; **Acc. w. Inf.** depending on arbitrabătur.

27 dolo, **Instrumental Abl.** — re renŏvet neve recurrat; clause of
purpose with ne and the Subjunctive.

28 ei cupĭdae obliviōnis, *to her desirous of forgetting;* cupĭdae is
in apposition to ei, and the **Gen.** obliviōnis depends on cupĭdae.
567. 1. — marĭti belongs to domus.

29 ocŭlis ejus occurrat, *should offer itself to her sight;* occurrĕre
being compounded with ob takes the **Dat.** *592.*

31 ventūrum, sc. esse.

32 a rege missos; the participle is best rendered by a *relative*
clause.

33 prima vespĕra; primus is often combined with a Substantive in order to denote that *part* of the thing which the Adjective
specifies: prima vespĕra, *at the first appearance of dark.* — provectăque in altum, sc. mare, *having proceeded out to the deep water.*

26.   1 onĕra harēnae pro pecunĭa involŭcris involūta, *loads of sand
which instead of the money had been packed into the cases;* invo-
lūcris, is **Instrumental Abl.**

2 lugubrĭque voce; **Abl. of Manner** without cum, *and with a plaintive voice.*

3 Acerbam ciet, *she invokes Acerbas.* — libens, the Adjective
instead of the Adverb. *550.*

6 olim, *hereafter, one day;* here of the future.

7 qui...subtraxĕrint, *who had taken away.* — quārum spe parricidĭum fecĕrit, *from the hope of which he (the king) had committed
parricide;* the Relative with the Subjunct. in a clause depending
upon an **Acc. w. Inf.**

8 subtraxĕrint takes the **Dat.** avaritĭae, to be translated by *from.*
588. — hoc metu omnĭbus injecto, *this fear having seized upon all.*

9 senatōrum in eam noctem praeparāta agmĭna, *the crowds of
senators who were ready for this night.*

10 sacris repetītis, *having recovered the sacred vessels.*

11 exsilĭo; the **Abl. of Manner** is often hardly to be distinguished
from that of *means.*

13 deōrum monĭtu; Verbal Abl. of Cause. *604.* — comĭtem se so- 26. cĭumque praebŭit, *offered himself as companion and ally;* prac-bēre, takes **two Acc.** *578.*

14 pactus, *having stipulated;* the perfect participle of a deponent verb may be used exactly as our perfect active participle.

16 accepta, sc. est. — virgĭnes admŏdum Cyprĭas, *very young Cyprian maidens;* raptas navĭbus impōni jubet, *ordered to be carried off AND put on board ship;* the Participle is best rendered by a co-ordinate sentence.

18 dum haec aguntur, *while these things are going on.*

19 impĭo bello, **Abl. of Means,** *with an impious war.*

20 aegre victus quiēvit, *he was only with difficulty restrained AND kept quiet.* — precĭbus matris deōrumque minis, **Instrum. Abl.** *605.*

21 canĕrent, *foretold;* since the responses of the oracles and prophets were usually sung in verse, canĕre signifies also *to foretell.* — urbis toto orbe auspicatissĭmae, *of a city founded under the most favorable auspices upon the whole earth.*

22 spatĭum respirandi fugientĭbus datum, *a breathing space was afforded to the fugitives.*

23 datum, sc. est. — delāta in Afrĭcae sinum, *having been carried into a bay of Africa.*

24 adventu and commercĭo are **Causal Abl.** depending on gaudentes, *rejoicing over. 604.*

25 empto loco, qui corĭo bovis tegi posset, *having bought as much ground as could be covered with the hide of an ox.* — qui for ut is, hence the Subjunctive.

26 in quo...reficĕre posset, *where she could refresh;* in quo for ut in eo. — fessos longa navigatiōne socĭos, *her companions weary of the long sea-voyage;* fessus takes the Abl. *604.*

27 quoad proficiscerētur, *until she would depart;* quoad, *until,* implying *purpose* or *futurity* takes the Subjunctive. *778.*

31 spe lucri, *from hope of profit;* **Causal Abl.**

33 instar civitātis, *an outline of a city.*

2 hortatīque sunt, urbem condĕrent, *and exhorted them to build* 27. *a city;* hortāri commonly takes ut with the Subjunctive; it may take the Subjunctive without ut. — ubi sedes sortīti essent, *where they had obtained settlements.*

3 Afros amor cepit, *a desire seized the Africans;* detineudi ad-vĕnas, depends on amor. — consentientĭbus omnĭbus, *by consent of all.* — statūto annŭo vectigāli, *a yearly tax being fixed.*

7 propter quod, *and therefore;* the relative instead of the demonstrative with a copulative particle.

9 auspicātam sedem, *a lucky foundation.*

10 ad opiniōnem novae urbis concurrentĭbus gentĭbus; the Abl. Abs: may be here rendered by a sentence with *when.*

11 magna facta, sc. est; the predicate agrees with the nearest word civĭtas, and is understood to popŭlus. *542.*

13 cujus virtus, *and its valor.* — rei publĭcae status, *the condition of the state.* — variis discordiārum casĭbus, *by various cases of dissension;* Abl. of Means.

15 cruenta sacrōrum religiōne, *bloody sacrifices;* Abl. depending on usi sunt. *626.*

18 aris admovēbant, *brought to the altars;* admovēre being compounded with ad takes the Dat. *592.* — pacem deōrum, depends on exposcentes. *580.*

19 pro quorum vita di rogāri maxĭme solent, *for whose life the gods are mostly and commonly supplicated;* the verb solēre may be conveniently rendered by the adverb *commonly* or *usually.*

C. Julius Caesar was born at Rome, July 12th, B. c. 100. By his valor and eloquence he soon acquired the highest reputation, and went through the usual course of political honors which the republic could bestow. Under the title and authority of a perpetual dictator he laid the foundation of the imperial constitution. But this provoked the hate of the liberal party, and on the Ides of March, B. c. 44, he was assassinated in the senate-house by a conspiracy under the lead of Brutus. In estimating the value of Caesar's writings it should be borne in mind that there are — strictly speaking — but two standard authors in the whole of the Roman literature: *Caesar* and *Cicero*.

---

10. *First landing in Britain.* Page

3 exigŭa parte aestātis relĭqua, *a small part of the summer being* 28. *left;* **Abl. Abs.** with an adjective instead of a participle. *836.*

4 matūrae sunt, *are early,* i. e., *set in early.*

5 omnĭbus fere Gallĭcis bellis, *nearly in all wars with Gaul. 673.* — inde, *from that quarter.* — administrāta, sc. esse, **Acc. w. Inf.** depending on intelligēbat.

7 si tempus anni ad bellum gerendum deficĕret, tamen arbitrabā- tur.., *if the season should be too late for carrying on war, still he believed;* one might have expected the Present deficiat here, the condition being represented as *possible. 788.* II. But frequently the Present Subjunctive of a future condition becomes Imperfect by the **Sequence of Tenses,** deficĕret being governed by arbitrabātur.

8 magno usŭi, *of great advantage;* **Dat.** to denote the *purpose* or *end. 595.* — si modo insŭlam adisset, *if he had only visited the island;* the Pluperfects adisset, perspexisset also depend on arbitra- bātur; si modo, *if only,* usually takes the **Indicative;** here the Sub- junctive is used in oratĭo oblīqua.

9 loca; only this form is used in the ordinary sense *"places". 191.*

Page

28. 10 quae omnĭa, *all of which.* — neque enim to be rendered with quisquam, *for no one.*

11 temĕre, *without good reason.* — neque quicquam, *and nothing.* — illo, *thither,* i. e., *to Britain.*

13 evocātis ad se mercatorĭbus, *having called the traders to him.*

14 esset, incolĕrent, habĕrent; all in the Subjunctive in the indirect question after reperīre potĕrat.

15 quem usum belli habĕrent, *in what way they carried on war.*

16 qui essent...idonĕi portus, *what suitable harbors there were.*

17 ad majōrum navĭum multitudĭnem idonĕi, *suitable for a great number of larger ships;* idonĕus takes the **Dat.** or ad w. **Acc.** *599.*

19 ad haec cognoscenda; ad with the **Gerundive** to denote *purpose.* *845.* — priusquam pericŭlum facĕret, *before making the trial;* priusquam has in narrative the same construction as *historical* cum. *779.*

20 idonĕum esse arbitrātus Gajum Voluscnum, *thinking Gaius Volusenus a fit person.* — cum navi longa, *with a galley,* a vessel propelled by a large number of oars.

21 huic mandat, ut revertātur, *he orders him to return;* verbs of *commanding* are followed by the **Dat.** with ut or ne. *738;* but jubĕo and veto take the **Acc. w. Inf.** *814.*

22 in Morĭnos, the people for the territory; the Morĭni occupied the nearest point to Britain.

24 quam..classem, *the fleet which;* the Antecedent classem incorporated into the relative sentence. *719.*

26 per mercatōres; the person considered as *means* or *instrument* is expressed by per with the **Acc.** *606.*

29. 1 qui polliceantur; the Subjunctive of *purpose* after qui. *792. 1.* obsĭdes dare; after the verbs *to promise, to hope,* &c., the Latins regularly use the **Fut. Inf.** with the **Acc.** of the pronoun expressed; but there are many instances of the **Pres. Inf.** instead of the Future, and also of the omission of the pronoun.

2 liberalĭter pollicĭtus, *having made liberal promises.*

3 ut..permanĕrent; ut with **Subjunct.** after hortāri. *758.*

7 magni habebātur, *was regarded as of great account,* **Gen.** of **Value.** *569.* — huic impĕrat, quas possit adĕat civitātes, *he orders him to visit what states he could;* the Subjunctives adĕat, hortĕtur, nuntĭet depend on ut, understood after impĕrat.

9 seque ventûrum (esse) nuntĭet, *and tell them that he is coming.* 29.

10 quantum ei facultātis dari potŭit, qui non audēret, *so far as opportunity could be given him since he did not venture;* the relative pronoun requires the Subjunctive when it denotes the *cause;* qui = cum is. *792.* II. — quantum facultātis, **Partitive Gen.** *566.* 6.

12 quaeque perspexisset, *what he had investigated;* the Subjunctive is used to express the belief of Voluscnus. The *historical* present renuntĭat is here followed by a *historical* tense, perspexisset, as usual.

14 in his locis, i. e., in the territory of the Morini. — navĭum parandārum causa; causa with the **Gen.** of **Gerund** or **Gerundive** to denote *purpose.* *843.*

15 morātur; the conjunction dum, *while, as,* is generally joined with the **Pres. Indic.** *734.*

16 qui se excusārent, *to apologize;* **Subjunctive of Purpose.** *792.* I. — de superiōris tempŏris consilĭo, *for their conduct of the past season.* — homĭnes barbări, *being barbarians = as they were barbarians.*

17 nostrae consuetudĭnis imperīti; the **Gen.** depends on the Adjective imperīti. *567.* 1.

18 fecissent; the Subjunctive is used to state the thoughts of another. *827.* — seque ea, quae imperasset, factūros pollicerentur; que connects pollicerentur to excusārent in the same construction; the **Acc. w. Inf.** se factūros (esse) after a verb of *promising.*

20 belli gerendi is to be joined to facultātem.

21 has tantulārum rerum occupatiōnes sibi Britannĭae anteponendas esse, *that engagements in such trifling affairs should be preferred to his expedition against Britain.* Britannĭae, the **Dative** depending on anteponendas *(592)* and equivalent to *his expedition against Britain.*

24 navĭbus circĭter octoginta onerarĭis coactis contractisque, *having brought together and concentrated about 80 ships of burden;* naves onerarĭae, *ships of burden,* opposed to naves longae, *galleys, ships of war.*

25 quot satis existimābat, *as many as he considered sufficient.* — ad duas legiōnes transportandas, *to carry across two legions.* *845.*

26 quod praetereă longārum navĭum habēbat, *all the galleys he had besides;* longārum navĭum is **Partitive Gen.** after quod. *566.* 6.

Page

29.   28 ex eo loco ab milĭbus passŭum octo, *eight miles from thence;* distance *how far* is put in the **Abl.**, commonly without any preposition; here ab is added. *681.*

29 vento tenebantur, quomĭnus possent, *were prevented by the wind from being able;* after verbs of *hindrance,* quomĭnus is used with the Subjunctive, where also ne, or if a negative precedes, quin may be used. *764.*

30 equitĭbus, *cavalry.* — relĭquum exercĭtum deducendum dedit; the **Gerundive** is used with the verb dare to express the *purpose* or *end* for which any thing is given. *841.*

30.   3 idonĕam ad navigandum tempestātem, *favorable weather for sailing;* the common construction of idonĕus is ad w. the **Acc.** *844.*

4 tertĭa fere vigilĭa, *about the third watch;* the third watch began at midnight; the Romans divided the night, from sunset to sunrise, into four equal watches. — solvit, supply naves, *he loosed the ships,* equivalent to the English expression, *he set sail* or *weighed anchor.*

5 se sequi jussit; se is here **Obj. Accusative,** *he ordered them to follow him.*

6 a quibus cum id; the Relative at the beginning of the sentence instead of a Demonstrative. — paulo tardĭus, *somewhat too tardily, rather tardily.* *705.*

7 hora diĕi circĭter quarta, *about the fourth hour of the day,* i. e., *about 10 o'clock in the morning.*

8 exposĭtas hostĭum copĭas armātas, *the forces of the enemy drawn up under arms.*

9 ita montĭbus angustis mare continebātur, *the sea was confined by mountains so close to it.*

11 ad egrediendum idonĕum locum, *a spot suitable for disembarking.*

12 dum relĭquae naves convenīrent; dum, *until,* takes the Subjunctive to denote the *design* in waiting at anchor. *778.*

13 ad horam nonam, *until the ninth hour,* i. e., *three o'clock in the afternoon.*

14 et quae ex Volusēno cognosset et quae fĭeri vellet; indirect questions depending upon ostendit.

15 monŭitque (ut rei militāris ratĭo, maximēque ut maritĭmae res postulārent, ut quae celĕrem atque instabĭlem motum habērent) ad nutum et ad tempus omnes res administrarentur, *and warned them*

that all things should be performed by them at a beck and at a 30.
*moment, as the principles of military discipline, and especially as
naval operations required, since they have a rapid and unstable
motion.* monŭit governs the Subjunctive without ut (administrarentur); ut, in the parenthesis, means *as*, and would govern the
Indicative, if not in oratio oblĭqua; the relative clause quae..habĕ-
rent is in the **Subjunctive** to denote the *cause;* in such sentences the
relative may be strengthened by ut or quippe. 792. II.

18 his dimissis, *when they were sent to their posts.* — et ventum
et aestum secundum, *both wind and tide favorable;* secundum belongs as well to ventum, as to aestum.

20 circĭter is here an adverb; milĭa passŭum septem, being the
Acc. of Distance *how far.* 681. — aperto ac plano littŏre, *where the
shore was open and level;* Abl. Absol.

22 praemisso equitātu et essedarĭis; the participle agrees with
the nearest noun and is to be understood to essedarĭis. — the essĕ-
dum was a two-wheeled war chariot, and the essedarĭus *the fighter
in a war chariot.*

23 quo genĕre, *a kind of force which,* is governed by uti, which
depends on consuērunt, for consuevērunt, from consuesco. 333.

24 relĭquis copĭis subsecūti, *having followed with the rest of their
troops;* the active participle, because subsĕqui is a Deponent Verb.
— nostros navĭbus egrĕdi prohibēbant, *endeavored to prevent our
men from disembarking;* after verbs of *hindering,* quomĭnus w. the
Subjunct. is generally used. 764; but prohibĕo is frequently followed
by the **Inf.**

26 in alto, *in deep water.*

27 militĭbus is to be taken with desiliendum, consistendum, pugnandum erat, *the soldiers had to leap, to maintain their position,
and to fight;* the **Dative** with the **Gerund** or **Gerundive** to denote the
person on whom the necessity rests. 596. — ignōtis locis, *in places
unknown to them;* Abl. to denote the place *where.* — impedītis
manĭbus, *with their hands engaged.*

28 gravi armōrum onĕre oppressis, is in apposition to militĭbus.

30 ex arĭdo, *from dry ground.*

31 omnĭbus membris expedīti, *having the free use of all their
limbs;* omnĭbus membris is the **Abl. of Limitation.** 608. — notissĭmis
locis, *in places which they knew perfectly;* opposed to ignōtis locis.

30.   32 equos insuefactos, *the horses trained to it.*

33 hujus genĕris puguae imperīti, *unskilled in this kind of battle;* pugnae depends on genĕris, and hujus genĕris on imperīti. *567. 1.*

31.   1 non eādem alacritāte et studĭo utebantur, *did not show the same alacrity and zeal;* Abl. depending on utebantur. *626.*

3 anīmum advertit, usually in one word, animadvertit; the **Perf. Indic.** is governed by ubi, *as soon as.* — naves longas is **Subject. Acc.** to removēri, incitāri, constitŭi; and hostes to propelli and submovēri; all these Passive Infinitives depend on jussit.

6 ad latus apertum hostīum constitŭi jussit, *ordered them to be stationed on the unprotected flank of the enemy.*   •

8 magno usŭi nostris fuit; both usŭi and nostris are governed by fuit; with the verb esse, besides the **Dative** of the *person,* another is used to denote the *purpose, intention, &c. 595.* — navīum figūra, remōrum motu, &c. permōti; the *moving cause* is often expressed by a participle, as, permōtus, *influenced, induced,* with the **Abl.**

12 qui decīmae legiōnis aquīlam ferēbat, *the eagle-bearer of the tenth legion.*

13 ut ea res legiōni felicīter evenīret, *that this undertaking might turn out successfully for the legion;* clause of *purpose* with ut.

15 meum officĭum praestitĕro, *I will promptly discharge my duty;* the **Perf. Fut.** is here used to denote the *speedy completion* of an act.

17 cohortāti inter se, *having exhorted each other,* i. e., *under mutual exhortations.* — ne tantum dedēcus admitterētur; ne (in a negative sense) is used with the **Subjunct.** after verbs of *exhorting.*

18 hos item ex proxīmis navĭbus cum conspexissent; supply milītes as subject.

11. On the habits of the Germans.

22 multum a consuetudīne Gallōrum diffĕrunt, *differ widely from the custom of the Gauls;* verbs compounded with dis nearly always take ā or ăb with the Abl. *621.*

23 druĭdes, the ministers of religion among the Gauls and Britons — qui rebus divīnis praesint; qui w. the **Subjunctive** to denote the *purpose,* for ut ii, *to preside over the religious rites.*

24 sacrificiis studēre, *to pay much attention to sacrifices.*

26 relĭquos ne fama quidem accepērunt, *of the rest they did not even know by hearsay.*

27 in studĭis rei militāris, *in military pursuits.*

30 in annos singŭlos, *for one year at a time;* time *for how long* is expressed by the Acc. w. in. 677.

31 gentĭbus cognationĭbusque, *to the tribes and families.* — qui una coiĕrint, *who should have united;* or *such as had united;* **Fut. Perf.**

32 quantum et quo loco visum est, *as much land and where they see fit.*

1 alĭo, *to a different quarter.* — ejus rei multas causas affĕrunt, 32. *they advance many reasons for this practice.* — ne adsidŭa consuetudĭnc capti, studĭum belli gerendi agricultūra commūtent, *that they might not, enslaved by long continued custom, divert their attention from war to agriculture;* this and the following clauses of *purpose* refer to transīre cogunt.

3 latos fines parāre, *to acquire extensive possessions.*

4 possessionĭbus expellant, *drive from their property;* after verbs of *removing* the **Abl. of Separation** is used, with or without a preposition. 620. — accuratĭus, *with greater care.* — ad frigŏra atque aestus vitandos; ad with the **Gerundive** expressing *purpose,* instead of ut w. the **Subjunct.** — vitandos agrees with aestus, and is to be understood to frigŏra.

5 ne qua oriātur pecunĭae cupidĭtas; qua for alĭqua; indefinite pronoun after ne. 758. — pecunĭae cupidĭtas is the **Object Gen.,** *greediness for money.* 566. 2.

7 aequitāte anĭmi plebem continĕant, *that they might control the mass by evenness of temper,* i. e., *by contentedness.* — cum quisque vidĕat, *since every one saw;* causal cum takes the **Subjunct.** 786. — cum potentissĭmis for cum opĭbus potentissimōrum, *with those of the mightiest.*

9 quam latissĭmas solitudĭnes, *deserts as extensive as possible.*

10 vastātis finĭbus, *by the desolation of their frontiers.* — proprĭum virtūtis, *a proof of valor.*

11 expulsos agris finitĭmos cedĕre, neque quemquam prope audēre consistĕre, *that,* or *when the neighbors, being driven from their estates, retire, and nobody dares to stay near them.*

12 hoc, *thereby.*

13 repentīnae incursiōnis timōre sublāto, *the fear of a sudden in-cursion being taken away.* — cum bellum civĭtas illātum defendit, *when a state repels a war that has been waged upon it.*

14 qui ei bello praesint; the Subjunctive clause denoting the *pur-pose,* the relative being equivalent to ut hi. 792. I.

15 ut vitae necisque potestātem habĕant, *so that they have power of life and death,* is a clause of *result.* — in pace, *in time of peace.* 673.

17 inter suos, *among their followers.*

18 latrocinĭa, quae fiunt, *robberies which are committed.*

19 juventŭtis exercendae ac desidĭae minuendae causa, *for the sake of exercising youth and diminishing idleness;* the **Gen.** of the **Gerund** or **Gerundive** with causa is a very common way of expressing *design.* 843.

20 ubi quis ex principĭbus dixit, *as soon as some one of the leaders said;* ubi takes the Perf. Ind. 737. II. — ubi, being a relative particle must be followed by quis. — ex principĭbus; the preposition ex is used instead of the **Part. Gen.**

21 qui sequi velint, profiteantur, *and that those who wish to follow him may give in their names;* **Subjunct.** in oratĭo oblīqua.

22 causam, *the enterprise.*

25 omnĭumque iis rerum postĕa fides derogātur, *and all credit in every thing is after this withheld from them;* verbs of *taking away* are followed by the **Dat.**, to be translated by *from.*

26 qui quaque de causa, *all persons who on any account what-ever.* — venĕrint, **Fut. Perfect.**

M. TULLIUS CICERO.

M. Tullius Cicero was born in the year of Rome 647, or about 105 years before Christ. His father who was of the equestrian order took great care of his education which was directed particularly with a view to the bar. In Greece he attended the Athenian orators and philosophers, and improved greatly both in eloquence and knowledge. From Athens Tully passed into Asia and after an excursion of two years returned to Italy. In his forty-third year Cicero was proclaimed consul. For his services in suppressing the conspiracy which had been formed by Catiline he was honored with the title of Pater Patriae or *Father of his Country*. Cicero's death happened on the 7th of December, in the sixty-fourth year of his age, about ten days after the first triumvirate. The extracts here given are from Cicero's philosophical writings.

12. Solon.

Page

5 scripsĕrit; the Subjunctive in a relative clause depending on an 33. **Acc. w. Inf.** *826.*

6 quod..simulavĕrit; as a rule, quod takes the **Indic.**, but the Subjunctive is used to express the thought of some other person. *782.* — quo tutior esset et prodesset; quo is a favorite *final* conjunction with *Comparatives*. *763.*

8 cur..constituisset; **Subjunct.** in indirect question. *801.* — qui necasset; the Subjunctive in a clause depending upon an **Acc. w. Inf.** *826.*

10 sapienter fecisse dicĭtur, *they say he acted sensibly;* **Nom. w. Inf.** *821.*

11 cum nihil sanxĕrit; cum, *whereas, since,* takes the **Subjunct.** *786.* — cum de eo nihil sanxĕrit, quod antĕa commissum non erat, *not having enacted a law against a crime which had not been committed heretofore.* — ne non tam prohibēre quam admonēre viderētur, *lest it should seem he had not so much forbidden as called attention to it;*

33. any verb used as, a verb of *willing* or *demanding* may have the construction with ut or ne denoting a *purpose*. *758.*

14 si qui; qui, after si, is an Indefinite Pronoun = alĭquis. *762.*

15 honestum illud Solōnis est, *that is an excellent thing of Solon.*

16 multa in dies addiscentem, *while learning much every day.* — qua voluptāte anĭmi nulla potest esse major, *a pleasure of the mind than which there can be certainly none greater;* the **Abl.** instead of quam with the same case as the thing compared must be regularly used in the Relative Clause. *610.*

17 prudentĭbus et bene institūtis; the **Dat.** of the indirect object, *in sensible and well-educated men.*

20 hoc illud est, quod Pisistrăto a Solōne responsum est, *this is the well-known answer Pisistratus got from Solon.*

22 cum illi quaerenti qua tandem spe fretus sibi tam audacĭter obsistĕret, respondisse tradĭtur: senectūte; *who as we are told, upon the former inquiring on what hope now he (Solon) relied to oppose him so boldly, replied "on old age".* — illi quaerenti, viz.: Pisistrăto, depends on respondisse. — qua spe fretus; fretus takes the **Abl.** *625.*

23 obsistĕret; the **Subjunct.** in an *indirect question.* — respondisse tradĭtur, **Nom. w. Inf.**, *he is said to have replied,* or, *replied, as we are told;* sometimes it is well to insert the verb of *saying* in a parenthetical clause.

24 quo se negat velle, &c., *in which he **says** that he does **not** wish;* the verb negāre is often conveniently translated *to say that not.*

25 dolōre et lamentis vacāre; vacāre, *to be void of,* takes the **Abl.** *622;* the same as carēre, *to be without,* in the following line.

26 **Hexameter.** $\underline{\prime}\ \cup\cup\ |\ \underline{\prime}\ \cup\cup\ |\ \underline{\prime}\ \cup\cup\ |\ \underline{\prime}\ \cup\cup\ |\ \underline{\prime}\ \cup\cup\ |\ \underline{\prime}\ \underline{\cup}$
Mors mea ne careat † lacrimis; linquamus amicis.

Pentameter. $\underline{\prime}\ \cup\cup\ |\ \underline{\prime}\ \cup\cup\ |\ \underline{\prime}\ \|\ \underline{\prime}\ \cup\cup\ |\ \underline{\prime}\ \cup\cup\ |\ \_$
Maerorem, ut celebrent funera cum gemitu.

This is an **Elegiac Distich** (*919*), consisting of a *Hexameter* followed by a *Pentameter.* In reading, the final syllable of maerō-rem is suppressed by Elision. *887.* — ne carĕat, linquămus, *let not be without, let us leave;* the **Subjunct.** is used to express an *exhortation* or *command;* **Imperative Subjunct.** *752.*

27 ut celĕbrent, clause of *result; so that they may celebrate.*

13. Leonidas.

2 mortes imperatoriae, *the death of generals;* in Latin the plural of abstract nouns occurs more frequently than in English; so mortes, because there were several generals. *694.*

6 anĭmo forti, *with good cheer;* Abl. of Manner.

7 alăcri magnōque anĭmo, *with active and lofty courage;* Abl. of Manner.

8 in quos Simonĭdes, supply ait, *in whose honor Simonĭdes says.*

```
 ⏑⏑│   ⏑⏑│   ⏑⏑│  ⏑⏑│   ⏑ ⏑│   ⏑
```
9 Hexameter. Dic, hospes, Spartae † nos te vidisse jacentes.

```
 ⏑⏑│_  ⏑ ⏑│ ‖   ⏑ ⏑│   ⏑ ⏑│ _
```
Pentameter. Dum sanctis patriae legibus obsequimur.

This is another **Elegiac Distich,** the epitaph of the three hundred brave Spartans who defended the Straits of Thermopylae. — nos te vidisse jacentes; nos is **Object Acc.** and te **Subject Acc.;** the context shows which is the real subject.

13 prae multitudĭne, *on account of the multitude;* prae is frequently used in the sense of *on account of,* implying an obstacle. *662.*

15 qualis tandem Lacaena? *what of that Spartan woman?*

17 ut esset qui non dubităret, *that there should be some one who would not hesitate;* non dubĭto, *I do not doubt,* takes quin; *766;* with the **Inf.** it means: *I do not hesitate.*

14. Themistocles.

21 belli quod cum Persis fuit, *of the Persian war.*

22 consilĭum rei publĭcae salutāre, *a plan which would be serviceable to the state.*

23 sed id sciri non opus esse, *but it was necessary that it should not be made public.* — postulāvit ut popŭlus alĭquem daret, *he demanded that the people should appoint a person;* verbs of *demanding* take ut.

24 quocum communicāret, *to whom he might communicate it;* quocum is for ut cum eo; accordingly, the verb is in the **Subjunct.** *792.* I. — huic ille, supply dixit.

25 quae subducta esset, *which was hauled ashore = which had gone into harbor;* the **Subjunct.** in oratio obliqua.

26 quo facto frangi Lacedaemoniōrum opes necesse esset, *and thus the power of the Lacedaemonians must of necessity be broken;*

Page

34. quo facto is **Abl. Abs.**, *this being done* = *thus;* the Subjunctive esset in oratīo oblīqua.

27 quod cum audisset, *having heard this;* the relative pronoun is to be translated by a demonstrative.

28 magna exspectatiōne, *amid the great expectation of all;* it is properly **Abl. Abs.**

29 adferret, the **Subjunct.** in oratīo oblīqua.

30 quod honestum non esset, *which was not honorable;* the Subjunctive is used to express the opinion of Aristides.

32 auctōre Aristīde, **Abl. Abs.**, but it may be rendered, *upon the authority of Aristides.*

35. 1 fertur, dicītur, *is said;* **Nom. w. Inf.** *821.* — incredibīli quadam magnitudīne consilii atque ingenii, *a man of an almost incredible amount of prudence and capacity;* **Abl. of Quality.** *615.*

2 ad quem = et ad eum.

5 se ei traditūrum (esse), *that he would teach him.*

6 dixisse illum doctōrem; the author here departs from the former construction of the **Nom. w. Inf.** and uses the **Acc. w. Inf.**; of course we must supply dicītur, *it is said;* it will greatly simplify the rendering of a passage like this, to drop the form of indirect discourse, inserting the verb *of saying* in a parenthetical clause: *as they say — a certain learned man came to him,* &c.

7 gratīus sibi illum esse factūrum, *he would do him a greater favor.*

8 si se oblivisci quam meminisse docuisset, *if he could teach him to forget rather than to remember.*

10 quod somnum capĕre non posset, *because* (as he said) *he could not find sleep;* quod takes the **Subjunct.** in oratīo oblīqua.

14 non sua sed patrīae glorīa, *not by his own but by his country's glory;* **Instrumental Abl.**

15 si ego Scriphīus essem &c.; the condition is *contrary to fact.* *788.* III.

18 collocāret; the **Subjunct.** in indirect question.

19 qui pecunīa egĕat, *who has no money* = *without money;* egĕo, takes the **Abl.** *622.*

15. Alexander the Great.

21 qua nocte ... eādem, for eādem nocte qua; the Antecedent
incorporated into the relative clause. *719*; begin with constat, *it
is well known.*

22 ex Olympiădo natum; Participles of *birth* take the **Abl.** with or
without ex. *604.* — atque ubi lucēre coepisset; ubi originally takes
the Indicative, but here the **Subjunct.** is used because it depends on
an **Inf.**; Attraction of Mood. *826.*

25 quod Diăna ... abfuisset domo; **Subjunct.** by Attraction of
Mood. *826.*

30 qui tuae virtūtis Homērum praecōnem invenĕris, *to have found
a proclaimer of your valor in Homer;* when qui = cum is, the
Subjunct. is employed. *792.* **II.**

31 nisi exstitisset; the condition is represented as *contrary to fact.*
788. **III.**

2 eōque vulnĕre..morerētur, *came near dying from this wound.* **36.**

3 adsīdens, *sitting up with him.* — secundum quiētem, *while
asleep, in a dream.*

4 visus ei dicĭtur draco radicŭlam ore ferre et dicĕre, *as they say,
the dragon appeared to him carrying a little root in its mouth, and
telling him;* **Nom. w. Inf.**; the verb of *saying* is best rendered in a
parenthetical clause.

5 quo illa loco nascerētur, *where it grew.*

6 ejus autem vim esse tantam; this **Acc. w. Inf.** depends on dicĕre.

7 ut.. sanāret; clause of *result* after tantam. *759.*

8 emisisse; translate this Infinitive depending upon dicĭtur (which
must of course be understood) by the Indicative. — qui quaercĕrent,
to seek; the subjunctive clause denoting the *purpose;* qui = ut ii.

9 Ptolemaeus sanātus dicĭtur; the predicate sanātus dicĭtur agrees
with Ptolemaeus, and is understood to multi milĭtes.

11 quiddam praesentĭens atque divīnans, *some touch of presage
and divination.*

13 in radicĭbus Caucăsi, *at the foot of the Causasus.*

14 quo..comburerētur, for ut eo comburerētur; the Relative with
the **Subjunct.** to denote the *purpose.*

15 O praeclārum discessum; the **Acc.** is used in *exclamations.* **585.**

36. 17 cumque eum rogăret, si quid vellet, ut dicĕret, *and when he asked him, if he wanted to say anything, to do so;* rogăre takes ut. *758.*

16. Dionysius, Tyrant of Syracuse.

24 qua pulchritudĭne urbem, quibus autem opĭbus praedĭtam servitŭte oppressam tenŭit civitâtem, *of what beauty was the city possessed, and moreover, how rich was the state which he held oppressed in slavery!* pulchritudĭne and opĭbus depend on praedĭtam *(623),* which belongs to both urbem and civitâtem.

26 sic scriptum accepĭmus, *we have so received it in writing,* i. e., *we are so informed.*

28 eundem tamen, *yet at the same time;* idem equivalent to an adverbial expression. *717.* — natûra, *from his natural disposition;* **Abl. of Limitation.**

·29 ex quo, *from this, for this reason.* — omnĭbus bene veritâtem intuentĭbus, *to all who look well into truth.*

30 vidēri necesse est miserrĭmum, *he must of necessity appear to be very wretched.* — ea quae, *those things which.*

31 ne tum quidem, cum omnia se posse censēbat, *not even at the time when he believed he could do anything = when he considered himself all-powerful.*

37. 1 cum, *though,* concessive conjunction with **Subjunct.** *769.* — honesto loco natus, *sprung from a decent family;* Participles of birth may take the **Abl.** with or without the preposition e, ex.

2 alĭus alĭo modo, *one in one way, and the other in another;* alĭus is used in a peculiar way with other cases of itself, where we use two sentences, with *one* and *another.* *729.* — abundâret aequalĭum familiaritatĭbus et conusetudĭne propinquōrum, *he had extensive and intimate acquaintance with his equals and ample social intercourse with his relatives;* abundâre, takes the **Abl.** *622.*

4 ex familĭis, *from the households;* familĭa, *the slaves in a household* (not = *family,* i. e., *wife and children*).

5 quibus .. detraxĕrat, *from whom he had taken away;* quibus is the **Dat.** of the *Indirect Object* to be rendered by *from.*

7 propter injustam dominâtus cupiditâtem, *in consequence of his iniquitous greed of power.*

10 sordĭdo atque ancillâri artificĭo, **Abl. of Manner;** *by the mean service of a handmaid.*

11 ab eis ipsis ferrum remōvit, *and even from them he removed* 37. *the iron,* i. e., *the razor;* verbs of *removing* require the **Abl.**; with persons the preposition a, ab must be used. *620.*

12 instituit ut, *he ordered that.*

13 candentĭbus juglandĭum putaminĭbus, **Instrum. Abl.**

17 cum fossam latam cubiculāri lecto circumdedisset, *having surrounded his resting place with a broad ditch;* circumdăre, takes a Dative with an Acc., or an Acc. with an Abl. *593.*

26 quia demonstravisset..quia approbavisset; quia, *because,* of itself is followed by the Indicative; here the **Subjunct.** is used in oratĭo oblīqua. — viam interimendi sui, *the way to kill him.*

28 eo facto sic doluit, *he was so sorry for his deed;* dolēre takes the **Causal Abl.** *604.* — nihil ut tulērit gravĭus in vita, *that nothing lay harder upon him during his whole life;* clause of *result* after sic ut. *759.*

29 quem, supply eum.

30 impotentĭum cupiditātes, *the passions of those who are not masters of themselves.*

31 quamquam, *notwithstanding.* — quam beātus esset; the **Subjunct.** in indirect question.

32 quidam ex ejus adsentatorĭbus, *one of his flatterers;* the preposition ex in a partitive sense.

2 negāretque unquam beatiōrem quemquam fuisse, *and said that* 38. *there had never been any luckier person;* negāre, *to say that not.*

5 in aurĕo lecto strato pulcherrĭmo textīli stragŭlo magnifĭcis operĭbus picto, *on a golden couch spread with a very fine textile fabric magnificently embroidered;* strato belongs to lecto; pulcherrĭmo textīli is **Instrumental Abl.** depending on strato; again, picto belongs to stragŭlo, and magnifĭcis operĭbus is the **Abl. of Means or Instrument** depending on picto.

8 eximĭa forma puĕros, *slaves of great beauty;* **Abl. of Quality.**

9 nutum illīus intuentes diligenter ministrāre, *awaiting his beck to attend upon him carefully.* — adĕrant, *there were also.*

13 saeta equīna aptum, *fastened with a horse-hair;* aptus is the Participle of apo, –ĕre, *to fasten.*

14 ut impendēret, clause of *result, so that it hung over.*

15 plenum artis argentum, *silver plate richly wrought* (lit. full of art); plenus takes the **Gen.** *567.*

38. 18 quod jam beātus nollet esse, *because,* as he said, *he did not want any longer to be happy;* quod takes the **Subjunct.** to express the intention of Damocles; jam with the negation in nollet is equivalent to *no longer.*

19 cui semper alĭqui terror impendĕat; the **Subjunct.** in a clause dependent on the **Inf.** esse. *826.*

21 Damōnem et Phintĭam ferunt hoc anĭmo fuisse ut, *as they say, Damon and Phintias entertained such sentiments towards each other that;* hoc anĭmo is **Abl. of Quality.**

24 commendandōrum suōrum causa, *for the sake of commending his family.* — vas factus sit alter ejus sistendi, depends on ut, *that the one became bail for the appearance of the other in court;* Clause of result. — vas ejus sistendi, *bail for his appearing in court.*

25 ut, si ille non revertisset, moriendum esset ipsi, *that if the former had not returned, the latter should die himself;* the **Subjunctives** of the **Imperf.** and **Pluperf.** are required by the Sequence of Tenses.

26 ad diem, *on the appointed day;* ad is used to denote a *fixed time. 629.*

27 tyrannus petīvit ut; verbs of *demanding* take ut. *758.* — se refers to tyrannus.

30 secundissĭmo vento, *with a very favorable wind.*

31 quam bona navigatĭo..detur, *what a fine voyage is given;* **Subjunct.** in indirect question.

33 homo acūtus, *the sharp fellow.* — bene planēque percepisset, *had learned this full well.*

39. 3 grandi pondĕre, *of great weight;* **Abl. of Quality.**

5 aestāte grave esse, &c., depends on cavillātus est, which implies dicens.

6 eīque lanĕum pallĭum injēcit, *and put on him a woollen cloak;* injicĕre, takes the **Dat.** *592.* — cum id esse aptum ad omne anni tempus dicĕret, *because, as he said, this was suitable to every season.*

8 neque enim convenīre bărbātum esse filĭum, &c., depending on an implied dicens, *for it was also not becoming in a son to have a beard.*

11 in quibus quod, for et quod in iis; the Relative instead of the

Page 39.

Demonstrative at the beginning of the sentence; in quibus quod inscriptum esset: Bonōrum Deōrum, *and because there was an inscription on them*, or, *because they bore the inscription "Of the good gods";* inscribĕre, takes in w. the **Abl.** *689.* — inscriptum esset, **Impers. Pass.** *423;* the **Subjunctive** is used in oratio oblīqua.

13 quae simulacrōrum porrectis manĭbus sustinebantur, *which were held up in the outstretched hands of the images.*

15 esse enim stultitĭam, a quibus bona precarēmur, ab eis porrigentĭbus et dantĭbus nolle sumĕre, *that it was a folly not to take willingly blessings from those whom we supplicate, when they present and give them;* this is a common Latin construction, the relative clause standing first; in English this is unusual; precarēmur is in the **Subjunct.** being dependent on the Inf. esse.

16 porrigentĭbus et dantĭbus; the Participles may be translated *when they offer and give them.*

17 cumdem, *likewise;* idem is here equivalent to an adverb. *717.* — haec quae dixi sublāta de fanis, *the above-mentioned objects which he had taken from the temples.*

19 exactāque pecunĭa, *having exacted the money.* — edixisse ut; verbs of *ordering* take ut. *758.* — ut quod quisque a sacris habēret, id ante diem certam in suum quidque fanum referret, *that before a certain day, each one should bring back what he possessed of the sacred objects, each one to its own temple.* — quod quisque a sacris; sometimes a, ab w. the **Abl.** is used instead of a Genitive.

21 ad impietātem in deos in homĭnes adjunxit injurĭam, *he added to impiety towards the gods injustice towards men;* words of kindred meaning are put side by side for the sake of *emphasis*, here in deos in homĭnes.

17. Socrates.

23 de Socrăte accepĭmus, *we have heard of Socrates.*

24 divīnum quiddam (quod daemonĭum appellat), *a divine something (which he called demon).*

25 cui semper ipse paruĕrit, *which he himself always obeyed;* the **Subjunct.** in a clause depending upon an **Acc. w. Inf.** — numquam impellenti, saepe revocanti; closely related to cui, *which however never impelled but often restrained him.*

26 quo quem auctōrem meliōrem quaerĭmus? The **Abl. of Comparison** must be regularly used in relative sentences. *610; and what better author are we looking for than he?*

39. 27 Xenophonti consulenti depends on ait. — sequereturne, *whether he should follow;* **Subjunct.** in indirect question.

28 quae sibi videbantur, *what seemed proper to himself.* — et nostrum quidem consilīum humānum est, *and our understanding is indeed human.*

30 ad Apollīnem censĕo referendum, *I believe we should refer to Apollo.*

31 de majorĭbus rebus, *about more important affairs.*

32 scriptum est, **Impers. Pass.**, *it has been communicated.*

40. 1 ocŭlum adligātum vidisset, *(when) he had seen his eye bound up.* — quid esset, *what was the matter;* **Subjunct.** in indirect question.

2 ambulanti ramŭlum adductum, ut remissus esset in ocŭlum suum recidisse, *that to him while walking a strained twig, when it was slackened, had recoiled into his eye.*

3 tum Socrătes, sc. ait.

4 cum utĕrer qua solĕo praesagitiōne divīna, *when I availed myself, as usual, of the divine presentiment.*

5 cum apud Delīum male pugnātum esset, **Impers. Pass.**, *when they had calamitously fought at Delium* = *after the defeat at Delium.*

7 ut ventum est in trivĭum, *when they had come to a cross road.* — eādem qua cetĕri (supply via), *by the same road as the rest;* the way *by which* is in the **Abl.** **688.**

8 quibus quaerentĭbus, *when they asked him.*

12 vult, *is of opinion.*

13 pusiōnem quemdam Socrătes interrŏgat quaedam, *Socrates asks an urchin sundry questions;* interrogāre takes **two Acc.** **581.**

16 eōdem pervenĭat quo (supply pervenīret) si geometrĭca didicisset, *he reaches the same point which he would reach, had he studied geometry;* the condition is *contrary to fact,* accordingly si with the **Imperf.** or **Pluperf. Subjunct.** is employed. **788.** III. — ex quo effĭci vult Socrătes, *whence Socrates means it to be understood that &c.*

18 cum ex eo esset quaesītum nonne, *when he was asked whether.*

21 ain tu? = aisne tu? *do you really mean so?* — an, *or;* sometimes the first part of an alternative question is omitted, and ăn alone asks a question. **798.**

Page

23 beātusne sit, *whether he is happy;* Subjunct. in indirect question. 40.
— an ego possim, *how could I;* Potential Subjunct. *750.*

24 cum ignōrem quam sit doctus, quam vir bonus, *since I do not know in how far he is a learned and good man.*

25 quid? tu in eo sitam vitam beātam putas? *why? do you think a happy life depends upon this?*

26 bonos beātos, imprŏbos misĕros, sc. esse.

32 quam si ei viderētur ediscĕret, *to learn it by heart, if it seemed good to him;* quam ediscĕret, the Subjunct. after the relative to denote *purpose;* quam for ut eam. *792.* I. — pro se, *in his behalf.*

33 non invītus, *not unwillingly,* i. e., *cheerfully.* In Latin as in English an assertion is sometimes made by denying the opposite, and the double negative is often stronger than the opposite positive.

2 quia non essent; the Subjunct. in oratĭo oblĭqua.   41.

5 quibus tantum statuēbant judĭces, damnārent an absolvĕrent, *whereby the judges only decided whether they would condemn or acquit.*

7 legĭbus, *according to the laws;* Abl. of Limitation. *608.* — ferre (sententĭam), *to give a vote.* — erat reo damnāto quasi poenae aestimatĭo, *a condemned culprit had, to some extent, a naming of his own punishment.*

8 et sententĭa cum judicĭbus darētur, *when it came to the jury to pass sentence;* lit. *when the sentence was given to the jury.*

9 interrogabātur reus quam quasi aestimatiōnem commeruisse se maxĭme confiterētur, *the defendant was asked what punishment he would confess he had properly deserved.*

13 qui honos apud Graecos maxĭmus habētur, *an honor which is considered the highest among the Greeks.*

15 capĭtis condemnārent; verbs of *condemning* with the Acc. of the *person* take the Gen. of the *punishment.* *570.*

16 apud Platōnem; apud with the name of an author means *in the writings of, in.* *630.* — Socrătes est dicens, *Socrates is introduced saying.*

19 Homerĭcum quemdam ejusmōdi versum, *some such verse of Homer.*

21 Hexameter. Tertia te Phthiae tempestas lacta locabit; *the*

Page

41. *third happy day will bring you to Phthia;* Phthia was the birth-place of Achilles; the meaning of the verse is, just as Achilles there-in says *"that in three days he will be home in Phthia, so you will be home in three days".*

28 duas esse vias &c.; this whole section down to esse faciendum is in the oratio oblīqua.

31 republīca violanda, *by betraying their country.*

32 eis devīum quoddam iter esse, *they had some by-way;* **Dat.** de-noting the *possessor.*

42. 1 quibusque fuisset minīma cum corporībus contagīo, *who had had least connection with their bodies.*

4 itāque commemŏrat, ut cycni cum cantu et voluptāte morian-tur, sic omnībus bonis et doctis esse faciendum, *and so he mentions that, just as swans die amid song and joy, so all good and learned men ought to do.* The oratio oblīqua is here resumed after comme-mŏrat; the intermediate clause qui non sine causa Apollīni dicāti sint, sed quod ab eo divinatiōnem habēre videantur qua providentes quid in morte boni sit, belongs to cycni, *the swans which are not without reason dedicated to Apollo, but because they seem to have from him a divination by which they foresee what a blessing there is in death.*

16 praeclāre id quidem, supply dixit. — qui permisĕrit et osten-dĕrit; the relative qui = cum is, to denote the *cause;* hence the **Subjunct.**, *because he was obliging to his friend and showed that he himself did not care about the whole affair.*

18. Demosthenes.

22 cumque ita balbus esset, *and although he was so stammering he stammered so badly;* concessive cum takes the **Subjunct.** 767.

23 cui studēret; the clause depends upon the **Subjunct.** esset, and is, therefore, itself in the **Subjunct.** — studēre takes the **Dat.** 589.

24 perfēcit meditando, *he brought it about by practising.*

25 cum spirītus ejus esset angustīor, *as his breath was rather short* = *as he was rather short of breath;* tantum continenda anīma in dicendo est adsecūtus, *he made up for it by arresting the cur-rent of air in speaking.*

26 ut una continuatiōne verbōrum binae ei contentiōnes vocis et remissiōnes continerentur, *so that in one continuous outflow of*

words two elevations and two depressions of the voice at a time 42.
were contained.

28 qui etĭam; the Relative for the Demonstrative.

29 summa voce, *at the top of his voice.*

30 uno spirĭtu, *in one breath.* — neque is, *and that not;* when a
quality is ascribed with emphasis to an object, Is with a copulative
particle is used. *715.*

31 adscensu ingredĭens ardŭo, *walking up a steep ascent.*

6 quid hoc levĭus? sc. est; *what could be sillier than this?* hoc, 43.
Abl. of Comparison.

8 sine actiōne, *without action,* i. e., *without a good delivery,* or
without the proper ornament of voice and gesture.

9 medĭocris hac instructus, *a middling one, if provided with it.*
— primas dare, *to give the first place.*

11 quo mihi melĭus etĭam illud ab Aeschĭne dictum vidēri solet,
*and the well-known saying of Aeschines commonly seems to me
still better than this;* quo is the **Abl. of Comparison,** for quam id; solet
is here best rendered by an Adverb, *commonly.*

12 qui cum, *the latter when;* the Relative instead of a Demonstrative.

13 propter ignominĭam judicĭi, *in consequence of a disgrace inflicted by the court,* **Subject. Gen.**

15 quam in Ctesiphontem contra Demosthĕnem dixĕrat, *which he,
as prosecutor of Ctesiphon, had pronounced against Demosthenes.*

17 pro Ctesiphonte, *as counsel for Ctesiphon.*

18 admirantĭbus omnĭbus, **Abl. Absol.**

19 quanto magis miraremĭni, *how much more would you have
been surprised;* the condition being represented as *impossible,* the
Imperf. or **Pluperf. Subjunct.** must be employed. *788.* III.

20 ex quo satis significāvit, quantum esset in actiōne, *hereby he
pointed out well enough how much lay in a good delivery.*

21 qui putārit (putavĕrit); qui = cum is, to denote cause, *since
he was of opinion.* *792.* II. — actōre mutāto, **Abl. Abs.** representing
a condition, *the speaker being changed,* i. e. *when delivered by another speaker. 833.*

19. The best sauce.

24 negāvit se umquam.., *he said he had never.*

25 scilĭcet, *the plain reason was.* — sitĭens, *being thirsty.*

26 esurĭens, *being hungry.* — cui cum peragranti Aegyptum cibarĭus panis datus esset, *when coarse bread had been given to him on his tour through Egypt.*

28 illo pane jucundĭus, *more delicious than that bread*; **Abl. of Comparison.**

29 contentĭus, *very vigorously;* contente (from contendĕre), *with great exertion.*

30 quo melĭus cenāret, *to have a better supper;* quo with the **Subjunct.** in clauses of *purpose,* especially with Comparatives. **703.**

31 opsonāre ambulando famem, *that he was purveying hunger,* i. e. *that he was getting up an appetite by walking;* opsonāre from Greek ὀψωνέω (ὄψον ὠνέομαι), *to go to market.* — ambulando, **Abl. of Means.**

32 in phiditĭis, *in the public meals of the Lacedaemonians.*

44. 4 ad Eurōtam, *on the banks of the Eurotas.*

7 ut quidquid objectum est; quidquid is used to express emphatically *anything whatever which.*

8 quod modo a natūra non sit aliēnum, *provided it is not contrary to their nature;* modo, *if only, provided,* takes the **Subjunct. 790.** — eo contentae, *satisfied with it;* contentus takes the **Abl.**

9 civitātes quaedam universae, *there are whole nations which.*

11 quos negat ad panem adhibēre quidquam praeter nasturtĭum, *of whom he says that they do not eat anything with their bread but water-cress.*

20. Burial service at Athens.

14 a Cecrōpe, *from the time of Cecrops.* — mos corpus terra humandi, *the custom of burying the body in the earth.*

18 quas inībant propinqui coronāti, *to which the relatives went decorated with garlands.*

19 apud quos, *in whose presence.*

20 justa confecta erant, *the customary rites were finished.*

23 apud Solōnem, *in the laws of Solon.*

24 "ne quis ea delĕat neve aliēnum infĕrat", *let no one destroy* **44.** *them or put in a stranger;* **Imperative Subjunct.** — poenãque est, *and it is punishable.* — si quis bustum violārit, dejecĕrit, fregĕrit, *if some one should mutilate, throw down or break a bust.* **788.** II.

26 post aliquanto, *shortly after.* — propter has amplitudĭnes sepulcrōrum, *in consequence of this magnificence of the tombs.*

29 neque id opĕre tectorio exornāri...licēbat, *nor was it allowed to adorn them with stucco;* the **Acc. w. Inf.** constructions depend on licēbat.

30 Hermas hos, quos vocant, *the so-called Hermae.*

6 civis tuendae civitātis peritissĭmus, *a citizen well versed in* **45.** *protecting the state;* perītus takes the **Gen.**

7 non solum poena, sed etiam tempŏre, *not only by punishment, but also by time,* i. e., *not only by establishing punishment, but also by fixing the time.* — ante lucem enim jussit efferri, *for he ordered funerals to take place before day-break.*

9 super terrae tumŭlum, *above the sepulchral mound.*

10 nolŭit quidquam statŭi, *he did not want,* i. e. *forbade anything to be placed.* — tribus cubĭtis non altiōrem, *not higher than three cubits.* **610.**

11 huic procuratiōni praefecĕrat, *to this charge he had appointed;* praeficĕre, *to set over, appoint,* takes the **Dat.** *592.*

21. Aratus of Sicyon.

16 clandestīno introĭtu, **Abl. of Means.**

22 quinquaginta annōrum possessiōnes, *a holding for fifty years.* — non nimis aequum, *not very fair.*

24 tenebantur, *were held in possession.*

25 judicāvit neque illis adĭmi nec his non satis fiĕri, quorum illa fuĕrant, oportēre, *he was of opinion that neither the latter should be deprived, nor those who had formerly possessed the property be without indemnification.*

26 quorum illa fuĕrant; the **Gen.** to denote that to which something belongs. *571.* — opus esse takes the **Abl.** *694.*

27 ad eam rem constituendam, *to fix this matter.*

30 alter refers to Ptolemaeum, hospĭtem suum, but is here incorporated into the relative clause, *the second who.*

1 quam, for cam. — adhibēre in consilĭum, *to consult one.*

3 alĭēna, *the property of others.*

4 aestimandis possessionĭbus, *by estimating the properties* = *by an estimate of the properties.*

5 possessionĭbus cedĕrent, *to give up their property;* possessionĭbus, **Abl. of Separation.** *620.*

6 quod tanti esset, *what was worth so much,* i. e., *an equivalent.*

7 perfectum est, ut omnes discedĕrent, *it was brought about that all came off.*

8 o virum magnum; **Acc. in exclamation.** *585.* — dignumque qui natus esset; after dignus, the Relative takes the **Subjunct.** *703. c.*

22. A remarkable dream.

11 Cum duo &c.; this whole section is in the oratĭo oblĭqua, depending on commemorātur.

14 qui ut cenāti quiescĕrent, *when after supper they retired to rest.* — concubĭa nocte, *during his first sleep.*

16 primo perterrĭtum somnĭo, *frightened by this first dream.*

17 idque visum pro nihĭlo habendum esse duxisset, *and had concluded that this vision should be regarded as nothing.*

19 quonĭam sibi vivo non subvenisset, *since he had not assisted him while alive.*

20 mortem suam ne inultam esse paterētur, *he would not allow his death to go unavenged.* — se interfectum in plaustrum a caupōne esse conjectum, *stating that, having been killed by the innkeeper, he had been thrust into a wagon;* this oratĭo oblĭqua depends on rogāre which implies dicens.

22 petĕre ut mane ad portam adesset, *he entreated him to be at the gate early in the morning.* — priusquam plaustrum ex oppĭdo exīret, *before the wagon could leave the city.* *719.*

23 hoc vero cum somnĭo commōtum, *the latter thoroughly roused by this dream.*

24 mane bubulco praesto ad portam fuisse, *waited at the gate early in the morning for the driver.*

26 re patefacta, *the deed being brought to light.*

Of Phaedrus, the Latin fabulist of the Augustan age, scarcely any accounts have been transmitted to us beyond occasional references, and of his personal history almost nothing is known beyond the fact that he was a slave who was brought from Thrace or Macedonia to Rome where he was freed by Augustus, as set forth in the title-page of the book: *Phaedri, Augusti liberti, fabularum Aesopiarum libri quinque*, containing 97 fables in Iambic verse.

---

23. *The wolf and the lamb.*

Page

3 Ad riv*um* eundem lupus et agnus venerant. — This is the most 47. common form of Iambic verse; it is called **Iambic Trimeter** or **Senarian**, and consists of three Iambic dipodies or six Iambic feet. Accordingly the formula of the verse is as follows:

$$\cup \overset{\prime}{} \cup \_ \mid \cup \overset{\prime}{} \cup \_ \mid \cup \overset{\prime}{} \cup \cup$$

In the Iambic Trimeter a Tribrach ($\cup \cup \cup$) may be substituted for any iambus except the last, as:

$$\cup \overset{\prime}{} \quad \cup \_ \mid \cup \quad \varpi \quad \cup \_ \mid \cup \overset{\prime}{} \cup \_$$

ad riv*um* eundem lupus et agnus venerant.

Likewise a Spondee ($\_ \_$) or its equivalent Anapaest ($\cup \cup \_$) or Dactyl ($\_ \cup \cup$) may be substituted for an Iambus in the odd places (1st, 3d, 5th foot). *922.*

4 super*ior*, *higher*, that is nearer the source of the river.

5 fauce impr*o*ba, **Abl. of Instrument** governed by incitātus; lit. *by his wicked throat;* i. e. *by his voracity.*

6 latro, *the robber*, i. e., *the wolf*. — jurg*ii* causam intulit, *picked a quarrel.*

7 mihi..bibenti, *for me while drinking* = *when I was drinking.*

8 lan*i*ger, *wool-bearing*, i. e., *the sheep*. — contra, *in turn*. — timens, *timidly;* the Participle translated adverbially; supply ait.

9 qui, old **Abl.** of qui, *in what way, how*. — quod quereris, *what you complain of.*

47. 12 male, ait, dixisti mihi, for: ait, maledixisti mihi; male and dixisti form one word; such a separation of a compound word into its parts is called **Tmesis.** *897.*

15 atque ita correptum lacĕrat, *and so he seizes AND tears him in pieces.*

17 fictis causis, *by fictitious causes.*

24. The frogs and their king.

19 aequis legĭbus, *under just laws.*

22 hic conspirātis factiōnum partĭbus, *some portions of the factions having entered into a conspiracy.*

25 grave omne insuĕtis onus est, *every burden is heavy when we are not accustomed to it.*

28 libĕris paludĭbus, *in their free swamps;* **Abl. of Place.**

48. 1 qui compescĕret, *who should restrain;* the relative = ut is, denoting *purpose,* with the verb following in the **Subjunct.**

3 missum quod &c. = quod tigillum missum, *and this log when sent down.* — vadi belongs to pavĭdum genus, *the timid population of the marshes.*

5 diutĭus, *somewhat long, a considerable time.*

7 explorāto rege, *having examined the king.*

8 timōre posĭto, *having dismissed their fear.*

9 lignumque supra, for: et supra lignum.

10 omni contumelĭa, *with all kind of contumely.*

12 inutĭlis quonĭam esset; the **Subjunctive** shows that this is what the frogs said.

17 adflictis ut succurrat, *that he should succor the wretched;* clause of *purpose.*

20 majus ne venĭat malum, *lest a greater evil may come;* clause of *purpose.*

25. The wolf and the crane.

24 deinde, to be pronounced dēinde (two syllables).

25 os devorātum fauce cum haerēret lupi, *when a bone which the wolf had devoured was sticking in his throat.*

26 singŭlos, supply amīcos, *his friends one by one.*

28 persuāsa est, *was persuaded;* this passive use of persuadĕo 48.
is not common and scarcely in accordance with the rule; verbs which
govern a **Dative** in the Active are used *only impersonally* in the
Passive; the usual construction would be: persuāsum est grui. *590.*

29 colli longitudĭnem, *his long neck.* See Note on **49.** 29.

30 medicīnam fecit lupo, *performed the operation on the wolf.*

32 ore quae e nostro caput abstulĕris; *transpose,* quae e nostro
ore, &c.; the relative quae is here equivalent to cum tu, *since you;*
accordingly it takes the **Subjunctive.** *792.* II.

33 et, *and yet;* et is often used in this sense.

26. *The ass and the lion in partnership.*

2 virtūtis expers verbis jactans glorĭam, is the subject of the sen- 49.
tence, *he who is without virtue and boasts of his fame (with words);*
expers takes the **Gen.** *567.* 1.

3 ignōtos, *those who do not know him.* — notis est derisŭi, *is a
derision to those who know him;* the **Dative** is used with esse to
denote the *purpose.* *595.*

4 asello comĭte, **Abl. Absol.**; a few substantives having a kind of
participial meaning take the construction of Ablative Absolute. *536.*

5 contexit illum frutĭce, *concealed him behind a shrub;* lit. *covered him with a shrub.*

7 auritŭlus; the ass is described by his length of ear.

10 quae dum = dum eae, sc. bestĭae.

12 qui, *this one=the lion.* — fessus caede; fessus takes the **Abl.** *604.*

13 tunc ille insŏlens, supply ait.

14 qualis vidĕtur opĕra tibi vocis meae? *how does my voice appear to aid you,* lit. *of what kind appears to you the help of my voice?*

15 insignis sic ut, *first rate so that;* ut introducing a clause of
result with the **Subjunct.** — nisi nossem, *had I not known;* nossem
for novissem. *333;* the condition being represented as *contrary to
fact* requires the **Imp.** or **Pluperf. Subjunct.** *788.* III.

27. *The fox and the crow.*

18 qui se laudāri gaudet, *he who takes pleasure in being praised;*
verbs of *emotion* may take the **Acc. w. Inf.** *815.*

49.   19 sera paenitentĭa, **Abl. Absol.**, *repentance being too late* = *when it is too late to repent.* — dat turpes poenas, *has to pay for it dishonorably.*

20 de fenestra raptum casĕum, *a cheese he had stolen from a window.*

21 comesse = comedĕre. **410.** — celsa resĭdens arbŏre, *perching on a lofty tree.*

23 O qui est nitor, *O what is the sheen!*

24 quantum decŏris, *how much grace;* **Partitive Gen.** after quantum. **566. c.**

28 avĭdis dentĭbus, *with her greedy teeth;* **Abl. of Means. 605.**

29 ingemŭit corvi deceptus stupor, *the stupid crow being deceived groaned;* the place of the Adjective, in case of a particular stress being laid upon it, is often supplied by a Substantive expressing the quality in the abstract, and the other Substantive is joined to it in the Genitive, as here, corvi stupor for corvus stupĭdus.

28. The aged lion.

32 ignāvis etĭam jocus est, *is the joke even of cowards.*

33 defectus annis et desertus virĭbus, *stricken in years and his strength gone;* annis is **Abl. of Limitation,** and virĭbus **Causal Ablative.**

34 spirītum extrēmum ducens, *breathing his last.*

50.   3 infestis cornĭbus, *with his dangerous horns.*

4 hostīle corpus, *the body of his enemy.*

6 at ille exspīrans, supply ait.—fortes indigne tuli mihi insultāre; **Acc. w. Inf.** after a verb of *emotion.* **815.**

7 te, natūrae dedĕcus, quod ferre cogor; begin with quod, *that I am compelled to endure you, monster of nature;* quod is used to introduce an explanatory cause; here it means, *the fact that, the circumstance that.* **784.**

29. The kite and the doves.

10 qui se committit homĭni tutandum imprŏbo, *he who commits himself for protection to a wicked man;* the **Gerundive** tutandum is used after committĕre, to denote *purpose.* **841.**

14 raptor, *the plunderer,* i. e., *the kite.*

16 quare sollicĭtum potĭus aevum ducĭtis? *why do you prefer to* 50. *lead a life of care?*

17 icto foedĕre, **Abl. Absol.**, *by making a league;* the use of the word icĕre, *to strike*, seems to have arisen from the notion of striking down the victim which formed part of the process observed in making treaties.

18 qui vos praestem; qui being equivalent to ut ego takes the **Subjunctive. 792. I.**

19 credentes, *full of confidence.*

20 qui, *this one*, for hic. — vesci singŭlas, supply columbas; vesci commonly takes the **Abl.** *626;* occasionally the **Accus.** is used, as here.

21 imperĭum exercēre, *to enforce one's power.*

22 de relicŭis una (supply inquit), *one of the rest said;* de is here used in a partitive sense.

30. The two mules.

25 fiscos, *money-bags;* fiscus was a basket of wicker-work for holding large quantities of money.

26 tumentes multo saccos hordĕo, *bags swollen with much grain.*

27 celsa cervīce emĭnet, *is conspicuous by his lofty neck.*

28 clarumque jactat collo tintinnabŭlum, *and shakes the tinkling bell on his neck.*

29 quiēto et placĭdo gradu, **Abl. of Manner.**

31 inter caedem ferro mulum saucĭant, *while beating him they wound the mule with a sword.*

1 me contemptum (supply esse); **Acc. w. Inf.** after a verb of *emotion.* 51.

3 hoc argumento, *by* or *according to this argument.*

4 porīclo obnoxĭae, *liable to danger;* obnoxĭus takes the **Dat.** *598.*

31. The dog and the wolf.

8 salutātum; the **Supine** (depending on restitērunt) denotes *a purpose.* **847.**

10 aut quo cibo fecisti tantum corpŏris? *or by what food have you gained so much flesh?* corpŏris depends on tantum. *366.* 6.

11 perĕo fame, *I perish with hunger, am starving.*

12 canis simplicĭter, supply ait. — eādem est condicĭo tibi, *you are in the same condition;* **Dative** to denote *possession.*

51. 15 tueāris et; the conjunction et here joins tucāris and sis; it does not often occur so far on in the sentence; generally it stands first, in poetry often in the second place, but seldom later.

19 et otiōsum largo satiāri cibo; the construction is : me otiōsum largo satiāri cibo quanto est facilĭus; **Aoo. w. Inf.** *811.*

21 a catēna collum detrītum cani, *the dog's neck being galled by the chain.*

22 unde hoc, amīce ? sc. inquit.

25 crcpuscŭlo; **Abl. of Time.** — qua visum est, *where I please.*

27 jactant familĭa; the **Plural** with the collective noun familĭa.

30 abīrc siquo est anĭmus, *if you have a mind to go somewhere;* quo, in the word siquo, is for alĭquo.

31 non planc est, *there is no liberty to do so absolutely* = *I cannot go quite where I please.*

32 liber ut non sim, *on condition that I be not free.*

32. The fox and the sour grapes.

52. 3 appetēbat, *kept aiming at;* the Imperfect is used to denote a repeated action. **735.**

6 vcrbis elĕvant, *they cry down.*

33. The ungrateful snake.

11 sinūquc fovit, *warmed it in his bosom.* — contra se ipse misc-rīcors, *compassionate against his own interest.*

13 hanc, sc. colŭbram. — alĭa, sc. colŭbra.

14 respondit, nc quis, *answered, (I did it) lest.*

34. The discontented stag.

16 laudātis; **Abl. of Comparison** for quam laudāta; the **regular** construction in prose would bc, haec narratĭo adsĕrit, saepe (ea) quae contempsĕris utiliōra invenīri quam laudāta.

25 retentis impedītus cornĭbus, *impeded by his entangled horns.*

27 voccm hanc edidisse dicĭtur, *he is said to have exclaimed thus.*

29 utilĭa mihi fuĕrint (ea), *how useful were to me those things.*

30 quantum luctus habuĕrint (ea), *how much grief they caused me;* luctus in the Genitive after quantum. *566.* o.

VOCABULARY.

NOTE. Changeable parts of words are printed in **bold-faced** type, so as to indicate the manner of forming the genitive, the gender endings, and the principal parts of verbs.

The –, simply added to a noun, indicates that the genitive is like the nominative.

(m.), (f.), (n.), (pl.) mean: masculine, feminine, neuter, plural, respectively.

The signs of quantity are given, unless the syllable is long by position (*26*), or contains a diphthong (*12*).

A.

ā, ăb, with abl., *from, of, by*

ăbăcŭs, -ī (m.), *a sideboard*

abdĭtŭs, -ă, -ŭm, *sequestered*

ăbĕō,-īrĕ, ăbĭī, ăbĭtŭm, *to move off, to get off*

abjĭcĭō, -ĕrĕ, abjēcī, abjectŭm, *to throw away*

ablĕgō, -ārĕ, -āvī, -ātŭm, *to send away*

abruptŭs, -ă, -ŭm, *broken;* abruptŭm, -ī (n.), *a precipice*

absolvō, -ĕrĕ, absolvī, absŏlūtŭm, *to acquit*

absŭm, ăbessĕ, āfŭī, (no sup), *to be away; to be wanting;* paulum, non longe abesse, *to be not far from;* domo abesse, *to be away from home*

absūmō, -ĕrĕ, absumpsī, absumptŭm, *to destroy, consume*

ăbundantĭă, -ac (f.), *abundance*

ăbundō, -ārĕ, -āvī, -ātŭm, *to abound, to be very numerous*

Ăbȳdŭs, -ī (f.), *Abydos,* a town in Mysia, on the narrowest point of the Hellespont

ăc, atquĕ, *and*

accēdō,-ĕrĕ, accessī, accessŭm, *to approach;* accēdit, *it is added*

accendō, -ĕrĕ, accendī, accensŭm, *to set on fire; rise to fury*

acceptŭs, -ă, -ŭm, *acceptable, welcome*

accessĭō, -ōnĭs (f.), *an increase*

accessŭs, -ūs (m.), *an approach*

accĭdō, -ĕrĕ, accĭdī, (no sup.), *to befall, happen*

accĭpĭō,-ĕrĕ, accēpī, acceptŭm, *to receive; to hear;* fama accipĕre,*to know by hearsay;* scriptum accipĕre, *to be informed;* pecunĭam accipĕre, *to take the money*

accūrātŭs, -ă, -ŭm, *careful;* accuratĭus, *with greater care*

ācĕr, -rĭs, -rĕ, *sharp, vigorous;* acerrĭma studĭa, *most acute studies;* acerrĭme, *most violently*

Ăcerbās, -ac (m.), *Acerbas,* Elissa's husband

ăcerbŭs, -ă,-ŭm, *sour; painful*

Ăchillēs, -ĭs (m.), *Achilles*

ăcĭēs,-ēī (f.), *line of battle, battle*

actĭŏ, -ōnĭs (f.), *an action;* of
an orator, *good delivery*
actŏr, -ōrĭs (m.), *a speaker*
ăcūmĕn, -ĭnĭs (n.), *keenness*
ăcūtŭs,-ă, -ŭm, *pointed, sharp;*
homo acūtus, *a sharper*
ăd, with acc., *at, to, against;
towards, by*
adclāmō, -ārĕ, -āvī, -ātŭm, *to
cry out*
addīcō, -ĕrĕ, addixī, addictŭm,
to sentence
addiscō, -ĕrĕ, addĭdĭcī, (no sup.),
to learn further, to learn more
addō, -ĕrĕ, addĭdī, addĭtŭm, *to
add*
addūcō, -ĕrĕ, adduxī, adduc-
tŭm, *to bring up*
adductŭs, -ă, -ŭm, *strained*
ădĕŏ, *so, to that degree*
ădĕō, -īrĕ, ădĭī, ădĭtŭm, *to approach;* ĭnsŭlam adīre, *to visit
an island;* contiōnem adīre, *to
go to the assembly*
adfĕrō, -rĕ, attŭlī, adlātŭm, *to
bring (up, to);* causas adferre,
to advance reasons
adfĭcĭō, -ĕrĕ, adfēcī, adfectŭm,
to treat,affect; often to be translated by a verb corresponding
to its ablative; verberĭbus ad-
fĭcĕre, *to flog;* verberĭbus servilĭbus adfĭci, *to be flogged by
a slave;* voluntariis verberĭbus
adfĭci, *to flog one's self*
adfīgō, -ĕrĕ, adfixī, adfixŭm,
to fasten to, nail to; cruci adfigĕre, *to crucify*
adflictŭs,-ă, -ŭm, *in a bad state,
distressed*
adflīgō, -ĕrĕ, adflixī, adflictŭm,
to strike down, shatter

adgrĕdĭŏr, -ī, adgressŭs sŭm, *to
set about; to assail, to approach; to address;* dolo adgrĕdi, *to take by surprise*
adhaerĕō, -ērĕ, adhaesī, adhae-
sŭm, *to adhere, be united with*
adhĭbĕō, -ērĕ, -ŭī, -ĭtŭm, *to
employ, use;* adhibēre in consilĭum, *to consult some one;* ad
panem adhibēre, *to eat with
the bread*
adhūc, *hitherto, still*
ădĭmō, -ĕrĕ, ădēmī, ădemptŭm,
to take away, deprive
ădĭpiscŏr, -ī, adeptŭs sŭm, *to
obtain, gain*
ădĭtŭs, -ūs (m.), *access; a landing place;* (pl.) *passages (for
entrance)*
adjĭcĭō, -ĕrĕ, adjēcī, adjectŭm,
to add to; tclum adjicĕre, *to
hurl a weapon*
adjungō, -ĕrĕ, adjunxī, adjunc-
tŭm, *to add to*
adjŭvō, -ārĕ, adjŭvī, adjūtŭm,
to assist
adlĭgātŭs, -ă, -ŭm, *bound up*
adlūdō,-ĕrĕ, adlūsī, adlūsŭm, *to
smile on*
admĭnistrātĭŏ, -ōnĭs (f.), *the ad-
ministration*
admĭnistrō, -ārĕ, -āvī, -ātŭm,
to manage, conduct, execute;
majestātem administrāre, *to
exercise the supreme power*
admīrātĭŏ, -ōnĭs (f.), *admiration*
admīrŏr, -ārī, -ātŭs sŭm, *to
wonder at, admire*
admittō, -ĕrĕ, admīsī, admis-
sŭm, *to admit;* in conspectum
admittĕre, *to admit to one's
presence*

admŏdŭm, *very;* admŏdum puer,
very young; with numerals,
about

admŏnĕō,-ērĕ,-ŭī, -ĭtŭm, *to re-
mind, suggest, call attention to*

admŏnĭtĭŏ, -ōnĭs (f.), *reminding*

admŏvĕō, -ērĕ, admōvī, admŏ-
tŭm, *to bring to*

adnătō, -ārĕ, -āvī, -ātŭm, *to
swim along*

ădŏlescō,-ĕrĕ, ădŏlēvī,ădultŭm,
to grow up

adquīrō, -ĕrĕ, adquīsīvī, adquī-
sītŭm, *to assume*

adrīdĕō, -ērĕ, adrīsī, adrīsŭm,
to laugh at

adscendō, -ĕrĕ, adscendī, ad-
scensŭm, *to ascend*

adscensŭs, -ŭs (m.), *an ascent*

adscrībō,-ĕrĕ,adscripsī, adscrip-
tŭm, *to join to;* sibi adscrībĕrĕ,
to apply to one's self

adsentātŏr, -ōrĭs (m.), *a flatterer*

adsĕquŏr, -ī, adsĕcūtŭs sŭm, *to
attain, reach, gain;*tantum ad-
sĕqui, *to make up for*

adsĕrō,-ĕrĕ, adsĕrŭī, adsertŭm,
to relate, assert

adsĭdens, -tĭs, *sitting near a
person*

adsĭdŭŭs, -ă, -ŭm, *constant*

adsignō, -ārĕ, -āvī, -ātŭm, *to
allot*

adspĭcĭō, see aspĭcĭō

adstō, -ārĕ, adstĭtī, (no sup.), *to
stand near*

adsŭcscō, -ĕrĕ, adsŭēvī, adsŭē-
tŭm, *to become accustomed*

adsŭm,ădessĕ, adfŭī, (no sup.), *to be
present, stand by; to be there;*
fides mortis adĕrat, *the news of
his death proved to be true*

adsūmō,-ĕrĕ, adsumpsī,adsump-
tŭm, *to assume;* in sociĕtātem
adsumĕrĕ, *to admit into one's
company*

ădŭlescens, -tĭs (m.), *a youth;
young*

ădŭlescentĭă, -ae (f.), *youth*

ădŭlescentŭlŭs, -ī (m.), *a very
young man*

ădultŭs, -ă, -ŭm, *grown up;* ac-
tas adulta, *full age*

ădūnātŭs, -ă, -ŭm, *united*

ădūrō, -ĕrĕ, ădussī, ădustŭm,
to singe off

advĕnă, -ae (m.), *a stranger*

adventō, -ārĕ, -āvī, -ātŭm, *to
approach;* of the day, *to dawn*

adventŭs, -ūs (m.), *a coming*

adversŭm } with acc., *against*
adversŭs }

adversŭs, -ă, -ŭm, *unfavorable,
disastrous;* ex adverso stare,
to face

advertō, -ĕrĕ, advertī, adversŭm, *to turn towards;* anĭmum
advertĕre, *to observe, perceive*

advŏcō, -ārĕ, -āvī, -ātŭm, *to
summon*

advŏlō, -ārĕ, -āvī, -ātŭm, *to fly
to, to hurry to*

Aeăcīdēs, -ae (m.), *an Aeacide,
a male descendant of Aeacus*

aedēs,-ĭs (f.), *a temple;* pl. *house,
palace*

aedĭfĭcĭŭm, -ī (n.), *a building*

aedĭfĭcō, -ārĕ, -āvī, -ātŭm, *to
build*

Aegĕūs, -ĕī (m.), *Aegeus,* king
of Athens, and father of Theseus

aegrĕ, *with difficulty*

Aegyptŭs, -ī (f.), *Egypt*

aemŭlātĭŏ, -ōnĭs (f.), *emulation*

Aeŏlĭdēs, -ŭm (f. pl.) insŭlae, *the Aeolic islands,* now *Lipari*

aequālĭs, -ē, *equal;* **subst.** *a contemporary*

acquālĭtĕr, *equally*

acquĭtās, -ātĭs (f.), *evenness;* animi acquĭtas, *evenness of temper*

acquō, -ārĕ, -āvī, -ātŭm, *to level, to make equal to;* acquāta patrimonĭa, *the equality of property*

acquŏr, -ĭs (n.), *the sea*

acquŭs, -ă, -ŭm, *even; fair;* aequum jus, *the same right;* acquae leges, *reasonable laws*

Acschĭnēs, -ĭs (m.), *the orator Aeschines,* rival to Demosthenes

Acscŭlāpĭŭs, -ī (m.), *Aesculapius,* deified after his death on account of his great knowledge of medicine

Acsōpŭs, -ī (m.), *Aesopus,* the Greek fabulist

acstās, -ātĭs (f.), *summer*

aestĭmātĭŏ, -ōnĭs (f.), *estimating*

acstĭmō, -ārĕ, -āvī, -ātŭm, *to estimate*

acstŭs,-ūs (m.), *heat; tide, surge*

aetās, -ātĭs (f.), *age;* aetātis privilegĭum, *privilege of seniority*

acternĭtās, -ātĭs (f.), *durability*

Acthĭōpĭă, -ae (f.), *Ethiopia,* a country in Africa

Actnă, -ae (f.), *Aetna,* the celebrated volcano of Sicily

acvŭm, -ī (n.), *an age;* sollicĭtum aevum agĕre, *to lead a life full of care*

Āfĕr, -rī (m.), *an African*

affĕrŏ, see adfĕrŏ

ăgĕ, *well then*

ăgĕr, -rī (m.), *a field, land; estate;* in agrum, *into the country*

aggrĕdĭŏr, see adgrĕdĭŏr

ăgĭtō, -ārĕ, -āvī, -ātŭm, *to drive (violently);* agitāri, *to be disturbed;* regnum agitāre, *to spend the reign;* facīnus agitāre, *to intend a crime*

agmĕn,-ĭnĭs (n.),*a line of march, an army;* agmīna senatōrŭm, *the crowds of senators*

agnoscŏ, -ĕrĕ, agnōvī, agnĭtŭm, *to recognize*

agnŭs, -ī (m.), *a lamb*

ăgō, -ĕrĕ, ēgī, actŭm, *to drive;* vitam agĕre, *to spend life;* victōrem agĕre, *to act as a conqueror;* inter plebem et senātum agĕre, *to manage between the people and senate;* in exsilĭum agĕre, *to banish;* de praemĭis agĭtur, *the question is concerning the rewards;* primos annos agĕre, *to spend the first years;* haec aguntur, *these affairs are going on;* perpetŭum exsilĭum agĕre, *to live in exile for life*

agrĭcultūră, -ae (f.), *husbandry*

ain' = aisnĕ? *do you mean?*

ăjō, *I say*

ălăcĕr, -rĭs, -rĕ, *lively, happy;* ălăcrĭŭs, *more briskly*

ălăcrĭtās, -ātĭs (f.), *liveliness, alacrity;* magna animōrum alacrĭtas, *high spirits*

Alcĭbĭădēs, -ĭs (m.), *Alcibiades*

ālēs, -ĭtĭs (m. & f.), *a bird*

Ălexandĕr,-rī (m.), *Alexander*

Ălexandrĭă, -ae (f.), *Alexandria*

ălĭēnō, -ārĕ, -āvī, -ātŭm, *to remove*

ălĭēnŭm, -ī (n.), *the property of others*

ălĭēnŭs, -ă, -ŭm, *belonging to others, strange, contrary to;* alienus (as a noun), *a stranger*

ălĭō, *in another direction, to a different quarter*

ălĭquandō, *sometime*

ălĭquantispĕr, *for some time*

ălĭquantō post, *some time after; shortly*

ălĭquĭs, ălĭquă, ălĭquĭd, ălĭquŏd, *some one, something (or other)*

ălĭtĕr, *otherwise*

ălĭŭs, -ă, -ŭd, *other (different);* nihil aliud, *nothing else;* alii ..alii, *some..others;* alii..alios, *one.. another;* alius alio modo, *some in this way and some in another*

allīgō, -ārĕ, -āvī, -ātŭm, *to fasten, chain up;* also written, adligo

allŏquĭŭm, -ī (n.), *a conversation*

ălō, -ĕrĕ, ălŭī, ălĭtŭm, *to feed;* of animals, *to keep*

altĕr, -ă, -ŭm, *other, second, one of two;* alter..alter, *the one..the other;* alteruter, *either*

altĕrŭtĕr, altĕrutră, altĕrutrŭm or altĕr ŭtĕr, altĕră ŭtră, altĕrŭm ŭtrŭm, *one of two*

altĭtūdō, -ĭnĭs (f.), *height, depth*

altŭs, -ă, -ŭm, *high;* altŭm, -ī (n.), *the deep sea;* in alto, *in deep water*

ămărŭs, -ă, -ŭm, *bitter*

ambĭtĭō, -ōnĭs (f.), *ambition;* ambitio vulgi, *paying court to the masses*

ambŭlō, -ārĕ, -āvī, -ātŭm, *to walk*

amīcĭtĭă, -ae (f.), *friendship*

ămĭcŭlŭm, -ī (n.), *a cloak*

ămīcŭs, -ī (m.), *a friend;* ămīcŭs, -ă, -ŭm, *loyal*

ămissĭō, -ōnĭs (f.), *a loss*

ămittō, -ĕrĕ, ămīsī, ămissŭm, *to lose*

Ammōn, -ĭs (m.), *Ammon, the supreme divinity of the Ethiopians*

ămō, -ārĕ, -āvī, -ātŭm, *to love*

ămŏr, -ōrĭs (m.), *love; an eager desire*

Amphictўōn, -ōnĭs (m.), *Amphictyon, a fabulous king of Attica*

amplĭtūdō, -ĭnĭs (f.), *magnificence*

amplĭŭs, *besides, more, further*

amplŭs, -ă, -ŭm, *splendid*

ampŭtō, -ārĕ, -āvī, -ātŭm, *to cut off*

ăn, *or, whether*

Ănaxĭlăŭs, -ī (m.), *Anaxilaus, tyrant of Sicily*

anceps, -ĭpĭtĭs, *wavering*

ancillārĭs, -ĕ, *of or belonging to a handmaid*

ancŏră, -ae (f.), *an anchor*

angustĭae, -ārŭm (f. pl.), *a narrow pass, defile;* angustiae maris, *narrow passages of the sea*

angustŭs, -ă, -ŭm, *narrow; close;* of breath, *short*

ănĭmă, -ae (f.), *breath, current of air*

ănĭmadvertō, -ĕrĕ, ănĭmadvertī, ănĭmadversŭm, *to observe, notice, perceive*

ănĭmōsŭs, -ă, -ŭm, *spirited*

ănĭmŭs, -ī (m.), *mind; courage;* anĭmo magnificentĭor, *more elevated in soul;* anĭmos frangĕre, *to break the spirits;* anĭmus minax, *animosity;* hoc anĭmo esse, *to entertain such sentiments*

annŭs, -ī (m.), *a year;* anni tempus, *a season*

annŭŭs, -ă, -ŭm, *for one year, yearly*

antĕ, with acc., *before;* adv., *before*

antĕā (adv.), *before, heretofore*

antēlūcānŭs, -ă, -ŭm, *that is or takes place before daybreak;* tempŏre antelucāno, *before daybreak*

antĕpōnō, -ĕrĕ, antĕpŏsŭī, antĕpŏsĭtŭm, *to prefer*

antīquĭtās, -ātĭs (f.), *antiquity*

antīquŭs, -ă, -ŭm, *ancient*

ānŭlŭs, -ī (m.), *a finger-ring*

anxĭē, *anxiously*

ăpĕr, -rī (m.), *a wild boar*

ăpertē, *openly, evidently*

ăpertŭs, -ă, -ŭm, *open;* latus apertum, *the unprotected flank*

Apollŏ, -ĭnĭs (m.), *Apollo*

appărātŭs, -ūs (m.), *a preparation;* pl. *supplies;* apparātus armōrum, conviviōrum, *preparation for war, for a banquet;* in medĭo hoc apparātu, *in the midst of this magnificence*

appārĕō, -ĕrĕ, -ŭī, -ĭtŭm, *to appear*

appăro, -ārĕ, -āvī, -ātŭm, *to prepare*

appellō, -ārĕ, -āvī, -ātŭm, *to call*

appellō, -ĕrĕ, appŭlī, appulsŭm, *to push ashore, to land;* classem appellĕre, *to land*

appĕtō, -ĕrĕ, appétīvī, appĕtītŭm, *to aim at*

approbō, -ārĕ, -āvī, -ātŭm, *to approve*

apprŏpinquō, -ārĕ, -āvī, -ātŭm, *to approach*

appulsŭs, -ūs (m.), *arriving;* appulsus terrae, *a landing*

aptŭs, -ă, -ŭm (from apō, -ĕrĕ), *fastened*

aptŭs, -ă, -ŭm, *suitable, fit*

ăpŭd, with acc., *by, at, among, with;* apud Xerxem, *at the court of Xerxes;* apud Platōnem, *in Plato;* apud quos, *in whose presence*

ăquă, -ae (f.), *water*

ăquĭlă, -ae (f.), *an eagle; a standard*

āră, -ae (f.), *an altar*

Ărabs, Ărăbĭs } (m.), *an Arabian*
Ărăbŭs, -ī }

Ărātŭs, -ī (m.), *Aratus of Sicyon*

Arbactŭs, -ī (m.), *Arbactus, an Assyrian prefect of Media*

arbĭtĕr, -rī (m.), *an umpire; an eye-witness*

arbĭtrĭŭm, -ī (n.), *the will*

arbĭtrŏr, -ārī, -ātŭs sŭm, *to believe, consider*

arbŏr, -ŏrĭs (f.), *a tree*

arcānŭm, -ī (n.), *a secret*

Arcās, -ădĭs (m.), *an Arcadian*

arcessō, -ĕrĕ, arcessīvī, arcessītŭm, *to summon*

Archĕlāŭs, -ī (m.), *Archelaus, king of Macedonia (400 B. C.)*

ardĕō, -ērĕ, arsī, arsŭm, *to burn*

ardŭŭs, -ă, -ŭm, *steep*

argentĕŭs, -ă, -ŭm, *of silver*

argentŭm, -ī (n.), *silver, plate*

Argī, -ōrŭm (pl. m.), *Argos*, the capital of Argolis

argŭmentŭm, -ī (n.), *a sign; an argument*

Arīaemĕnēs, -ĭs (m.), *Ariaemenes*, son of Dareus

Arīdaeŭs,-ī (m.), *Aridaeus*, half-brother of Alexander

ărīdŭs, -ă, -ŭm, *dry;* ărīdŭm, -ī (n.), *dry ground*

Aristŏmăchē, -ēs (f.), *Aristomache*, wife of Dionysius

Ăristŏtĕlēs, -ĭs (m.), *Aristotle*

armă, -ōrŭm (n. pl.), *arms*

armătŭs, -ă, -ŭm, *armed, in arms;* subst., *an armed man*

armō,-ārĕ, -āvī, -ātŭm, *to arm*

ars, -tĭs (f.), *an art, accomplishment; cunning;* ars memorīae, *the art of remembering*

Artăphernēs, -ĭs (m.), *Artaphernes*, brother of Dareus

Artĕmīsĭă, -ae (f.), *Artemisia*, queen of Halicarnasus

artĭfex, -ĭcĭs (m.), *a master*

artĭfĭcĭŭm, -ī, (n.), *a service*

arx, -cĭs (f.), *a citadel*

Ascălōnĭŭs, -ī (m.), *an Ascalonian*, inhabitant of Ascalon

ásellŭs, -ī (m.), *an ass*

Asĭă, -ae (f.), *Asia*

ăsĭnŭs, -ī (m.), *an ass*

aspĕr, -ă, -ŭm, *sharp;* aspĕra vita, *a life full of hardships*

aspĭcĭō,-ĕrĕ, aspexī, aspectŭm, *to look at, behold*

assūmō, see adsūmō

Assўrĭŭs, -ī (m.), *an Assyrian*

astŭs, -ūs (m.), *craft;* astu, *cunningly*

Astўägēs, -ĭs (m.), *Astyages*, last king of the Medians

ăt, *but; for at least*

Athēnae, -ārŭm (f. pl.), *Athens*

Athēnĭensĭs, - (m.), *an Athenian*

atquĕ, *and*

atquī, *nevertheless*

Atrĕbătēs,-ŭm (m. pl.), *the Atrebates*, a people in Gallia Belgica

attĕrō, -ĕrĕ, attrīvī, attrītŭm, *to impair*

Atthĭs, -ĭdĭs (f.), *Atthis*, daughter of king Cranaus

Attĭcŭs, -ī (m.), *an Athenian*

attingō, -ĕrĕ, attĭgī, attactŭm, *to touch, reach*

attrĭbŭō, -ĕrĕ, attrĭbŭī, attrĭbūtŭm, *to assign, allot*

auctŏr, -ōrĭs (m.), *an author;* auctor auxilĭī, *the source of assistance;* auctor belli, *the originator of the war;* auctor sententĭae, *the adviser of an opinion;* auctōre Aristīde, *upon the advice of Aristides*

auctōrĭtās, -ātĭs (f.), *authority, influence*

audācĭă, -ae (f.), *boldness*

audācĭtĕr, *boldly*

audĕō,-ērĕ, ausŭs sŭm, *to dare, venture*

audĭō, -īrĕ, -īvī, -ītŭm, *to hear*

aufĕrō, -rĕ, abstŭlī, ablātŭm, *to take away from, to withdraw*

augĕō, -ērĕ, auxī, auctŭm, *to augment, increase*

aurĕŭs, -ă, -ŭm, *golden*

aurĭtŭlŭs, -ī (m.), *a long-eared animal, an ass*

aurŭm, -ī (n.), *gold*

Auruncŭlējŭs, -ī (m.), *Aurunculeius*

auspĭcătŭs, -ă, -ŭm, *lucky;* auspicăta sĕdes, *lucky foundation;* male auspicătus, *evil begun;* auspicatissĭmus, *founded under the most favorable auspices*

auspĭcĭŭm, -ī (n.), *an augury;* auspicĭis, *under the guidance*

auspĭcŏr, -ārī, -ātŭs sŭm, *to begin*

aut, *or;* aut..aut, *either..or*

autĕm, *but*

auxĭlĭărĭs, -ĕ, *assisting;* auxĭlĭārēs,-ĭŭm (m. pl.), *auxiliaries*

auxĭlĭŭm, -ī (n.), *assistance;* auxilĭum ferre, *to bring assistance;* in auxilĭum venīre, *to come to assistance;* communĭa auxilĭa, *common sources of aid;* auxilĭa, *auxiliary troops*

ăvārĭtĭă, -ae (f.), *avarice*

āversŏr, -ārī, -ātŭs sŭm, *to avoid*

ăvĭdŭs, -ă, -ŭm, *eager, greedy;* avĭdus vini, *fond of the cup*

ăvītŭs, -ă, -ŭm, *derived from a grandfather, ancestral;* avītus mos, *a hereditary custom*

ăvŏlŏ, -ārĕ, -āvī, -ātŭm, *to fly away*

ăvuncŭlŭs, -ī (m.), *an uncle*

ăvŭs, -ī (m.), *a grandfather*

B.

Băbўlŏn, -ĭs (f.), *Babylon,* the chief city of the Babylo-Assyrian empire

Băbўlŏnĭă, -ae (f.), *Babylonia,* the land named after its capital

Bactrĭānŭs, -ī (m.), *a Bactrian*

balbŭs, -ă, -ŭm, *stammering*

barbă, -ae (f.), *a beard*

barbărŭs, -ă, -ŭm, *barbarous*

barbātŭs, -ă, -ŭm, *bearded*

bĕātŭs, -ă, -ŭm, *happy*

bellĭcōsŭs, -ă, -ŭm, *warlike*

bellĭcŭm, -ī (n.), *a signal;* bellĭcum canĕre, *to give the signal for an attack*

bellŭm, -ī (n.), *war*

bĕnĕ, *well;* bĕnĕ planēque, *full well*

bĕnĕfĭcĭŭm, -ī (n.), *a kindness*

bestĭă, -ae (f.), *a beast, an animal*

bĭbŏ, -ĕrĕ, bĭbī, bĭbĭtŭm, *to drink*

bĭformĭs, -ĕ, *two-shaped*

bīnī, -ae, -ă, *two*

bĭs, *twice*

bĭtūmĕn, -ĭnĭs (n.), *mineral pitch*

blandĭens, -tĭs, *flattering*

blandŭs, -ă, -ŭm, *insinuating*

Boeōtĭă, -ae (f.), *Boeotia*

bŏnĭtăs, -ātĭs (f.), *goodness*

bŏnŭm, -ī (n.), *a blessing, good*

bŏnŭs, -ă, -ŭm, *good;* bonus auctor, *a trusty author*

bōs, bŏvĭs (m.), *an ox*

brĕvĭs, -ĕ, *short;* brevi, *in a short time*

brĕvĭtĕr, *in a few words*

Brĭtannĭă, -ae (f.), *Great Britain*

Brĭtannŭs, -ī (m.), *a Briton*

bŭbulcŭs, -ī (m.), *a driver*

bŭbŭlŭs, -ă, -ŭm, *belonging to an ox;* caput bubŭlum, *an ox-head*

bustŭm, -ī (n.), *a bust*

Byrsă,-ae (f.), *Byrsa,* the citadel of Carthage

C.

căcūmĕn, -ĭnĭs (n.), *the top*

cădāvĕr, -ĭs (n.), *a corpse*

cădō,-ĕrĕ, cĕcĭdī, cāsūm, *to fall*

caecātŭs, -ă, -ŭm, *blinded*

caedēs,-ĭs (f.), *a murder,slaughter; a beating;* caedem edĕre, *to bring forth a defeat, to cause a slaughter;* inter caedem, *in the course of beating*

caedō, -ĕrĕ, cĕcīdī, caesūm, *to slay;* flagellis caedĕre, *to whip, scourge*

caelātŭs, -ă, -ŭm, *engraved;* argentum aurumque caelātum, *gold and silver plate*

caelŭm, -ī (n.), *heaven*

Caesăr, -ărĭs (m.), *Caesar*

Călānŭs, -ī (m.), *Calanus,* name of an Indian

calcĕŭs, -ī (m.), *a shoe*

calcō, -ārĕ, -āvī, -ātŭm, *to trample upon*

calcŭlŭs, -ī (m.), *a pebble*

callĭdŭs, -ă, -ŭm, *cunning, sly*

calx, -cĭs (f.), *the heel*

Cambȳsēs, -ĭs (m.), *Cambyses,* father of Cyrus

campŭs, -ī (m.), *a field*

candens, -tĭs, *red-hot*

cănĭs, - (f.), *a dog;* canis femĭna, *a she-dog*

cănō, -ĕrĕ, cĕcĭnī, cantŭm, *to sing;* of oracles, *to foretell;* bellĭcum canĕre, *to give the signal for an attack*

cantŭs, -ūs (m.), *a song*

căpessō, -ĕrĕ, căpessīvī, căpessītŭm, *to take to;* pugnam, proelĭum capessĕre, *to engage in a fight*

căpillŭs, -ī (m.), *the hair*

căpĭō, -ĕrĕ, cēpī, captŭm, *to take, seize; to hold; to take prisoner;* somnum capĕre, *to find sleep;* captus, *enslaved*

căpĭtālĭs, -ĕ, *capital;* capitāle esse coepit, *it began to be a capital crime*

captīvĭtās, -ātĭs (f.), *captivity*

captīvŭs, -ă, -ŭm, *captured*

căpŭt, -ĭtĭs (n.), *the head;* judicĭum capĭtis, *trial for life;* capĭtis damnāre, *to condemn to death;* cenae caput, *the chief dish of the meal*

carcĕr, -ĭs (m.), *a prison*

cărĕō,-ĕrĕ,-ŭī, (no sup.), *to want, be in want*

cărō, carnĭs (f.), *flesh*

Carthāgĭnĭensĭs, - (m.), *a Carthaginian*

căsă, -ae (f.), *a hut*

cāsĕŭs, -ī (m.), *cheese*

castĭgātĭō, -ōnĭs (f.), *reproof*

castră, -ōrŭm (n. pl.), *a camp*

castŭs, -ă, -ŭm, *guiltless*

cāsŭs, -ūs (m.), *a fall, calamity;* casus gravis, *a heavy downfall;* casus discordiārum, *cases of dissension*

cătēnă, -ae (f.), *a chain*

cătervă, -ae (f.), *a heap*

Cătĭnĭensēs,-ĭŭm (m. pl.), *the Catinienses,* inhabitants of Catina

Caucăsŭs, -ī (m.), *the Caucasus*

caupō, -ōnĭs (m.), *an innkeeper;* ad caupōnem devertĕre, *to put up at an inn*

causă, -ae (f.), *a cause;* causam probāre, *to approve an enterprise;* causā, **w. gen.**, *for the sake of* căvĕō, -ērĕ, cǎvī, cautŭm, *to be on one's guard, beware*

căvernă, -ae (f.), *a hollow, cavity*

căvillōr, -ārī, -ātŭs sŭm, *to jest*

Cĕcrops, -ŏpĭs (m.), *Cecrops, first king of Athens*

cĕdō, -ĕrĕ, cessī, cessŭm, *to give way, retreat, retire;* possessionĭbus cedĕre, *to give up one's property*

cĕlĕbĕr, -rĭs, -rĕ, *celebrated*

cĕlĕbrĭtās, -ātĭs (f.), *a great number*

cĕlĕbrō, -ārĕ, -āvī, -ātŭm, *to celebrate*

cĕlĕr, -ĭs, -ĕ, *quick*

cĕlĕrĭtās, -ātĭs (f.), *speed, quick-*

cĕlĕrĭtĕr, *quickly* [*ness*

celsŭs, -ă, -ŭm, *lofty*

cēnă, -ae (f.), *a dinner*

cēnātŭs, -ă, -ŭm, *having dined, after dinner*

cēnō, -ārĕ, -āvī, -ātŭm, *to dine*

censĕō, -ērĕ, censŭī, censŭm, *to express one's opinion; to assent; to believe*

centŭm, *a hundred*

cēră, -ae (f.), *wax; a tablet (*to write upon*)*

Cĕrămīcŭs, -ī (m.), *Ceramicos, the pot market*

cernō, -ĕrĕ, crēvī, crētŭm, *to see*

certāmĕn, -ĭnĭs (n.), *a contest;* certamĭna Olympĭca, *the Olympic games*

certātĭm, *emulously, eagerly*

certĕ, *certainly, assuredly*

certō, -ārĕ, -āvī, -ātŭm, *to contend (*cum, *against*)*

certŭs, -ă, -ŭm, *sure, certain;* certus modus, *a fixed measure;* certiōrem facĕre, *to inform*

cervix, -īcĭs (f.), *mostly in the* pl., *the neck, nape*

cervŭs, -ī (m.), *a stag*

cessĭm, *backward;* cessim ire, *to stay behind*

cētĕrŭm, *but*

(cētĕrŭs), -ă, -ŭm, *all the other, the rest*

Chărĭādēs, -ĭs (m.), *Chariades, an Athenian general in the Peloponnesian war*

Chărillŭs, -ī (m.), *Charillus, cousin of Lycurgus*

Chărybdĭs, - (f.), *Charybdis, a whirlpool between Italy and Sicily, and opposite to the rock Scylla*

cĭbărĭŭs, -ă, -ŭm, *pertaining to food;* cibarĭus panis, *black bread*

cĭbŭs, -ī (m.), *food*

cĭĕō, -ērĕ, cĭvī, cĭtŭm, *to rouse;* bellum ciĕre, *to stir up battle;* Acerbam ciet, *she invokes Acerbas*

circă, **with acc.**, *around, about*

circĭtĕr, *about*

circŭm, **with acc.**, *round about*

circumdō, -ārĕ, circumdĕdī, circumdātŭm, *to surround*

circumspĭcĭō, -ĕrĕ, circumspexī, circumspectŭm, *to look around*

circumstō, -ārĕ, circumstĕtī, (**no sup.**), *to surround*

circumvĕnĭō, -īrĕ, circumvēnī, circumventŭm, *to surround*

cĭtō, *quickly, in a short time*

cĭtō, -ārĕ, -āvī, -ātŭm, *to quicken;* citāto cursu, *at a quick run;* citāto impĕtu, *with rapid motion*

cīvīlĭs, -ĕ, *of a citizen, civil*

cīvĭs, – (m. & f.), *a citizen, fellow-citizen*

cīvĭtās, -ātĭs (f.), *a state; a city*

clādēs, -ĭs (f.), *a defeat*

clăm, *secretly*

clāmĭtō, -ārĕ, -āvī, -ātŭm, *to cry out*

clāmŏr, -ōrĭs (m.), *shouting*

clandestīnŭs, -ă, -ŭm, *clandestine, secret*

clārŭs, -ă, -ŭm, *famous, of renown, remarkable;* clarum tintinnabŭlum, *the tinkling bell*

classĭs, – (f.), *a fleet*

claudō, -ĕrĕ, clausī, clausŭm, *to shut, close*

Cŏcălŭs, -ī (m.), *Cocalus, an ancient king of Sicily*

coctŭs, -ă, -ŭm, *cooked; baked;* later coctus, *a brick*

Cōdrŭs, -ī (m.), *Codrus, the last king of Athens*

cŏĕō, -īrĕ, cŏĭī, cŏĭtŭm, *to come together;* in se coīre, *to dash against each other;* una coīre, *to unite*

coepī, coepissĕ, *to begin*

coeptă, -ōrŭm (n.pl.), *an undertaking*

coeptŭs, -ă, -ŭm, *begun*

cŏercĕō, -ērĕ, -ŭī, -ĭtŭm, *to hold together;* matrimonĭa coercēre, *to restrain their wives*

cōgĭtō, -ārĕ, -āvī, -ātŭm, *to think*

cognātĭō, -ōnĭs (f.), *kindred; relatives*

cognātŭs, -ī (m.), *a kinsman*

cognōmĭnō, -ārĕ, -āvī, -ātŭm, *to surname, name*

cognōscō, -ĕrĕ, cognōvī, cognĭtŭm, *to know, to learn; to in-*

vestigate; causam cognoscĕre, *to investigate a case*

cōgō, -ĕrĕ, cŏēgī, cŏactŭm, *to bring together, to compel*

cŏhortŏr, -ārī, -ātŭs sŭm, *to exhort*

collaudō, -ārĕ, -āvī, -ātŭm, *to praise*

collĭgō, -ĕrĕ, collēgī, collectŭm, *to collect*

collĭs, – (m.), *a hill*

collŏcō, -ārĕ, -āvī, -ātŭm, *to place;* filĭam collocāre, *to give one's daughter in marriage*

collŏquĭŭm, -ī (n.), *a conversation*

collŏquŏr, -ī, collŏcūtŭs sŭm, *to parley, confer; to speak to;* colloquendi copĭa, *opportunity of a conference*

collŭm, -ī (n.), *the neck*

cŏlō, -ĕrĕ, cŏlŭī, cultŭm, *to till, cultivate;* amicitĭam colĕre, *to cultivate friendship*

cŏlŭbră, -ae (f.), *a snake*

cŏlumbă, -ae (f.), *a dove, pigeon*

cŏlŭmellă, -ae (f.), *a pillar*

cŏlumnă, -ae (f.), *a column*

cŏlŭs, -ī (f.), *a distaff*

combūrō, -ĕrĕ, combussī, combustŭm, *to burn wholly*

cŏmĕdō, -ĕrĕ, cŏmēdī, cŏmēsŭm (cŏmestŭm), *to eat*

cŏmēs, -ĭtĭs (m. & f.), *a companion*

commĕātŭs, -ūs (m.), *provisions*

commĕmŏrō, -ārĕ, -āvī, -ātŭm, *to make mention of, to relate*

commendō, -ārĕ, -āvī, -ātŭm, *to commend*

commercĭŭm, -ī (n.), *trade;* commercĭum mutuārum rerum, *trade by exchange of goods* commĕrĕŏ, -ērĕ, -ŭī, -ītŭm, *to deserve* [*soldier*

commīlītŏ, -ōnĭs (m.), *a fellow-soldier*

committŏ, -ĕrĕ, commīsī, commissŭm, *to commit, intrust;* salūtem committĕre, *to intrust one's safety;* proelĭum committĕre, *to commence a battle; to fight a battle;* se committĕre, *to intrust one's self*

Commĭŭs, -ĭ (m.), *Commius*

commŏdŏ, *well*

commŏdŭm, -ĭ (n.), *interest*

commŏdŭs, -ă, -ŭm, *convenient*

commŏtŭs, -ă, -ŭm, *thoroughly roused*

commŏvĕŏ, -ērĕ, commōvī, commōtŭm, *to move (thoroughly)*

commūnĭcŏ, -ārĕ, -āvī, -ātŭm, *to impart; to communicate*

commūnĭs, -ĕ, *common*

commūtŏ, -ārĕ, -āvī, -ātŭm, *to change*

compărŏ, -ārĕ, -āvī, -ātŭm, *to compare*

compellŏ, -ĕrĕ, compŭlī, compulsŭm, *to drive; to compel*

compensātĭŏ, -ōnĭs (f.), *exchange, barter*

compescŏ, -ĕrĕ, compescŭī, (no sup.), *to restrain*

complūrĕs, -ă, *several*

concēdŏ, -ĕrĕ, concessī, concessŭm, *to concede;* in imperĭum concedĕre, *to consent to the government*

concĭlĭŭm, -ĭ (n.), *an assembly; a company*

concinnē, *elegantly*

concĭpĭŏ, -ĕrĕ, concēpī, conceptŭm, *to take in;* fraudem concipĕre, *to commit a crime*

concĭtŏr, -ōrĭs (m.), *an exciter*

concordans, -tĭs, *harmonizing*

concordĭă, -ac (f.), *concord, harmony*

concors, -dĭs, *united in heart;* concordi anĭmo, *of one mind*

concŭbĭŭs, -ă, -ŭm, *belonging to the time of sleep;* concubĭa nocte, *in the first sleep*

concŭpiscŏ, -ĕrĕ, concŭpīvī, concŭpītŭm, *to covet*

concurrŏ, -ĕrĕ, concurrī (concŭcurrī), concursŭm, *to rush together*

concursŭs, -ūs (m.), *a rush, a gathering*

condemnŏ, -ārĕ, -āvī, -ātŭm, *to condemn*

condĭcĭŏ, -ōnĭs (f.), *an option, a condition;* condicĭo ponĭtur, *a choice is left*

condĭmentŭm, -ĭ (n.), *a spice*

condĭŏ, -īrĕ, -īvī, -ītŭm, *to season*

condĭtŏr, -ōrĭs (m.), *a founder*

condŏ, -ĕrĕ, condĭdī, condĭtŭm, *to found, build;* moenĭa condĕre, *to build walls;* (of the dead) *to bury*

confectŭs, -ă, -ŭm, *worn out*

confĕrŏ, -rĕ, contŭlī, collātŭm, *to bring together, to unite;* collātis virĭbus, *with united forces;* se conferre, *to betake one's self*

confessĭŏ, -ōnĭs (f.), *a confession*

confĭcĭŏ, -ĕrĕ, confēcī, confectŭm, *to end, finish*

confīdŏ, -ĕrĕ, confīsŭs sŭm, *to trust, confide*

confĭtĕŏr, -ērī, confessŭs sŭm, *to confess*

confluō, -ĕrĕ, confluxī, conflu-
xŭm, *to flock together*
confŏdĭo, -ĕrĕ, confŏdī, confos-
sŭm, *to stab, pierce*
confŭgĭō, -ĕrĕ, confŭgī, (no sup.),
to take refuge
congrĕdĭŏr, -ī, congressŭs sŭm,
to engage
congressĭŏ, -ōnĭs (f.), *an attack*
conjectŭră, -ae (f.), *a conjecture*
conjĭcĭō, -ĕrĕ, conjēcī, con ec-
tŭm, *to throw, to thrust into*
conjungō, -ĕrĕ, conjunxī, con-
junctŭm, *to connect*
conjunx (conjux), conjŭgĭs (f., *a
wife;* conjŭgem ducĕre, *to
marry*
conjūrātĭŏ, -ōnĭs (f.), *a conspiracy*
conlīdō, -ĕrĕ, conlīsī, conlīsŭm,
to dash together
conpellō, -ĕrĕ, conpŭlī, conpul-
sŭm, *to compel*
conpendĭŭm, -ī (n.), *a short cut*
conpĕs, -ĕdĭs (f.), *a fetter*
conpōnō, -ĕrĕ, conpŏsŭī, conpŏ-
sĭtŭm, *to get up*
conprĕhendō, -ĕrĕ, conprĕhendī,
conprĕhensŭm, *to seize*
conquīsītŭs, -ă, -ŭm, *select,
choice*
consanguĭnĕŭs, -ī (m.), *a kinsman, relative*
conscendō, -ĕrĕ, conscendī, con-
scensŭm, *to mount;* navem
conscendĕre, *to go on board
ship*
consciscō, -ĕrĕ, conscīvī, conscī-
tŭm, *to procure;* mortem sibi
consciscĕre, *to bring death
upon one's self*
conscĭŭs, -ī (m.), *an accomplice*

consectŏr, -ārī, -ātŭs sŭm, *to
pursue*
consĕnescō, -ĕrĕ, consĕnŭī, (no
sup.), *to grow old*
consentĭō, -īrĕ, consensī, consen-
sŭm, *to agree*
consĕquŏr, -ī, consĕcūtŭs sŭm,
*to obtain, to reach; to follow,
overtake*
consĕrō, -ĕrĕ, consĕrŭī, conser-
tŭm, *to·join;* manum conserĕre, *to join battle*
consĭlĭŭm,-ī (n.), *a plan, design,
deliberation, skill;* humănum
consilĭum, *human understanding;* supĕriōris tempŏris consilĭum, *a purpose of former
times;* magnitūdo consilĭi,
amount of prudence
consistō, -ĕrĕ, constĭtī, (no sup.),
to stand (still), halt; in fluctĭbus consistĕre, *to maintain the
position among the waves;*
consistens in loco, *standing
still in one place;* consistĕre
in, *to consist in*
consōlŏr, -ārī, -ātŭs sŭm, *to
console*
consōpĭō, -īrĕ, -īvī, -ītŭm, *to
lull to sleep;* somno consopīri,
to fall asleep
conspectŭs,-ūs (m.), *sight, view;*
in conspectum admittĕre, *to admit to one's presence*
conspĭcĭō, -ĕrĕ, conspexī, con-
spectŭm, *to see*
conspīrātĭŏ,-ōnĭs (f.), *a conspiracy*
conspīrō, -ārĕ,-āvī, -ātŭm, *to
enter into a conspiracy*
constantĭă, -ae (f.), *self-com-
mand*

constĭtŭō, -ĕrĕ, constĭtŭī, con-
tĭtūtŭm, *to appoint;* rem constituĕre, *to arrange an affair,
fix a matter;* navem constituĕre,
to moor or *station a ship;*
supplicĭum constituĕre, *to im-
pose a punishment;* concor-
dĭam constituĕre, *to establish
harmony*

constō, -ārĕ, constĭtī, (no sup.),
to stand fast, consist; constat,
it is an established fact

consŭescō, -ĕrĕ, consŭēvī, con-
sŭētŭm, *to accustom one's self*

consŭētŭdŏ, -ĭnĭs (f.), *a custom;*
consuetūdo propinquōrum, *social intercourse of relatives*

consŭlō, -ĕrĕ, consŭlŭī, consul-
tŭm, *to consult;* reipublĭcae
consulĕre, *to consult the interest of the state;* sibi consulĕre,
*to consult one's own interest;
to take care of one's self*

consummō, -ārĕ, -āvī, -ātŭm,
to consummate, complete

consūmō, -ĕrĕ, consumpsī, con-
sumptŭm, *to consume;* opĕram
consumĕre, *to take pains*

consurgō, -ĕrĕ, consurrexī, con-
surrectŭm, *to stand up for*

contāgĭŏ, -ōnĭs (f.), *connection*

contāmĭnō, -ārĕ, -āvī, -ātŭm,
to contaminate

contĕgō, -ĕrĕ, contexī, contec-
tŭm, *to cover up, conceal*

contemnō, -ĕrĕ, contempsī, con-
temptŭm, *to despise*

contemptŭs, -ūs (m.), *contempt*

contendō, -ĕrĕ, contendī, contentŭm, *to make for; to exert
one's self;* proficisci contendit,
he hastens to start

contentĭŏ, -ōnĭs (f.), *a contest;*
contentĭo vocis, *an elevation of
the voice*

contentĭŭs, *very vigorously*

contentŭs, -ă, -ŭm, *contented*

conterrĭtŭs, -ă, -ŭm, *alarmed*

contestŏr, -ārī, -ātŭs sŭm, *to
invoke*

contĭnĕŏ, -ērĕ, -ŭī, contentŭm,
to contain; plebem, rempublĭ-
cam continēre, *to control the
people;* anĭmam continēre, *to
arrest the current of air;* continēri (pass.), *to be bounded,
confined*

contingō, -ĕrĕ, contĭgī, contac-
tŭm, *to fall to one's lot;* con-
tingit, *it happens*

contĭnŭātĭŏ, -ōnĭs (f.), *a continuous outflow*

contĭnŭŭs, -ă, -ŭm, *uninter-
rupted*

contĭŏ, -ōnĭs (f.), *an assembly*

contĭōnŏr, -ārī, -ātŭs sŭm, *to
harangue*

contrā, with acc., *against;* contra
Gallĭam, *over against Gaul;*
contra, adv., *just the contrary,
on the other side, in return*

contrăhō, -ĕrĕ, contraxī, con-
tractŭm, *to collect, concentrate;* pestem contrahĕre, *to
generate a plague;* auxilĭa contrahĕre, *to collect forces;* naves contrahĕre, *to concentrate
ships*

contrārĭŭs, -ă, -ŭm, *opposite*

contrōversĭă, -ae (f.), *a dispute,
question*

contŭmax, -ācĭs, *insolent;* as a
noun, *a refractory child*

contŭmēlĭă, -ae (f.), *contumely*

convălescō, -ĕrĕ, convălŭī, (no
sup.), *to gain strength*

convĕnă, -ae (m. & f.), *coming
together;* pl., *runaway stran-
gers*

convĕnĭō, -īrĕ, convĕnī, conven-
tŭm, *to agree; to come together, to assemble;* convĕnit,
it is becoming

convertō, -ĕrĕ, convertī, conver-
sŭm, *to turn*

convexŭm, -ī (n.), *a hollow*

convīcĭŭm, -ī (n.), *railing, hard
speeches*

convīvĭŭm, -ī (n.), *a feast, banquet*

convīvŏr, -ārī, -ātŭs sŭm, *to
take meals together*

convŏcō, -ārĕ, -āvī, -ātŭm, *to
call together*

convulnĕrō, -ārĕ, -āvī, -ātŭm,
to wound severely

cōpĭă, -ae (f.), *abundance;* copĭa
colloquendi, *opportunity of a
conference;* copĭae, -ārŭm,
forces; property

cŏquō, -ĕrĕ, coxī, coctŭm, *to
cook*

cŏrĭŭm, -ī (n.), *a hide*

cornū, -ūs (n.), *a horn;* ramōsa
cornŭa, *antlers*

cŏrōnă, -ae (f.), *a wreath*

cŏrōnō, -ārĕ, -āvī, -ātŭm, *to
crown*

corrĭpĭō, -ĕrĕ, corrĭpŭī, correp-
tŭm, *to seize*

corruptŭs, -ă, -ŭm, *corrupt*

corpŭs, -ŏrĭs (n.), *a body*

corvŭs, -ī (m.), *a crow*

cōtīdĭānŭs, -ă, -ŭm, *daily*

Cottă, -ae (m.), *Cotta,* a Roman
surname

Crănăŭs, -ī (m.), *Cranaus,* king
of Athens

crēdens, -tĭs, *full of confidence*

crēdō, -ĕrĕ, crēdĭdī, crēdĭtŭm,
to credit, believe, intrust; ne-
mīni credĕrc, *to trust no one*

crēdŭlŭs, -ă, -ŭm, *credulous;*
convivĭa credŭla, *trusting ban-
quets*

crĕmō, -ārĕ, -āvī, -ātŭm, *to
burn*

crĕō, -ārĕ, -āvī, -ātŭm, *to
create;* magistrātus, duces creāre, *to appoint magistrates,
leaders*

crĕpuscŭlŭm, -ī (n.), *twilight*

crescō, -ĕrĕ, crēvī, crētŭm, *to
grow; to make progress, im-
prove*

Crētă, -ae (f.), *Crete*

Crītō, -ōnĭs (m.), *Crito,* a friend
of Socrates

crŭcĭātŭs, -ūs (m.), *torture*

crūdēlĭs, -ĕ, *cruel*

crūdēlĭtās, -ātĭs (f.), *cruelty*

crŭentŭs, -ă, -ŭm, *bloody*

crŭŏr, -ōrĭs (m.), *gore*

crūs, -ūrĭs (n.), *a leg*

crux, crŭcĭs (f.), *a cross*

Ctĕsĭphōn, -ontĭs (m.), *Ctesiphon,* a friend of Demosthenes

cŭbĭcŭlārĭs, -ĕ, *pertaining to a
sleeping chamber;* lectus cubi-
culāris, *a bed*

cŭbĭcŭlŭm, -ī (n.), *a chamber*

cŭbĭtŭm, -ī (n.), *a cubit*

culmĕn, -ĭnĭs (n.), *a roof*

cultŭs,-ūs (m.), *cultivation,care;*
literārum cultus, *the cultivation of science*

cultŭs, -ă, -ŭm, *cultivated;* cultĭus, *more elegantly*

cŭm, **with abl.**, *with*

cŭm, **conjunction**, *when, as; though*

cunctŏr, -ārī, -ātŭs sŭm, *to delay, hesitate*

cunctŭs, -ă, -ŭm, *all (together)*

cŭpĭdĭtās, -ātĭs (f.), *eagerness; ambition; greed;* cupĭdītas fugiendi, *desire to flee;* imperĭi cupīdītas, *ambition for power;* cupĭdītas pecunĭae, *eagerness for money;* cupiditātes impotentĭum, *the passions of those who are not master of themselves*

cŭpĭdŭs, -ă, -ŭm, *desirous*

cŭpĭō, -ĕrĕ, cŭpīvī, cŭpītŭm, *to wish*

cŭr, *why*

cūrō, -ārĕ, -āvī, -ātŭm, *to take care of, care for; to have (a thing done); to order*

currŭs, -ūs (m.), *a chariot*

cursŭs,-ūs (m.), *a run, a course;* cursum tenēre, *to hold on one's way;* cursus ad Eurōtam, *running on the banks of the Eurotas;* cursus levis, *nimble running*

custōdĭă, -ae (f.), *protection, care;* custodĭa corpŏris, *lifeguard;* custodĭa divitiārum, *the keeping of riches;* custodĭa publĭca, *the public prison*

custōs, -ōdĭs (m. & f.), *a guard*

Cyclōpēs, -ŭm (m. pl.), *the Cyclops,* **a** gigantic race of Sicily

cycnŭs, -ī (m.), *a swan*

Cўnĕgīrŭs, -ī (m.), *Cynegirus,* an Athenian who distinguished himself in the battle of Marathon

Cўprĭŭs, -ă, -ŭm, *Cyprian*

Cўprŭs, -ī (f.), *the island of Cyprus*

Cўrŭs, -ī (m.), *Cyrus,* first king of Persia

D.

daemŏnĭŭm, -ī (n.), *a demon*

damnō, -ārĕ, -āvī, -ātŭm, *to find guilty, condemn*

damnŭm, -ī (n.), *a loss*

Dămŏclēs, -ĭs (m.), *Damocles,* a courtier of the tyrant Dionysius

Dāmōn, -ōnĭs (m.), *Damon,* a Pythagorean in the time of Dionysius

Dārĕŭs, -ī (m.), *Dareus,* the name of several Persian kings

dē, **with abl.**, *from; of* (partitive); *concerning, about;* victorĭa de Persis, *a victory over the Persians*

dēbĕō, -ērĕ, -uī, -ĭtŭm, *to owe; to be obliged;* **pass.** *be owing, due*

dēcēdō,-ĕrĕ, dēcessī, dēcessŭm, *to depart, to die*

dĕcĕm, *ten*

dēcernō, -ĕrĕ, dēcrēvī, dēcrētŭm, *to decree;* classem decernĕre, *to determine upon the building of a fleet*

dēcĭens centum milĭa, 1.000.000

dĕcĭmŭs, -ă, -ŭm, *the tenth*

dēcĭpĭō,-ĕrĕ, dēcēpī, dēceptŭm, *to deceive*

dēclāmō, -ārĕ, -āvī, -ātŭm, *to declaim*

dēclārō, -ārĕ, -āvī, -ātŭm, *to declare, manifest*

dĕcŏrō, -ārĕ, -āvī, -ātŭm, *to distinguish, decorate*

dĕcrĕtŭm, -ī (n.), *a decree*

dĕcurrō, -ĕrĕ, dĕcurrī (dĕcŭ-currī), dĕcursŭm, *to run down*

dĕcŭs, -ŏrĭs (n.), *grace*

dĕdĕcŭs, -ŏrĭs (n.), *disgrace; infamy;* natūrae dĕdĕcus, *monster of nature*

dĕdītĭŏ, -ōnĭs (f.), *a capitulation*

dĕdītŭs, -ă, -ŭm, *given*

dĕdūcō, -ĕrĕ, dĕduxī, dĕductŭm, *to draw down;* copīas dĕdu-cĕre, *to march the troops;* in agrum deducĕre, *to bring into the country;* auxilĭa dĕducĕre, *to withdraw troops* [*tion*

dĕfectĭŏ, -ōnĭs (f.), *a revolt, de*-fec-dĕfectŭs, -ă, -ŭm, *stricken in*

dĕfendō, -ĕrĕ, dĕfendī, dĕfen-sŭm, *to protect from;* bellum defendĕre, *to repel a war*

dĕfĕrō, -rĕ, dĕtŭlī, dĕlātŭm, *to bring;* deferre ad, *to bring before;* rem deferre, *to make a report;* inde deferre, *to draw from thence;* in Afrĭcae sinum dēlātus, *having been carried into a bay of Africa*

dĕfĭcĭŏ, -ĕrĕ, dĕfēcī, dĕfectŭm, *to fail;* tempus anni defĭcit, *the season is too late*

dĕflăgrō, -ārĕ, -āvī, -ātŭm, *to burn down*

dĕflens, -tĭs, *weeping*

dĕflŭō, -ĕrĕ, dĕfluxī, dĕfluxŭm, *to glide down*

dĕformĭs, -ĕ, *disfigured*

dĕfungŏr, -ī, defunctŭs sŭm, *to have done with, to discharge;* (morte) defungi, *to die*

dĕgō, -ĕrĕ, dĕgī, (no sup.), *to spend (time);* vitam degĕre, *to pass one's life*

dĕgustō, -ārĕ, -āvī, -ātŭm, *to taste*

dĕin, dĕindĕ, *then, after, thereupon*

dĕinceps, *after that*

dĕjĭcĭŏ, -ĕrĕ, dĕjēcī, dĕjectŭm, *to throw down*

dĕlātŭs, -ă, -ŭm, *having been carried*

dĕlectō, -ārĕ, -āvī, -ātŭm, *to delight*

dĕlectŭs,-ă,-ŭm, *selected, choice*

dĕlĕō, -ĕrĕ, dĕlēvī, dĕlētŭm, *to destroy, annihilate*

dĕlībĕrō, -ārĕ, -āvī, -ātŭm, *to deliberate*

dĕlīgō, -ĕrĕ, dĕlēgī, dĕlectŭm, *to appoint; to choose, select*

dĕlītŭs, -ă, -ŭm, *smeared over*

Dēlĭŭm, -ī (n.), *Delium, a small place in Boeotia*

Delphī, -ōrŭm (m. pl.), *Delphi, the famous city of the oracle of Apollo*

Delphĭcŭs, -ă, -ŭm, *Delphic*

dēlūbrŭm,-ī (n.),*a shrine, temple*

dēmandō, -ārĕ, -āvī, -ātŭm, *to intrust;* insŭlae demandăre, *to send to an island for safety*

Dēmărătŭs, -ī (m.), *Demaratus*

dēmentĭă,-ae (f.), *insanity, madness*

Dēmētrĭŭs, -ī (m.), *Demetrius, the name of several Greeks*

dēmittō,-ĕrĕ, dēmīsī, dēmissŭm, *to let down*

dēmō, -ĕrĕ, dempsī, demptŭm, *to take off, away*

dēmonstrō, -ārĕ, -āvī, -ātŭm, *to demonstrate, point out*

Dēmŏphŏŏn, -ontĭs (m.), *Demophoon,* son of Theseus

Dēmosthěnēs, -ĭs (m.), *Demos-thenes*, 1. an Athenian general, 2. the most celebrated of the Grecian orators

dēmŭm, *at last*

dēnīquě, *in fine*

dens, -tĭs (m.), *a tooth; tusk*

dēnuntĭō, -ārě, -āvī, -ātŭm, *to give notice*

dēnŭō, *again*

dēpōnō, -ěrě, dēpŏsŭī, dēpŏsĭtŭm, *to give up;* in terra deponěre, *to put on shore*

dērīsŭs, -ūs (m.), *derision*

dērŏgō, -ārě, -āvī, -ātŭm, *to withhold;* fidem derogāre, *to withhold the credit*

descendō, -ěrě, descendī, descensŭm, *to go down, to come down*

dēsěrō, -ěrě, dēsěrŭī, dēsertŭm, *to abandon, forsake;* bellum deserěre, *to give up war*

dēsertōr, -ōrĭs (m.), *a runaway*

dēsertŭs, -ă, -ŭm, *forsaken;* desertus virĭbus, *his strength gone*

dēsīděrō, -ārě, -āvī, -ātŭm, *to require*

dēsĭdĭă, -ae (f.), *sloth*

dēsīdō, -ěrě, dēsēdī, (no sup.), *to sink, to tumble down*

dēsĭlĭō, -īrě, dēsĭlŭī, dēsultŭm, *to jump down*

despērātĭō, -ōnĭs (f.), *hopelessness*

despĭcĭō, -ěrě, despexī, despectŭm, *to despise*

destĭnō, -ārě, -āvī, -ātŭm, *to destine*

destĭtŭō, -ěrě, destĭtŭī, destĭtŭtŭm, *to forsake*

destĭtūtŭs, -ă, -ŭm, *disappointed*

dēsŭm, děessě, dēfŭī, (no sup.), *to be wanting, to fail*

dētěgō, -ěrě, dētexī, dētectŭm, *to expose*

dēterrěō, -ērě, -ŭī, -ĭtŭm, *to deter*

dētĭněō, -ērě, dětĭnŭī, dētentŭm, *to keep back*

dētorquěō, -ērě, dētorsī, dētortŭm, *to turn away*

dētrăhō, -ěrě, dētraxī, dētractŭm, *to take away*

dētrītŭs, -ă, -ŭm, *galled*

Deucălĭōn, -ōnĭs (m.), *Deucalion*, son of Prometheus, famous on account of the deluge

děŭs, -ī (m.), *God*

dēvertō, -ěrě, dēvertī, dēversŭm, *to put up*

dēvincō, -ěrě, dēvīcī, dēvictŭm, *to defeat*

dēvĭŭs, -ă, -ŭm, *out of the way;* iter devĭum, *a by-way*

dēvŏrō, -ārě, -āvī, -ātŭm, *to devour*

dextěr, -ă, -ŭm, *right;* dextra, sc. manus, *the right hand*

Dĭānă, -ae (f.), *Diana*, the daughter of Jupiter

dīcō, -ěrě, dixī, dictŭm, *to say, call;* jus dicěre, *to pronounce judgment, to administer justice*

dīcō, -ārě, -āvī, -ātŭm, *to dedicate*

dictĭtō, -ārě, -āvī, -ātŭm, *to say*

dictŭm, -ī (n.), *a saying*

dĭēs, -ēī (m. & f.), *a day;* in dies, *from day to day;* ad diem, *on the appointed day* diffĕrō, –rĕ, distŭlī, dīlātŭm, to defer; differre a, to be different from; multum differre, to differ widely

diffĭcĭlĭs, –ĕ, difficult

difficultās, –ātĭs (f.), a difficulty

diffīsŭs, –ă, –ŭm, distrusting

diffūsŭs, –ă, –ŭm, diffused

dĭgĭtŭs, –ī (m.), a finger

dignĭtās, –ātĭs (f.), a position, dignity; imperatorĭa dignĭtas, generalship

dignŭs, –ă, –ŭm, worthy, worth

dīlābŏr, –ī, dīlapsŭs sŭm, to scatter

dīlātĭŏ, –ōnĭs (f.), a putting off, postponement

dīlĭgens, –tĭs, careful; diligenter, carefully; comp. diligentĭus, superl. diligentissĭmc

dīlĭgentĭă, –ae (f.), diligence

dīlĭgō, –ĕrĕ, dīlexī, dīlectŭm, to esteem highly; to like

dīmensĭŏ, –ōnĭs (f.), a measuring

dīmĭcō, –ārĕ, –āvī, –ātŭm, to fight; dimicātum est, there was a contest

dīmittō, –ĕrĕ, dīmīsī, dīmissŭm, to let go, dismiss

Dĭŏnȳsĭŭs, –ī (m.), Dionysius, the name of two tyrants of Syracuse

dīrĭmō, –ĕrĕ, dīrĕmī, dīremptŭm, to separate

dīrĭpĭŏ, –ĕrĕ, dīrĭpŭī, dīreptŭm, to plunder

dīrŭs, –ă, –ŭm, fearful

discēdō, –ĕrĕ, discessī, discessŭm, to depart, to separate; a bello discedĕre, to lay down arms; sine querella discedĕre, to come off without complaint

discessŭs, –ūs (m.), a departure

disciplīnă, –ae (f.), discipline

discō, –ĕrĕ, dĭdĭcī, (no sup.), to learn

discordĭă, –ae (f.), disagreement, discord, dissension

dīsertŭs, –ă, –ŭm, eloquent

displĭcĕō, –ĕrĕ, –ŭī, –ĭtŭm, to displease

dispŭtō, –ārĕ, –āvī, –ātŭm, to discuss

dissensĭŏ, –ōnĭs (f.), difference of opinion

dissĕrō, –ĕrĕ, dissĕrŭī, dissertŭm, to discourse

dissĭmŭlō, –ārĕ, –āvī, –ātŭm, to dissemble; dissĭmŭlātŭs, –ă, –ŭm, concealed

dissĭpō, –ārĕ, –āvī, –ātŭm, to scatter

dissŏlūtŭs, –ă, –ŭm, loose

dissolvō, –ĕrĕ, dissolvī, dissŏlūtŭm, to abolish (of laws)

distrăhō, –ĕrĕ, distraxī, distractŭm, to draw (in different directions)

distrĭbŭō, –ĕrĕ, distrĭbŭī, distrĭbūtŭm, to divide, distribute

dĭū, for a long time; dĭūtĭŭs, somewhat long, a considerable time

dīversŭs, –ă, –ŭm, contrary, opposite, different

dīvĕs, –ĭtĭs, rich

dīvĭdō, –ĕrĕ, dīvīsī, dīvīsŭm, to divide

dīvīnātĭŏ, –ōnĭs (f.), divination

dīvīnō, –ārĕ, –āvī, –ātŭm, to divine; quiddam divīnans, some touch of divination

dīvīnŭs, –ă, –ŭm, divine; divīnum quiddam, a divine something

dĭvĭtĭae, –ārŭm (f. pl.), *riches*

dō, –ārĕ, dĕdĭ, dătŭm, *to give;* terga dare, *to turn the back;* sententiam judicibus dare, *to charge a jury;* se dare, *to give one's self up;* primas dare, *to give the first place;* poenas dare, *to suffer punishment;* veniam dare, *to forgive*

dŏcĕō, –ērĕ, dŏcŭī, doctŭm, *to teach; to show*

doctŏr, –ōrĭs (m.), *a teacher*

doctŭs, –ă, –ŭm, *learned*

dŏcŭmentŭm, –ī (n.), *a lesson, an example*

dŏlendŭs, –ă, –ŭm, *deplorable*

dŏlĕō, –ērĕ, –ŭī, (no sup.), *to be grieved, to lament, to rue for*

dŏlŏr, –ōrĭs (m.), *pain, grief*

dŏlōsŭs, –ă, –ŭm, *cunning*

dŏlŭs, –ī (m.), *a trick, wile;* per dolum, *deceitfully*

dŏmestĭcŭs, –ă, –ŭm, *belonging to a family, domestic, private;* domesticus judex, *a family judge*

dŏmĭnātĭō, –ōnĭs, (f.), *dominion*

dŏmĭnātŭs, · ūs (m.), *dominion*

dŏmĭnŭs, –ī (m.), *a lord, master*

dŏmō, –ārĕ, dŏmŭī, domĭtŭm, *to subdue*

dŏmŭs, –ūs (f.), *a house;* domi, *at home;* domum, *home;* domo, *from home*

dōnĕc, *until*

dōnŭm, –ī (n.), *a gift, present*

Dōrĭensēs, –ĭŭm (m. pl.), *the Dorians*

Dōrĭs, –ĭdĭs (f.), *Doris,* wife of Dionysius

dormĭō, –īrĕ, –īvī, –ītŭm, *to sleep*

dōs, dōtĭs (f.), *a dowry*

drăcŏ, –ōnĭs (m.), *a dragon, a sort of serpent*

Drăcō, –ōnĭs (m.), *Draco,* the Athenian lawgiver

Drŭĭdēs, –ŭm (m. pl.), *the Druids,* priests and wise men of the Gauls

dŭbĭtātĭō, –ōnĭs (f.), *hesitation;* sine dubitatione, *promptly*

dŭbĭtō, –ārĕ, –āvī, –ātŭm, *to doubt, hesitate*

dŭbĭŭs, –ă, –ŭm, *doubtful, undecided;* dubius consilii, *wavering in opinion*

dŭcentī, –ae –ă, *two hundred*

dūcō, –ĕrĕ, duxī, ductŭm, *to lead; to deem, to conclude;* conjūgem ducĕre, *to marry;* in numĕro ducĕre, *to count among;* aevum sollicitum ducĕre, *to lead a life of care*

dulcēdŏ, –ĭnĭs (f.), *delightfulness, charm*

dulcĭs, –ĕ, *sweet*

dŭm, *while, as long as; until*

dŭŏ, –ae, –ŏ, *two;* duodequadraginta, *thirty eight*

duplex, –ĭcĭs, *double*

dūrō, –ārĕ, –āvī, –ātŭm, *to last*

dūrŭs, –ă, –ŭm, *hard, hardy*

dux, dūcĭs (m.), *a leader;* ducem praeponĕre, *to put in command*

E.

ē, see ex

ēbrĭĕtās, –ātĭs (f.), *drunkenness*

ēdīcō, –ĕrĕ, ēdixī, ēdictŭm, *to order*

ēdiscō, –ĕrĕ, ēdĭdĭcī, (no sup.), *to learn by heart*

ēdĭtŭs, –ă, –ŭm, *elevated*

ĕdŏ, -ĕrĕ, ĕdī, ēsŭm, *to eat*

ēdŏ, -ĕrĕ, ēdĭdī, ēdĭtŭm, *to
give out;* caedem edĕre, *to
bring forth a defeat; to cause a
slaughter;* oratiōnem edĕre, *to
deliver an oration;* vocem
edĕre, *to exclaim*

ēdŭcō, -ārĕ, -āvī, -ātŭm, *to
bring up*

ēdūcō, -ĕrĕ, ēduxī, ēductŭm, *to
march out, to lead out*

effĕrō, -rĕ, extŭlī, ēlātŭm, *to
carry out* (for burial); *to bury*

effĭcĭō, -ĕrĕ, effĕcī, effectŭm, *to
make, work out, effect, complete;* efficĭtur, *it follows, it is
understood*

effĭgĭēs, -ēī (f.), *an image*

ĕgĕō, -ĕrĕ, -ŭī, (no sup.), *to be in
want*

ēgĕrō, -ĕrĕ, ēgessī, ēgestŭm, *to
bring out* (in heaps); *to discharge*

ĕgŏ, *I*

ēgrĕdĭŏr, -ī, ēgressŭs sŭm, *to go
out, march out;* navĭbus egrĕdi,
to land, to disembark; in proclĭum egrĕdi, *to march out to
battle*

ēgrĕgĭŭs, -ă, -ŭm, *excellent;*
multa egregĭa, *many excellent
deeds*

ēlăbōrō, -ārĕ, -āvī, -ātŭm, *to
elaborate, work out*

Ēleusīnĭŭs, -ă, -ŭm, *Eleusinian*

Ēleusīs, -īnĭs (f.), *Eleusis,* a
very ancient city of Attica

ēlĕvō, -ārĕ, (no perf.), -ātŭm, *to
disparage, make light of;* verbis elevāre, *to cry down*

ēlĭgō, -ĕrĕ, ēlēgī, ēlectŭm, *to
choose, pick*

Ēlissă, -ae (f.), *Elissa,* another
name for *Dido,* the celebrated
foundress of Carthage

ēlŏgĭŭm, -ī (n.), *a saying*

ēlŏquentĭă, -ae (f.), *eloquence*

ēlūdō, -ĕrĕ, ēlūsī, ēlūsŭm, *to
baffle*

ēmĭcō, -ārĕ, ēmĭcŭī, ēmĭcātŭm,
to shine forth

ēmĭnĕō, -ĕrĕ, -ŭī, (no sup.), *to be
conspicuous*

ēmittō, -ĕrĕ, ēmīsī, ēmissŭm, *to
send forth; to let go*

ĕmō, -ĕrĕ, ĕmī, emptŭm, *to buy*

emptĭō, -ōnĭs (f.), *a purchase*

ēnascŏr, -ī, ēnātŭs sŭm, *to grow
up*

ĕō, īrĕ, īvī, ĭtŭm, *to go, march*

ĕō, *to that place, thither*

Ēphĕsĭŭs, -ă, -ŭm, *Ephesian,*
pertaining to Ephesus in Asia
Minor

Ēpĭdaurŭs, -ī (f.), *Epidaurus,* a
city in Argolis

ĕpistŭlă, -ae (f.), *a letter*

ĕpŭlae, -ārŭm (f. pl.), *a (sumptuous) feast, a repast;* conqui-
sitissĭmae epŭlae, *the choicest
dishes*

ĕpŭlŏr, -ārī, ĕpŭlātŭs sŭm, *to
feast upon*

ĕquĕs, -ĭtĭs (m.), *a horseman;*
equĭtes, *cavalry*

ĕquĭdem, *I for my part*

ĕquīnŭs, -ă, -ŭm, *of a horse;*
sacta equīna, *a horse-hair*

ĕquĭtātŭs, -ūs (m.), *cavalry*

ĕquŭs, -ī (m.), *a horse*

ērādō, -ĕrĕ, ērāsī, ērāsŭm, *to
scrape off*

Ērechtheūs,-ĕī (m.),*Erechtheus,*
an ancient king of Athens

ergastŭlŭm, -ī (n.), *a workhouse*
ergō, *therefore*
ērĭpĭō, -ĕrĕ, ērĭpŭī, ēreptŭm, *to set free, deliver*
ēructō, -ārĕ, -āvī, -ātŭm, *to throw up*
ērŭdĭō, -īrĕ, -īvī, -ītŭm, *to instruct*
ērŭdītŭs,-ă,-ŭm, *accomplished, learned*
ērŭō, -ĕrĕ, ērŭī, ērŭtŭm, *to drag* escă, -ae (f.), *food* [*out*
essĕdārĭŭs, -ī (m.), *a charioteer, one who fights from an essedum*
estō, *let it be so; well*
ēsŭrĭens, -tĭs, *hungry*
ĕt, *and*
ĕtĭăm, *also, even*
etsī, *although*
Eurōpă, -ae (f.), *Europe*
Eurōtās, -ae (f.), *Eurotas, a river in Laconia*
Eurўmĕdōn, -ontĭs (m.), *Eurymedon, an Athenian general*
ēvĕhŏr, -ī, ēvectŭs sŭm, *to ride, sail out*
ēvĕnĭō, -īrĕ, ēvēnī, ēventŭm, *to turn out, happen*
ēventŭs, -ūs (m.), *an issue, success*
ēvŏcō, -ārĕ, -āvī, -ātŭm, *to summon, call out*
ēvŏlō, -ārĕ, -āvī, -ātŭm, *to rush out*
ex (before vowels and consonants), ē (before consonants),w. abl., *out of, from out of, on the side of; in accordance with*
exaestŭō, -ārĕ, -āvī, -ātŭm, *to boil up*
exardescō, -ĕrĕ, exarsī, exarsŭm, *to be incensed*

exaudĭō,-īrĕ,-īvī,-ītŭm,*to hear*
excēdō, -ĕrĕ, excessī, excessŭm, *to depart*
excīdō, -ĕrĕ, excīdī, excīsŭm, *to extirpate*
excĭpĭō,-ĕrĕ,excēpī, exceptŭm, *to catch; to take up*
excūsō, -ārĕ, -āvī, -ātŭm, *to apologize, to plead in defense*
exemplŭm, -ī (n.), *an example*
excō, -īrĕ, -ĭī, -ĭtŭm, *to go out, march off; ex urbe exīre, to leave the city*
exercĕō, -ĕrĕ, -ŭī, -ĭtŭm, *to exercise, practice; regna exercēre, to tyrannize;* imperĭum exercēre, *to enforce the power*
exercĭtātŭs, -ă, -ŭm, *practised*
exercĭtŭs, -ūs (m.), *an army*
exĭgō, -ĕrĕ, exēgī, exactŭm, *to exact;* puerĭtĭam exigĕre, *to spend one's boyhood*
exĭgŭŭs, -ă, -ŭm, *small*
exīmĭŭs,-ă,-ŭm, *extraordinary*
exĭmō, -ĕrĕ, exēmī, exemptŭm, *to take from*
exintĕrātŭs,-ă, -ŭm, *eviscerated*
existĭmō, -ārĕ, -āvī, -ātŭm, *to believe, suppose*
exĭtĭŭm, -ī (n.), *destruction*
exĭtŭs, -ūs (m.), *an outlet, exit*
exornō, -ārĕ, -āvī, -ātŭm, *to adorn*
exōrō, -ārĕ, -āvī, -ātŭm, *to beg earnestly*
expĕdītŭs, -ă, - ŭm, *unimpeded, free;* omnĭbus membris expedītus, *having the free use of all one's limbs;* motus ad usum expeditĭor, *movement quicker for use,* i. e., *more easy to be managed*

expellō, -ĕrĕ, expŭlī, expulsŭm,
to drive out

expĕrĭmentŭm, -ī (n.), a trial,
experiment

expĕrĭŏr, -īrī, expertŭs sŭm, to
try, experience

expĕrrectŭs,-ă, -ŭm, awakened

expers, -tĭs, having no share in

expĭō, -ārĕ, -āvī, -ātŭm, to ex-
piate

expĭlō, -ārĕ, -āvī, -ātŭm, to
plunder

explōrō, -ārĕ, -āvī, -ātŭm, to
explore, examine

expōnō, -ĕrĕ, expŏsŭī, expŏsĭ-
tŭm, to expose, to explain; copĭas exponĕre, to draw up
forces

exposcō, -ĕrĕ, expŏposcī, (no
sup.), to implore

expŏsĭtĭŏ, -ōnĭs (f.), an exposing

expugnō, -ārĕ, -āvī, -ātŭm, to
take by storm; to subdue

exsĕcrŏr, - ārī, -ātŭs sŭm, to
curse

exsĭlĭŭm, -ī (n.), exile

exsistō, -ĕrĕ, exstĭtī, (no sup.), to
rise, exist

exspectātĭŏ, -ōnĭs (f.), expectation

exspectō, -ārĕ, -āvī, -ātŭm, to
expect, to wait; non exspec-
tāto, without waiting any
longer; non exspectandus, unexpected; exspectāre in ancŏris,
to wait at anchor

exspīrō,-ārĕ,-āvī,-ātŭm, to die

exstinguŏ,-ĕrĕ, exstinxī, exstinc-
tŭm, to put out, to undo; pass.,
to die

exstirpō, -ārĕ, -āvī, -ātŭm, to
root out

exstō, -ārĕ, exstĭtī, (no sup.), to
be extant, to exist

exstrŭō, -ĕrĕ, exstruxī, exstruc-
tŭm, to erect; mensae exstru-
ebantur, the tables were heaped

exsŭl, -ĭs (m.), an exile

exsŭlō, -ārĕ, -āvī, -ātŭm, to
live in exile

extemplō, forthwith

externŭs, -ă, -ŭm, external,
foreign

exterrĭtŭs, -ă, -ŭm, greatly terrified

extollō, -ĕrĕ, (no perf. & sup.), to
elevate; in majus extollĕre, to
exaggerate

extrā, with acc., outside of

extrăhō, -ĕrĕ, extraxī, extrac-
tŭm, to draw out

extrēmŭs, -ă, -ŭm, last

extundō, -ĕrĕ, extŭdī, extūsŭm,
to strike out; frontem extundĕre, to knock out the brains

F.

făbellă, -ae (f.), a short fable, a
tale

făbrĭcō, -ārĕ, -āvī, -ātŭm, to
build

făbŭlă, -ae (f.), a fable, story

făbŭlōsŭs, -ă, -ŭm, fabulous

făcĭlĭs, -ĕ, easy; facĭle, easily

făcĭlĭtās, -ātĭs (f.), facility, readiness

facillĭmē, very easily

făcĭnŭs, -ŏrĭs (n.), a deed; a
crime

făcĭō, -ĕrĕ, fēcī, factŭm, to do,
make; certiōrem facĕre, to inform; classem facĕre, to build
a fleet; conspiratiōnem facĕre,
to form a conspiracy; iter

facĕre, *to travel;* bellum facĕre, *to wage war;* sacra facĕre, *to sacrifice*

factĭō, –ōnĭs (f.), *a faction, party*

factĭtō, –ārĕ, –āvī, –ātŭm, *to practice;* studiōsc factitāre, *to be fond of*

factŭm, –ī (n.), *a deed, action, transaction*

făcultās, –ātĭs (f.), *opportunity, chance*

fallācĭă, –ae (f.), *deceit, trickery*

fallō, –ĕrĕ, fĕfcllī, falsŭm, *to deceive*

falx, –cĭs (f.), *a sickle*

fāmă, –ae (f.), *fame, report, rumor; public opinion, renown;* famā, *by hearsay*

fămēs, –ĭs (f.), *hunger; a famine*

fămĭlĭă, –ae (f.), *the slaves in a household; the family servants*

fămĭlĭārĭs, –ĕ, *familiar;* (subst.) *an intimate friend*

fămĭlĭārĭtās, –ātĭs (f.), *intimacy, friendship; acquaintance*

fānŭm, –ī (n.), *a temple*

fās, indecl. *allowable, lawful, right*

fastīdĭō, –īrĕ, –īvī, –ītŭm, *to loathe, despise*

fastīgĭŭm, –ī (n.), *a top, summit*

fătīgō, –ārĕ, –āvī, –ātŭm, *to weary;* fatigātus, *wearied*

fātŭm, –ī, (n.), *fate*

faux, –cĭs (f.), usually faucēs (pl.), *jaws; a defile, narrows;* imprŏba faux, *voracity*

făvŏr, –ōrĭs (m.), *favor, good will*

fēlĭcĭtās, –ātĭs (f.), *good fortune;* nascendi felicitas, *a lucky circumstance of birth*

fēlīcĭtĕr, *successfully*

fēlix, –īcĭs, *lucky, happy*

fēmĭnă, –ae (f.), *a wife, woman, female;* canis femīna, *a she-dog*

fĕnestră, –ae (f.), *a window*

fĕră, –ae (f.), *a wild beast*

fĕrax, –ācĭs, *productive, fruitful*

fĕrē, *almost, nearly*

fĕrĭtās, –ātĭs (f.), *fierceness*

fermē, *about, nearly*

fĕrō, –rĕ, tŭlī, lātŭm, *to carry, bear;* auxilĭum ferre, *to bring assistance;* legem ferre, alĭquid ferre, *to make a motion, propose a law;* gravĭter ferre, *to be annoyed, take ill, amiss;* indigne ferre, *to take ill;* in sublīme ferri, *to be borne high in the air;* sententĭam ferre, *to give one's vote;* ferunt, *they say;* fertur, *it is said;* fructum ferre, *to bear fruit*

fĕrōcĭtās, –ātĭs (f.), *fierceness*

ferrŭm, –ī (n.), *iron, a sword, a razor*

fĕrŭs, –ă, –ŭm, *wild;* subst. ferus, *a wild beast, especially a lion*

fervens, –tĭs, *foaming*

fessŭs, –ă, –ŭm, *weary*

fictŭs, –ă, –ŭm, *fictitious*

fīdēlĭs, –ĕ, *faithful*

fīdēs, –ĕī (f.), *(good) faith, faithfulness;* summa fide, *conscientiously;* fides pacis, *the promise of peace;* spectāta fides, *tried honesty;* fidem servāre, *to keep a promise;* fidem habēre, *to believe;* fides mortis adest, *the news of the death proves to be true;* fidem popŭli Romāni sequi, *to seek the protection of the*

Roman people; in fidem recipĕre, *to receive under protection;* fidem derogāre, *to withhold the credit*

fīdūcĭă, –ae (f.), *confidence*

fīdŭs, –ă, –ŭm, *faithful, trusty*

fīgūră, –ae (f.), *the form*

fīlĭă, –ae (f.), *a daughter*

fīlĭŭs, –ī (m.), *a son*

fingō,–ĕrĕ, finxī, fictŭm, *to feign*

fīnĭō, –īrĕ, –īvī, –ītŭm, *to limit*

fīnĭs, – (m.), *a boundary, end*

fīnĭtĭmŭs, –ă,–ŭm, *neighboring;* as subst., *a neighbor*

fīō, fĭĕrī, factŭs sŭm, *to be made or done, to become; to be brought about;* certiōrem fĭĕri, *to be informed*

firmō, –ārĕ, –āvī, –ātŭm, *to strengthen, confirm;* firmāre in or ad, *to animate to*

fiscŭs, –ī (m.), *a money-bag*

fistŭlă,–ae (f.), *a pipe; a canyon; a passage*

flăgellŭm, –ī (n.), *a whip, rod*

flăgĭtĭŭm, –ī (n.), *a disgrace*

flăgĭtō, –ārĕ, –āvī, –ātŭm, *to demand*

flammă, –ae (f.), *a flame*

flātŭs, –ūs (m.), *a blowing* ⌊*for*

flĕō, –ĕrĕ, flēvī, flētŭm, *to weep*

flōrĕō,–ĕrĕ,–ŭī, (no sup.), *to flour-*

flōs, flōrĭs (m.), *a flower* [*ish*

fluctŭs, –ūs (m.), *a wave, tide*

flūmĕn, –ĭnĭs (n.), *a river*

foedĭtās, –ātĭs (f.), *horribleness;* foedĭtas morientĭum, *the horrible sight of the dying*

foedŭs, –ă, –ŭm, *ignominious*

foedŭs, –ĕrĭs (n.), *a league;* foedus īcĕre, *to make a league*

fons, –tĭs (m.), *a spring*

fŏrĕ, **Fut. Inf.** of sum and fio

fŏrĕm, **Subj. Imperf.** of sum and fio

fŏrĭs,– (f.), & fŏrēs,–ĭŭm, *a door*

formă, –ae (f.), *shape, form, appearance;* insignis, eximĭa forma, *great beauty*

formātŭs, –ă, –ŭm, *informed*

forsĭtăn, fortassĕ, *perhaps*

fortĕ, *by chance*

fortĭs, –ĕ, *brave, courageous, gallant;* fortĭus, *with greater courage*

fortūnă, –ae (f.), *fortune; fate;* fortūna privāta, *private condition*

fortūnātŭs, –ă, –ŭm, *happy*

fŏrŭm, –ī (n.), *a market-place*

fossă –ae (f.), *a ditch, trench*

fŏvĕō, –ĕrĕ, fōvī, fōtŭm, *to warm, hug*

frăgĭlĭs, –ĕ, *brittle, fragile*

frangō, –ĕrĕ, frēgī, fractŭm, *to break*

frātĕr, –rĭs (m.), *a brother*

frāternŭs, –ă, –ŭm, *brotherly*

fraus, fraudĭs (f.), *fraud; a crime*

frĕmĭtŭs, –ūs (m.), *roaring*

frēnŭm, –ī (n.), *a bridle, reins*

frĕquentĕr, *often*

frĕquentĭă, –ae (f.), *a large num-*

frĕtŭm, –ī (n.), *straits* [*ber*

frĕtŭs, –ă, –ŭm, *relying*

frīgĭdŭs, –ă, –ŭm, *cold*

frīgŭs, –ŏrĭs (n.), *cold*

frons, –tĭs (f.), *the forehead;* a frontĭbus, *in front;* frontem extundĕre, *to knock out the brains*

fructŭōsŭs, –ă, –ŭm, *productive*

fructŭs, –ūs (m.), *fruit;* fructum ferre, *to bear fruit*

frūgālĭtās, –ātĭs (f.), *frugality*

frūgēs, –ŭm (f. pl.), *fruit*

frŭmentŭm, –ī (n.), *corn*

frŭŏr, –ī, frŭītŭs (fructŭs) sŭm, *to enjoy*

frustrā, *in vain; without cause*

frustŭm, –ī (n.), *a piece, morsel*

frŭtex, –ĭcĭs (f.), *a shrub*

fŭgă, –ae (f.), *flight; banishment*

fŭgĭō, –ĕrĕ, fŭgī, (no sup.), *to flee;* fugientes, *those endeavoring to escape*

fŭgĭtō, –ārĕ, –āvī, –ātŭm, *to flee from*

fulgens, –tĭs, *glittering*

fulgŏr, –ōrĭs (m.), *glitter*

fulmĕn, –ĭnĭs (n.), *a thunderbolt*

fulmĭnĕŭs, –ă, –ŭm, *belonging to lightning, flashing*

fŭmŭs, –ī (m.), *smoke*

fundă, –ae (f.), *a sling*

fundāmentŭm, –ī (n.), *a foundation;* fundamenta jacĕrĕ, *to lay the foundation*

fundō,–ĕrĕ, fūdī, fūsŭm, *to rout;* sanguĭnem fundĕre, *to shed blood*

fundŭs, –ī (m.), *a piece of land;* fundus imus, *the lowest bottom*

fūnŭs, –ĕrĭs (n.), *a funeral*

fūr, fūrĭs (m.), *a thief*

fŭrō,–ĕrĕ, (no perf. & sup.), *to rage, to be mad*

fŭrŏr, –ōrĭs (m.), *madness*

furtĭm, *stealthily, secretly*

fŭtūrŭs, –ă, –ŭm, *future*

G.

Gājŭs, –ī (m.), *Gaius*

Gallĭă, –ae (f.), *Gaul*

Gallĭcŭs, –ă, –ŭm, *Gallic*

gaudĕō, –ĕrĕ, gāvīsŭs sŭm, *to rejoice*

Gĕlō, –ōnĭs (m.), *Gelo,* tyrant of Sicily

gĕlū, –ūs (n.), *cold* [Sicily

gĕmĭtŭs, –ūs (m.), *groaning*

gĕnĕr, –ī (m.), *a brother-in-law*

gĕnĕrō, –ārĕ, –āvī, –ātŭm, *to produce*

gĕnĭtŭs, –ă, –ŭm, *born*

gens, –tĭs (f.), *a tribe, a nation*

gĕnŭs, –ĕrĭs (n.), *a race, kind;* genus Stratōnis, *the family of Strato;* genus urbis, *the stock of the city*

gĕōmetrĭcă,–ōrŭm (n. pl.), *geometry*

Germānŭs, –ī (m.), *a German*

germĕn, –ĭnĭs (n.), *a germ*

gĕrō, –ĕrĕ, gessī, gestŭm, *to carry, wear;* bellum gerĕre, *to wage war;* res gerundae, *public business;* res gestae, *exploits, achievements*

gestĭō, –īrĕ, –īvī, –ītŭm, *to long*

gignō, –ĕrĕ, gĕnŭī, gĕnĭtŭm, *to beget, to bear;* pass., *to be born*

glădĭŭs, –ī (m.), *a sword*

gliscens, –tĭs, *kindling* [noun

glōrĭă, –ae (f.), *glory, fame,* re-

glōrĭŏr,–ārī, –ātŭs sŭm, *to boast*

glōrĭōsŭs, –ă, –ŭm, *glorious*

grădātĭm, *step by step*

grădŭs,–ūs (m.), *a degree; step;*

Graecĕ, *in Greek* [stage

Graecĭă, –ae (f.), *Greece*

Graecŭs, –ă, –ŭm, *Greek*

grandĭs, –ĕ, *great, heavy;* grandis pecunĭa, *an immense amount of money*

grassŏr, –ārī, –ātŭs sŭm, *to rage*

grātĭă, –ae (f.), *favor, gratitude;* gratĭam fingĕre, *to feign friendship;* gratĭam quaerĕre, trahĕre, *to seek, to gain favor*

grātŭs, -ă,-ŭm, *grateful, accept-*
able; gratĭus facĕre, *to do ɔ*
greater favor
grăvātŭs, -ă, -ŭm, *loaded*
grăvĭs, -ĕ, *heavy, oppressive;*
gravis imāgo, *a grievous im-*
age; graviōra bclla, *severer*
wars; gravis casus, *a heavy*
downfall; gravcm pati, *to be in-*
dignant at, to be greatly em-
bittered against
grăvĭtĕr, *heavily, seriously;* gra-
vĭtcr ferre, *to be annoyed*
grĕmĭŭm, -ī (n.), *the lap*
grex, grĕgĭs (f.), *a herd; crowd*
grŭĭs, - (f.), *a crane*
gŭlă, -ae (f.), *the gullet*
Gўlippŭs, -ī (m.), *Gylippus,* general of the Spartans in Sicily
Gythĕŭm, -ī (n.), *Gytheum,* a
seaport in Laconia

H.

hăbĕō,-ērĕ, -ŭī, -ĭtŭm, *to have,*
hold, possess; to consider,
think; habēri pro, *to be con-*
sidered as; fidem habēre, *to*
believe; magni habēre, *to con-*
sider of great importance; pro
nihĭlo habēre, *to regard as*
nothing; obvĭum habĕrc, *to meet*
hăbĭlĭs, -ĕ, *easy* (of shoes)
hăbĭtŭs, -ūs (m.), *dress;* deformis habĭtu, *deformed by his*
dress; habĭtus squalōris, *the*
appearance of squalor
haerĕō, -ērĕ, haesī, haesŭm, *to*
stick at; to hesitate
Hălĭcarnāsŭs, -ī (f.), *Halicarna-*
sus, a city of great antiquity in
Asia Minor
Hămilcăr, -ărĭs (m.), *Hamilcar*

hărēnă, -ae (f.), *sand*
hărĭŏlŭs, -ī (m.), *a soothsayer*
Harpăgŭs, -ī (m.), *Harpagus,* a
Median nobleman
haud, *not*
haustŭs, -ūs (m.), *a draught*
herclĕ, hercŭlĕ, *by Hercules*
Hercŭlēs, -ĭs (m.), *Hercules*
hērēdĭtās, -ātĭs (f.), *an inherit-*
ance
hērēs, -ēdĭs (m. & f.), *an heir*
Hermae, -ārŭm (m. pl.), *the*
Hermae
hesternŭs -ă, -ŭm, *of yesterday*
hībernŭs, -ă, -ŭm, *winter-*
hĭc, haec, hŏc, *this; the latter,*
the former
hĭc, **adv.,** *here*
hĭcms, -ĕmĭs (f.), *winter*
Hīmĕră, -ac (f.), *Himera*
hinc, *here, on this side; from*
here, hence
Hipparchŭs,-ī (m.), *Hipparchus,*
& Hippĭās, -ac (m.), *Hippias,*
sons of Pisistratus
hīstŏrĭă, -ae (f.) *history*
hŏdĭĕ, *to-day*
hŏdĭernŭs, -ă, -ŭm, *to-day's*
Hŏmĕrĭcŭs, -ă, -ŭm, *belonging*
to Homer, Homeric
Hŏmĕrŭs, -ī (m.), the Greek poet
Homer
hŏmō, -ĭnĭs (m.), *man, human*
being; pl., *people*
hŏnestŭs, -ă, -ŭm, *honorable,*
noble, excellent; honestĭus, *with*
more honor
hŏnŏr, -ōrĭs (m.), *an honor,*
dignity; esteem, regard
hŏnŏrātŭs, -ă, -ŭm, *respected*
hŏră, -ae (f.), *an hour* (twelfth
part of daylight or night, the

first hour being, say, 6 A. M. or
P. M.); horae meridiānae, *noon*
hordĕŭm, -ī (n.), *grain*
horrendŭs, -ă, -ŭm, *horrible*
hortŏr, -ārī, -ātŭs sŭm, *to exhort, urge*
hospēs, -ĭtĭs (m.), *a stranger,
guest, friend*
hospĭtĭŭm, -ī (n.), *hospitality;* in
hospitĭo, *at a friend's*
hostīlĭs, -ĕ, *of an enemy, hostile*
hostĭs, - (m. & f.), *an enemy*
hūc, *hither;* huc accēdit, *to this
is added*
hūmānĭtās, -ātĭs (f.), *human
nature;* pia humanĭtas, *kind
feelings*
hūmānŭs, -ă, -ŭm, *human*
hŭmīlĭs, -ĕ, *low;* humiliōrcs, *the
weaker ones*
hŭmō, -ārĕ, -āvī, -ātŭm, *to
bury;* terra humāre, *to inter*
hūmŏr, -ōrĭs (m.), *a liquid,
moisture*
hydrŭs, -ī (m.), *a snake*
Hyrcānī, -ōrŭm (m. pl.), *the
Hyrcanians* on the Caspian Sea

I.

ĭbĭ, *there*
īcō, -ĕrĕ, īcī, ictŭm, *to strike,
hit;* foedus icĕre, *to make a
league*
ictŭs, -ūs (m.), *a stroke, blow*
idcircō, *therefore*
ĭdĕm, ĕădĕm, ĭdĕm, *the same; at
the same time, likewise*
ĭdĕŏ, *on that account* [venient
ĭdōnĕŭs, -ă, -ŭm, *suitable,* con-
ĭgĭtŭr, *therefore*
ignāvŭs, -ă, -ŭm, *coward*
ignĭs, - (m.), *fire*

ignōmĭnĭă, -ae (f.), *a disgrace;*
ignominĭa judicĭi, *a disgrace
inflicted by the court; contempt
of court*
ignōrō, -ārĕ, -āvī, -ātŭm, *not
to know, be unacquainted with*
ignōtŭs, -ă, -ŭm, *unknown; he
who does not know*
Ilĭās, -ădĭs (f.), *Iliad*
illĕ, illă, illŭd, *that; he, she, it;
the former; the latter;* illud,
that well-known saying
illĕcĕbrae, -ārŭm (f. pl.), *attraction*
illĭc, *there*
illĭcĭō, -ĕrĕ, illexī, illectŭm, *to
allure, entice*
illō, illūc, *thither*
Illўrĭcŭs, -ă, -ŭm, *Illyrian*
ĭmāgō, -ĭnĭs (f.), *an image*
imbĕr, -rĭs (m.), *a shower,
storm*
imberbĭs, -ĕ, *beardless*
ĭmĭtātĭŏ, -ōnĭs (f.), *imitation*
ĭmĭtŏr, -ārī, -ātŭs sŭm, *to imi-
tate*
immĭnĕō, -ĕrĕ, (no perf. & sup.), *to
threaten*
immŏlō, -ārĕ, -āvī, -ātŭm, *to
sacrifice*
immortālĭs, -ĕ, *immortal*
immortālĭtās, -ātĭs (f.), *immor-
tality*
impătĭentĭŭs, *beyond endurance*
impĕdĭmentŭm, -ī (n.), *hindrance, impediment*
impĕdĭō, -īrĕ, -īvī, -ītŭm, *to
hinder, impede;* manĭbus impedītis, *with their hands engaged*
impellō,-ĕrĕ, impŭlī, impulsŭm,
to push on, instigate, impel

impend**ĕō**,-**ērĕ**, (**no perf. & sup.**), to
hang over, to be impending,
to threaten
impĕrăt**ŏr**, -**ōrĭs** (m.), a com-
mander, general; emperor
impĕrătōrĭ**ŭs**,-**ă**,-**ŭm**, belonging
to a general; dignĭtas imperatorĭa, generalship; mors imperatorĭa, a general's death
impĕrīt**ŭs**,-**ă**, -**ŭm**, unpractised,
unskilled, ignorant
impĕrĭ**ŭm**, -**ī** (n.), dominion,
government, empire; imperĭum
paternum, his father's dominion; imperĭum regis, the king's
order; justitĭa imperiōrum, the
justice of commands; imperĭum temptāre, to make an attempt on the government; imperĭum orbis, empire of the
world; imperĭum exercēre, to
enforce the power
impĕr**ō**, -**ārĕ**, -**āvī**, -**ātŭm**, to
give commands, to command,
order; obsĭdes imperāre, to
order to furnish hostages
impĕtr**ō**, -**ārĕ**, -**āvī**, -**ātŭm**, to
obtain, get
impĕt**ŭs**, -**ūs** (m.), violence; an
attack; citāto impĕtu, with
rapid motion
implĕt**ās**, -**ātĭs** (f.), impiety
impĭ**ŭs**, -**ă**, -**ŭm**, impious
implĕ**ō**,-**ērĕ**, implēvī, implētŭm,
to fill
implōr**ō**, -**ārĕ**, -**āvī**, -**ātŭm**, to
call upon for aid, to beseech
impōn**ō**, -**ĕrĕ**, impŏsŭī, impŏsĭ-
t**ŭm**, to put in; navĭbus impo-
nĕre, to put on board
impŏtens, -**tĭs**, not master of
one's self

impressĭ**ō**, -**ōnĭs** (f.), an attack
imprīmĭs, see inprīmis
imprŏb**ŭs**, -**ă**, -**ŭm**, wicked
imprōvīs**ō**, unawares, unexpect-
impūber, -**ĭs**, under age   [edly
impūn**ē**, without punishment
im**ŭs**,-**ă**,-**ŭm**, the lowest, deepest
ĭn,with acc., into, to, towards, for,
against; in Ctesiphontem, as
prosecutor of Ctesiphon; with
abl., in, amongst, in the case of
ĭnambŭlans, -**tĭs**, walking
incendĭ**ŭm**, -**ī** (n.), a fire, con-
flagration
incend**ō**, -**ĕrĕ**, incendī, incen-
s**ŭm**, to set on fire, to fire; in-
cens**ŭs**, -**ă**, -**ŭm**, burnt out;
of the mind, incensed
ĭncert**ŭs**, -**ă**, -**ŭm**, uncertain,
doubtful
incĭd**ō**, -**ĕrĕ**, incĭdī, incāsŭm, to
fall into, to chance upon
incĭt**ō**, -**ārĕ**, -**āvī**, -**ātŭm**, to
urge; naves incitāre, to set the
ships in rapid motion; equum
incitāre, to spur on a horse
inclīn**ō**, -**ārĕ**, -**āvī**, -**ātŭm**, to
incline
inclĭt**ŭs**, -**ă**, -**ŭm**, celebrated, re-
nowned
inclūd**ō**, -**ĕrĕ**, inclūsī, inclūs**ŭm**,
to shut up
incognĭt**ŭs**, -**ă**, -**ŭm**, unknown
incŏl**ă**, -**ae** (m.), an inhabitant
incŏl**ō**, -**ĕrĕ**, incŏlŭī, incultŭm,
to inhabit
incŏlŭmĭs,-**ĕ**,unhurt,unharmed,
safe
inconpŏsĭt**ŭs**, -**ă**, -**ŭm**, disor-
dered
incrĕbresc**ō**, -**ĕrĕ**, incrĕbrŭī, (**no**
sup.), to gain ground

incrĕdĭbĭlĭs, -ĕ, *passing belief,*
incredible
incrēmentŭm, -ī (n.), *increase*
incumbō, -ĕrĕ, incŭbŭī, incŭbĭ-
tŭm, *to hasten*
incursĭŏ, -ōnĭs (f.), *an incursion*
indĕ, *there, thence; from thence;*
hinc..inde, *here..there*
indĭcĭŭm, -ī (n.), *an indication,*
information
indignātĭŏ,-ōnĭs (f.),*indignation*
indignē ferrĕ, *to take ill, to be in-*
dignant at
indignŏr, -ārī, -ātŭs sŭm, *to be*
indignant at
indignŭs, -ă, -ŭm, *unworthy,*
disgraceful; undeserving
indoctŭs, -ă, -ŭm, *untaught*
indŏlēs, -ĭs (f.), *disposition, tal-*
ent, temper
indŭbĭtātŭs, -ă, -ŭm, *without*
doubt
indulgentĭă, -ae (f.), *indulgence*
Indŭs, -ī (m.), *an Indian* [*try*
industrĭă,-ae (f.), *energy, indus-*
industrĭŭs, -ă, -ŭm, *industri-*
ous, active
ĭnĕō, -īrĕ, ĭnĭī, ĭnĭtŭm, *to enter*
upon; consilĭum inīre, *to form*
a plan; epŭlas inīre, *to go to a*
repast
ĭnermĭs,-ĕ, *unarmed, defenseless*
ĭners, -tĭs, *silly, simple*
ĭnexpĭăbĭlĭs, -ĕ, *inexpiable*
infāmĭă, -ae (f.), *a disgrace, in-*
famy
infans,-tĭs(m.&f.),*an infant,child*
infēlix, -īcĭs, *calamitous*
infĕrī, -ōrŭm (m. pl.), *the gods*
below, the lower world
infĕrĭae, -ārŭm (f. pl.), *sacri-*
fices (in honor of the dead)

infĕrĭŏr,-ŭs,*lower, further down*
infĕrō,-rĕ, intŭlī, illātŭm, *to bear*
in, to carry in or upon, to in-
flict; bellum inferre, *to make*
war upon; venalĭa inferre, *to*
offer for sale; jurgĭi causam inferre, *to pick a quarrel*
infestŭs, -ă, -ŭm, *implacable;*
dangerous
inflātŭs, -ă, -ŭm, *puffed up*
ingĕmiscō,-ĕrĕ,ingĕmŭī,(no sup.),
to groan
ingĕnĭŭm, -ī (n.), *mind, talents,*
character, disposition; inge-
nĭum mite, *mild disposition*
ingens,-tĭs, *gigantic,vast,great;*
ingens pugnandi anĭmus, *an*
eager desire for the combat
ingĕnŭŭs, -ă, -ŭm, *free-born;*
ingenŭus homo, *a gentleman;*
ingenĭa ingenŭa, *natural dis-*
position of a freeman
ingrātŭs, -ă, -ŭm, *ungrateful*
ingrĕdĭŏr, -ī, ingressŭs sŭm, *to*
step in, enter; to march; to
walk up
ĭnhĭbĕō, -ĕrĕ,-ŭī, -ĭtŭm, *to re-*
strain; inhibēre remis, *to row*
a ship backwards
ĭnĭtĭŭm, -ī (n.), *a beginning;*
initĭa (pl.), *sacred mysteries*
inĭquŭs, -ă, -ŭm, *unfair, unjust*
injĭcĭŏ, -ĕrĕ, injĕcī, injectŭm,
to throw into; to throw over;
metum injĭcĕre, *to strike one*
with fear; pallĭum injĭcĕre, *to*
put on a cloak
injūrĭă, -ae (f.), *a wrong, out-*
rage, injury; injustice
injustŭs, -ă, -ŭm, *unjust, iniq-*
uitous, severe
inlĕcĕbrae, see illĕcĕbrae

inlustrĭs, -ĕ, *bright, famous*

inlŭvĭēs, -ēī (f.), *an inundation;*
inluvĭes aquārum, *a deluge*

inmĕrītō, *without cause, unde-
servedly*

inmortālĭs, see immortālis

innŏcens, -tĭs, *innocent*

innoxĭŭs, -ă, -ŭm, *innocent*

innŭmĕrŭs, -ă, -ŭm, *innumer-
able*

ĭnŏpĭă, -ae (f.), *want, scarcity*

ĭnŏpīnans, -tĭs, *not expected,
unaware*

ĭnŏpīnātŭs, -ă, -ŭm, *unexpected*

ĭnops, -ŏpĭs, *without means*

inpressĭō, -ōnĭs (f.), *an attack.*
Written also impressĭo

inprīmĭs, *chiefly, especially*

inquăm, *quoth I, I say*

inquĭnō, -ārĕ, -āvī, -ātŭm, *to
defile*

inrumpō, -ĕrĕ, inrūpī, inrup-
tŭm, *to rush into, burst into*

inscendō, -ĕrĕ, inscendī, inscen-
sŭm, *to step upon*

inscītĭă, -ae (f.), *unexperience*

inscrībō, -ĕrĕ, inscripsī, inscrip-
tŭm, *to write on, inscribe*

insĕquŏr, -ī, insĕcūtŭs sŭm, *to
follow up, pursue*

insĕrō, -ĕrĕ, insĕrŭī, insertŭm,
to put into

insĭdĭae, -ārŭm (f. pl.), *an am-
bush, snare*

insĭdĭōsŭs, -ă, -ŭm, *treacherous,
insidious*

insignĭs, -ĕ, *prominent, extraordinary;* insignis oratĭo, *extraordinary style of speech;*
insignis forma, *great beauty*

insĭlĭō, -īrĕ, insĭlŭī, insultŭm,
to leap upon

insŏlens, -tĭs, *insolent, arrogant*

insŏlĭtŭs, -ă, -ŭm, *unaccustomed,
unfamiliar*

inspĭcĭō, -ĕrĕ, inspexī, inspec-
tŭm, *to look at*

inspīrātŭs, -ă, -ŭm, *inspired*

instăbĭlĭs, -ĕ, *unsteady*

instăr, indecl., *as good as;* instar
civitātis, *an outline of a city*

instĭtŭō, -ĕrĕ, instĭtŭī, instĭtūtŭm, *to set up, arrange, in-
stitute;* leges instituĕre, *to
frame* or *enact laws;* herĕdem
instituĕre, *to appoint one heir*

instĭtūtŭm, -ī (n.), *an establishment;* instĭtūta, *institutions;*
instĭtūtis uti, *to have institutions*

instĭtūtŭs, -ă, -ŭm, *educated;*
bene instĭtūtus, *well-bred*

instructŭs, -ă, -ŭm, *provided*

instrūmentŭm, -ī (n.), *a means;*
instrumenta bellōrum, *imple-
ments of war*

instrŭō, -ĕrĕ, instruxī, instruc-
tŭm, *to draw up (in battle
array);* bellum instruĕre, *to
make preparations for war;*
odĭa instruĕre, *to occasion
hatred*

insŭĕfactŭs, -ă, -ŭm, *trained to*

insŭĕtŭs, -ă, -ŭm, *not accustomed to, unusual*

insŭlă, -ae (f.), *an island* [sult

insultō, -ārĕ, -āvī, -ātŭm, *to in-

insŭsurrō, -ārĕ, -āvī, -ātŭm, *to
whisper to*

intĕgĕr, -ră, -rŭm, *unchanged,
fresh, virtuous;* ex intĕgro,
anew

intellĕgō, -ĕrĕ, intellexī, intellec-
tŭm, *to observe, to see clearly*

intentŭs, -ă, -ŭm, *intent*

intĕr, with acc., *between, among; in the midst of; inter se, among themselves, with one another; inter eaedem, in the course of beating*

intercĭpĭŏ, -ĕrĕ, intercēpī, interceptŭm, *to cut off, intercept*

intercludŏ, -ĕrĕ, interclūsī, interclūsŭm, *to cut off*

interclūsŭs, -ă, -ŭm, *cut off*

interdiŭ, *in daytime*

interdŭm, *sometimes*

intĕreă, *meanwhile* [*derer*

interfectŏr, -ōrĭs (m.), *a murinterficĭŏ, -ĕrĕ, interfēcī, interfectŭm, to kill*

intĕrĭm, *meanwhile*

intĕrĭmŏ, -ĕrĕ, intĕrēmī, interemptŭm, *to kill, slay*

intĕrĭtŭs, -ūs (m.), *destruction*

interjĭcĭŏ, -ĕrĕ, interjēcī, interjectŭm, *to cast between; tempore interjecto, some time having intervened*

intermiscĕŏ, -ĕrĕ, intermiscŭī, intermixtŭm, *to intermingle*

internuntĭŭs,-ī (m.), *a messenger*

interpellŏ, -ārĕ, -āvī, -ātŭm, *to hinder*

interrŏgātĭŏ, -ōnĭs (f.), *a question*

interrŏgŏ, -ārĕ, -āvī, -ātŭm, *to ask, question*

interrumpŏ, -ĕrĕ, interrūpī, interruptŭm, *to break down*

intersternŏ, -ĕrĕ, interstrāvī, interstrātŭm, *to lay between*

intră, with acc., *within; intra tricesimum annum, within thirty and forty*

intrinsĕcŭs, *on the inside*

intrŏ, -ārĕ, -āvī, -ātŭm, *to penetrate*

intrŏĭtŭs, -ūs (m.), *an entrance*

intŭĕŏr, -ērī, intŭĭtŭs sŭm, *to look at, observe; nutum intuēri, to await the beck*

inultŭs, -ă, -ŭm, *unavenged*

inūsĭtātŭs, -ă, -ŭm, *unusual, novel*

inūtĭlĭs, -ĕ, *useless*

invādŏ, -ĕrĕ, invāsī, invāsŭm, *to attack; naves invadĕre, to seize the ships; rempublicam invadĕre, to seize the government*

invĕnĭŏ, -īrĕ, invēnī, inventŭm, *to invent, find*

inventĭŏ, -ōnĭs (f.), *invention; (of laws) framing*

invĭcĕm, *mutually, each other*

invictŭs,-ă, -ŭm, *unconquered; invincible*

invĭdĕŏ, -ērĕ, invīdī, invīsŭm, *to envy*

invĭdĭōsŭs, -ă, -ŭm, *spiteful, malicious*

invĭŏlātŭs, -ă, -ŭm, *unhurt*

invīsŭs, -ă, -ŭm, *hated, detested*

invītŏ, -ārĕ, -āvī, -ātŭm, *to invite*

invītŭs,-ă,-ŭm, *unwilling;* non invītus, *cheerful(ly)*

invŏlūcrŭm, -ī (n.), *a case*

involvŏ, -ĕrĕ, involvī, invŏlūtŭm, *to pack up*

Īŏnēs, -ŭm (m. pl.), *the Ionians*

ipsĕ, -ă, -ŭm, *self*

īră, -ae (f.), *anger*

īs, ĕă, ĭd, *he, she, it; that;* eo minus, *the less*

istĕ, -ă, -ŭd, *that of yours*

ĭtă, *so;* non ita, *not so, not so very; not quite*

Ĭtălĭă, -ae (f.), *Italy*

ĭtăquĕ, *and so, consequently, therefore*

ĭtĕm, *just so, likewise*

ĭtĕr, ĭtĭnĕrĭs (n.), *a journey, march, road;* iter felicĭus, *a luckier march;* iter terrestre, *a land journey;* iter facĕre, *to* Ĭtĕrŭm, *again*   [*travel*

J.

jăcĕō, -ērĕ, -ŭī, (no sup.), *to lie (prostrate)*

jăcĭō,-ĕrĕ, jēcī, jactŭm, *to hurl, throw;* of foundations, *to lay*

jactō, -ārĕ, -āvī, -ātŭm, *to throw, toss; to boast;* tintinnabŭlum jactăre, *to shake the bell;* frusta jactăre, *to cast morsels to*

jactŭs, -ŭs (m.), *a throw, cast*

jăcŭlŭm, -ī (n.), *a javelin*

jăm, *already, now, by this time;* jam non, *no more, no longer;* the translation of jam is often inadmissible in English.

jŏcans, -tĭs, *in jest*

jŏcŭs, -ī (m.), *joking*

jŭbĕō, -ērĕ, jussī, jussŭm, *to bid, order*

jŭcundŭs, -ă, -ŭm, *pleasant, delicious;* jŭcundĭus, *more deliciously*   [*man*

jŭdex, -ĭcĭs (m.), *a judge, jury-*

jŭdĭcĭŭm, -ī (n.), *a judgment, decision, sentence; a court;* judicĭo, *by discretion;* judicĭum capĭtis, *trial for life*

jŭdĭcō, -ārĕ, -āvī, -ātŭm, *to judge; to think, consider*

juglans, -dĭs (f.), *a walnut*

jungō, -ĕrĕ, junxī, junctŭm, *to join*

Jūnĭŭs, -ī (m.), *June*

Juppĭtĕr, Jŏvĭs (m.), *Jupiter,* the supreme God; Gr. Ζεύς

jurgĭŭm, -ī (n.), *a quarrel;* in jurgĭo, *in the heat of dispute;* jurgĭi causam inferre, *to pick a quarrel*

jūs, jūrĭs (n.), *right, justice, authority;* jus humănum, *human law* — jūs, jūrĭs (n.), *broth*

jūs jūrandŭm, jūrĭs jūrandī (n.), *an oath*

justĭtĭă, -ae (f.), *justice*

justŭs, -ă, -ŭm, *just;* justă, -ōrŭm (n.pl.), *customary rites*

jŭvĕnĭs, - (m.), *a young man*

jŭventŭs, -ūtĭs (f.), *youth*

jŭvō, -ārĕ, jūvī, jūtŭm, *to assist*

juxtā, with acc., *beside, according to;* juxta praeceptum, *according to the order*

L.

lăbellŭm, -ī (n.), *a small vessel*

lăbŏr, -ōrĭs (m.), *toil, labor, exertion, trouble;* labor militĭae, *the toil of military service;* labor quaerendi, *acquisitive disposition*

lăbōrĭōsŭs, -ă, -ŭm, *troubled*

lăbōrō, -ārĕ, -āvī, -ātŭm, *to suffer from, to be in distress;* nihil laborăre, *not to care about*

lăc, lactĭs (n.), *milk*

Lăcaenă, -ae (f.), *a Spartan woman*

Lăcĕdaemōn, -ŏnĭs (f.), *the city of Lacedaemon*

Lăcĕdaemŏnĭŭs, -ī (m.), *a Lacedaemonian*

lăcĕrō, -ārĕ, -āvī, -ātŭm, *to lacerate, tear in pieces*

Lăchēs, -ētĭs (m.), *Laches*, an Athenian general

lăcrĭmă, -ae (f.), *a tear*

lăcrĭmō, -ārĕ, -āvī, -ātŭm, *to shed tears, to weep*

lăcŭnăr, -ārĭs (n.), *a ceiling*

laedō, -ĕrĕ, laesī, laesŭm, *to injure, insult*

laetŭs, -ă, -ŭm, *glad, joyful*

Lămăchŭs, -ī (m.), *Lamachus*, an Athenian general

lămentă, -ōrŭm (n. pl.), *lamentation*

lămentābĭlĭs, -ĕ, *attended with lamentation*

lămentātĭŏ, -ōnĭs (f.), *lamentation*

Lampōnĭŭs, -ī (m.), *Lamponius*, an Athenian general

lānĕŭs, -ă, -ŭm, *woollen*

lānĭgĕr, -ă, -ŭm, *wool-bearing*, i. e. *a sheep*

lār, lārĭs (m.), *a household god*

largŭs, -ă, -ŭm, *ample, abundant*

lascīvĭă, -ae (f.), *wantonness;* per lasciviam, *from wantonness*

lătĕbră, -ae (f.), *a hiding-place*

lătĕō, -ĕrĕ, lătŭī, (no sup.), *to lie hid, to be hidden*

lătĕr, -ĭs (m.), *a brick*

lātrātŭs, -ūs (m.), *barking*

lātrō, -ōnĭs (m.), *a highwayman*

lātrō, -ārĕ, -āvī,-ātŭm, *to bark*

lātrōcĭnĭŭm, -ī (n.), *robbery (on the highway)*

lātŭs, -ă, -ŭm, *broad, wide;* lati fines, *extensive possessions;* quam latissimae solitudines, *deserts as extensive as possible*

lătŭs, -ĕrĭs (n.), *a side, flank*

laudō, -ārĕ, -āvī, -ātŭm, *to praise*

laus, -dĭs (f.), *praise, glory*

lectŭs, -ī (m.), *a couch*

lectŭs, -ă, -ŭm, *picked*

lēgātŭs, -ī (m.), *an envoy;* in the Roman army, *a lieutenant*

lĕgĭŏ, -ōnĭs (f.), *a legion* (at the time of Caesar consisting of 10 cohorts of from 300 to 360 men each)

lĕgō,-ĕrĕ, lēgī, lectŭm, *to pick, choose, gather; read;* vitae sortem legĕre, *to choose a condition of life*

lĕŏ, -ōnĭs (m.), *a lion*

Lĕōnĭdās, -ae (m.), *Leonidas*, a king of Sparta, † 480

lĕpŭs, -ŏrĭs (m.), *a hare*

lĕvĭs, -ĕ, *light, silly;* levis cursus, *nimble running*

lex, lēgĭs (f.), *a law; a condition*

lĭbens, -tĭs, *willing(ly)*

lĭbĕr, -rī (m.), *a book*

lĭbĕr, -ă, - ŭm, *free*

lĭbĕrālĭtĕr, *generously*

lĭbĕrī, -ōrŭm (m. pl.), *children*

lĭbĕrō, -ārĕ, -āvī, -ātŭm, *to deliver*

lĭbertās, -ātĭs (f.), *freedom*

lĭbīdŏ, -ĭnĭs (f.), *pleasure;* libidines, *passions*

Lĭbyă, -ae (f.), *Libya, Africa*

lĭcentĭă, -ae (f.), *license; leave*

lĭcĕt, -ĕrĕ, lĭcŭĭt, lĭcĭtŭm est, *it is left free, one may; it is lawful*

lignĕŭs, -ă, -ŭm, *wooden*

lignŭm, -ī (n.), *wood, log*

līmĕn, -ĭnĭs (n.), *a threshold*

līmŭs, -ī (m.), *mud* [leave

linquō, -ĕrĕ, līquī, (no sup.), *to*

līquŏr, -ōrĭs (m.), *a liquid; water*
līs, lītĭs (f.), *a suit at law*
littĕră, -ae (f.), *a letter* (character
of the alphabet); pl. littĕrae,
*letter, epistle; letters, studies,
science*
lītŭs, -ŏrĭs (n.), *a shore*
lŏcō, -ārŏ, -āvī, -ātŭm, *to
place, bring*
Lŏcrensĭs, – (m.), *a Locrian*, inhabitant of Locri
Lŏcrī, -ōrŭm (m. pl.), *Locri*, a
city in the territory of the
Bruttii
lŏcŭplēs, -ētĭs, *rich, wealthy*
lŏcŭs, -ī (m.), *a place, position,
spot;* loca, *regions;* honesto
loco natus, *sprung from decent
family*
longē, *far, distant, by far*
longĭtūdŏ, -ĭnĭs (f.), *length;* colli
longitūdo, *a long neck*
longŭs, -ă, -ŭm, *long;* navis
longa, *a ship of war, galley*
lŏquŏr, -ī, locūtŭs sŭm, *to speak,
talk*
lūcĕō, -ērĕ, luxī, (no sup.), *to
shine;* lucet, *the day dawns*
Lūcĭŭs, -ī (m.), *Lucius*, a Roman
name, usually represented by L.
lŭcrŭm, -ī (n.), *profit, gain*
luctŏr, -ārī, -ātŭs sŭm, *to
wrestle, struggle, fight*
luctŭs, -ūs (m.), *mourning, grief*
lūdō, -ĕrĕ, lūsī, lūsŭm, *to play,
sport;* pila ludĕrc, *to play ball*
lūgĕō, -ērĕ, luxī, (no sup.), *to
be in mourning, to bewail*
lūgŭbrĭs, -ĕ, *plaintive*
lūnă, -ae (f.), *the moon;* Luna,
the moon-goddess
lŭpŭs, -ī (m.), *a wolf*

lux, lūcĭs (f.), *light;* ante lucem,
before daybreak; luce, *during
the day*
luxŭrĭă, -ae (f.), *luxury*
Lўcurgŭs, -ī (m.), *Lycurgus*, the
lawgiver of the Spartans
Lўsĭăs, -ae (m.), *Lysias*, an
Athenian orator

M.

Măcĕdō, -ŏnĭs (m.), *a Macedonian*
Măcĕdŏnĭă, -ae (f.), *Macedonia*
măcĭēs, -ēī (f.), *leanness, thin-
ness*
maerŏr, -ōrĭs (m.), *grief, mourning*
Măgī, -ōrŭm (m. pl.), *the Magi,*
priestly caste in Persia
măgĭcŭs, -ă, -ŭm, *magic*
măgĭs, *more*   [*ter*
măgistĕr, -rī (m.), *a teacher, mas-
măgistrātŭs, -ūs (m.), *a magis-
trate*
magnĭfĭcentĭă, -ae (f.), *magnificence*
magnĭfĭcŭs, -ă, -ŭm, *magnif-
icent, grand*
magnĭtūdŏ, -ĭnĭs (f.), *bigness,
greatness, size;* magnitūdo animi, *magnanimity;* magnitūdo
consilii et ingenii, *amount of
prudence and capacity*
magnŭs, -ă, -ŭm, *great, large,
big;* magni habēre, *to consider
of great importance;* magna
voce, *with a loud voice*
mājestās, -ātĭs (f.), *majesty;* majestātem administrāre, *to exercise supreme power*
mājŏr, -ŭs, *greater, more important;* majōres, *ancestors;* in
majus extollĕrc, *to exaggerate*

mălĕ, *badly;* male auspicări, *to begin unfortunately;* cum male pugnátum esset, *after the defeat*

mălĕdĭcō, -ĕrĕ, mălĕdixī, mălĕdictŭm, *to speak evil against, revile*

mălĕfĭcŭs, -ă, -ŭm, *wicked*

mălītĭă, -ae (f.), *malice*

mălō, mallĕ, mălŭī, (no sup.), *to wish rather; to prefer*

mălŭm, -ī (n.), *an evil, adversity, calamity;* malum discordĭae, *the seed of discord*

mandātŭm,-ī (n.), *a commission*

mandō, -ārĕ, -āvī, -ātŭm, *to commit, to order*

mānĕ, *(in good time)in the morning, early in the morning*

mānĕō, -ĕrĕ, mansī, mansŭm, *to remain*

mănĭfestŭs -ă, -ŭm, *manifest*

mănŭbĭae, -ārŭm (f. pl.), *spoils*

mănŭs,-ūs (f.), *the hand; a band (of men); force;* manum conserĕrĕ, *to join battle*

Mărăthōnĭŭs,-ă,-ŭm,*Marathonian*

Mardōnĭŭs, -ī (m.), *Mardonius*

mărĕ, -ĭs (n.), *the sea*

mărīnŭs, -ă, -ŭm, *belonging to the sea, sea-;* commĕātus marīnus, *provisions by sea*

mărītĭmŭs,-ă,-ŭm, *sea-;* ora marĭtĭma, *the seashore;* res marĭtĭmae, *naval operations*

mărītŭs, -ī (m.), *a husband*

mātĕr, -rĭs (f.), *a mother*

mātĕrĭă, -ae (f.), *material*

mātĕrnŭs, -ă, -ŭm, *maternal*

mātrĭmōnĭŭm, -ī (n.), *marriage;* in matrimonĭum tradĕre, *to marry;* matrimonĭa (pl.), *wives*

mātrōnă, -ae (f.), *a lady*

mātūrō, -ārĕ, -āvī, -ātŭm, *to accelerate*

mātūrŭs, -ă, -ŭm, *ripe;* matūra hiems, *an early winter*

mātūtīnŭs, -ă, -ŭm, *of the morning;* matutīnum tempus, *the morning hours*

maxĭmĕ, *especially; properly*

maxĭmŭs, -ă,-ŭm, *greatest;* maxĭmus natu, *oldest;* maxĭma vox, *a very loud voice*

Mĕdī, -ōrŭm (m. pl.), *the Medes;* Media,the country of the Medes

mĕdĭcīnă, -ae (f.), *an operation*

mĕdĭŏcrĭs, -ĕ, *middling, indifferent; ordinary;* non mediŏcris, *not common* [tice

mĕdĭtŏr,-ārī,-ātŭs sŭm,*to prac-*

mĕdĭŭs,-ă, -ŭm, *middle;* medĭo tempŏrĕ, *in the meantime;* medĭo noctis, *at midnight*

Mĕgără, -ae (f.), *Megara*

Mĕgărensēs, -ĭŭm (m. pl.), *the Megarenses*

mĕlĭŏr, -ŭs, *better*

membrŭm, -ī (n.), *a member*

mĕmĭnī, -issĕ, *to remember*

mĕmŏr, -ĭs, *mindful*

mĕmŏrăbĭlĭs, -ĕ, *remarkable*

mĕmŏrĭă, -ae (f.), *memory, recollection;* memorĭa nomĭnis, *remembrance of his name;* ars memorĭae, *the art of remembering*

Mĕnăpĭī, -ōrŭm (m. pl.), *the Menapii,* a people of Belgic Gaul

Mĕnō, -ōnĭs (m.), *Menon,* a dialogue of Plato

mens, -tĭs (f.), *the mind, disposition, understanding;* tristĭor mens, *deeper affection* mensă, -ae (f.), *a table*

mensĭs, – (m.), *a month*

mentĭō, -ōnĭs (f.), *a mentioning*

mentĭŏr, -īrī, -ītŭs sŭm, *to lie, tell a lie*

mercātŏr, -ōrĭs (m.), *a merchant*

mercēs, -ēdĭs (f.), *pay, reward*

Mercūrĭŭs, -ī (m.), *Mercurius*

mĕrĕō, -ērĕ, -ŭī, -ĭtŭm, *to deserve*

mergō, -ĕrĕ, mersī, mersŭm, *to sink*

mĕrīdĭānŭs, -ă, -ŭm, *midday-;* horae meridiānae, *noon*

mĕrĭtō, *deservedly*

mĕrĭtŭm, -ī (n.), *a merit, desert*

merx, -cĭs (f.), *ware*

mĕtŭendŭs, -ă, -ŭm, *dreadful, shocking*

mĕtŭō, -ĕrĕ, -ī, (no sup.), *to fear*

mĕtŭs, -ūs (m.), *fear;* metus religiōnis, *religious awe*

Mīcȳthŭs, -ī (m.), *Micythus,* name of a Sicilian

mīgrātĭō, -ōnĭs (f.), *a removal*

mīgrō, -ārĕ, -āvī, -ātŭm, *to migrate*

mīlĕs, -ĭtĭs (m.), *a soldier*

mīlĭtĭă, -ae (f.), *military service*

millĕ, indecl., *one thousand*

Miltĭădēs, -ĭs (m.), *Miltiades*

mīlŭŭs, -ī (m.), *a kite*

mĭnae, -ārŭm (f. pl.), *threats, menaces*

mĭnax, -ācĭs, *threatening;* anĭmus minax, *animosity*

Mĭnervă, -ae (f.), *Minerva*

mĭnĭmĕ, *by no means, not at all*

mĭnĭmŭs, -ă, -ŭm, *least*

mĭnistĕr, -rī (m.), *a minister, servant*

mĭnistĕrĭŭm, -ī (n.), *a service*

mĭnistrātŏr, -ōrĭs (m.), *an attendant*

mĭnistrō, -ārĕ, -āvī, -ātŭm, *to attend, wait upon*

mĭnŏr, -ŭs, *less, smaller*

mĭnŭō, -ĕrĕ, mĭnŭī, mĭnūtŭm, *to weaken, diminish;* controversīas minuĕre, *to settle disputes;* desidĭam minuĕre, *to remove sloth*

mĭnŭs, *less;* nihĭlo minus, *not a whit the less*

mīrācŭlŭm, -ī (n.), *a miracle, wonder*

mīrandŭs, -ă, -ŭm, *wonderful*

mīrŏr, -ārī, -ātŭs sŭm, *to admire, be surprised, wonder at*

mīrŭs, -ă, -ŭm, *wonderful*

miscĕō, -ērĕ, miscŭī, mixtŭm, *to mix;* civitātem miscēre, *to disturb the state*

mĭsĕr, -ă, -ŭm, *wretched, miserable, sad*

mĭsĕrĭcordĭă, -ae (f.), *pity, compassion*

mĭsĕrĭcors, -dĭs, *compassionate*

mītĭgō, -ārĕ, -āvī, -ātŭm, *to soothe*

mītĭs, -ĕ, *mild*

mittō, -ĕrĕ, mīsī, missŭm, *to send, let go, throw;* malum discordĭae mittĕre, *to sow the seed of discord*

mŏdĕrātĭō, -ōnĭs (f.), *moderation*

mŏdĕrātŭs, -ă, -ŭm, *moderate;* moderatĭus, *more moderately*

mŏdŏ, *only*

mŏdŭs, -ī (m.), *a measure, manner, size;* hoc modo, *in this way;* nullo modo, *by no means;* ejus modi versum, *some such verse*

moenĭă, -ĭŭm (n. pl.), *(city) walls*

mōlēs, -ĭs (f.), *a mass*

mōlĭŏr, -īrī, -ītŭs sŭm, *to undertake*

mōmentŭm, -ī (n.), *a moment, short space*

mŏnĕō, -ērĕ, -ŭī, -ĭtŭm, *to admonish, warn*

mŏnĭtŭs, -ūs (m.), *an admonition*

mons, -tĭs (m.), *a mountain*

monstrŭm, -ī (n.), *a monster*

mŏnŭmentŭm, -ī (n.), *a monument*

Mŏrīnī, -ōrŭm (m. pl.), *the Morini*, a people of Gaul

mŏrĭŏr, -ī, mortŭŭs sŭm, *to die; to be in a dying state*

mŏrŏr, -ārī, -ātŭs sŭm, *to delay, tarry*

mors, -tĭs (f.), *death*

morsŭs, -ūs (m.), *a bite; the teeth*

mortālĭs, -ĕ, *mortal*

mortĭfĕr, -ă, -ŭm, *deadly, fatal*

mortŭŭs, -ă, -ŭm, *dead*

mōs, mōrĭs (m.), *custom, way;* mores, *character, manners, morals*

mōtŭs, -ūs (m.), *a motion, movement;* terrae motus, *an earthquake*

mŏvĕō, -ērĕ, mōvī, mōtŭm, *to move, affect;* arma movēre, *to take up arms;* seditiōnem movēre, *to stir up a sedition;* possessiōnem movēre, *to disturb a possession*

mox, *soon*

mŭlĭĕbrĭs, -ĕ, *womanish*

mŭlĭĕr, -ĭs (f.), *a woman* [an

mŭlĭercŭlă, -ae (f.), *a little wom-*

multĭtŭdŏ, -ĭnĭs (f.), *a large body, great number, crowd, multitude*

multŭs, -ă, -ŭm, *many*

mūlŭs, -ī (m.), *a mule*

mundŭs, -ī (m.), *the world*

mūnĭceps, -cĭpĭs (m. & f.), *a citizen*

mūnītĭŏ, -ōnĭs (f.), *fortifying, a fortification, intrenchment*

mūnŭs, -ĕrĭs (n.), *a gift*

mūrŭs, -ī (m.), *a wall*

mūtō, -ārĕ, -āvī, -ātŭm, *to change*

mūtŭŭs, -ă, -ŭm, *mutual;* mutuārum rerum commercĭum, *trade by exchange of goods*

Muttŏ, -ōnĭs (m.), *Mutto*, king of Tyre

Mycălē, -ēs (f.), *Mycale*, a promontory and city in Ionia

N.

năm, namquĕ, *for*

nanciscŏr, -ī, nactŭs sŭm, *to get, to find*

narrātĭŏ, -ōnĭs (f.), *a tale*

narrō, -ārĕ, -āvī, -ātŭm, *to relate*

nascŏr, -ī, nātŭs sŭm, *to be born, to be produced; to take origin from;* of plants, *to grow;* felicītas nascendi, *the lucky circumstance of birth;* ordo nascendi, *priority of birth*

nasturtĭŭm, -ī (n.), *watercress*

nātĭŏ, -ōnĭs (f.), *a nation*

nātū, *in age;* maxĭmus natu, *oldest*

nātūră, -ae (f.), *nature, natural quality*

nātūrālĭs, -ĕ, *natural*

nātŭs, -ă, -ŭm, *old* (so and so
many years); honesto loco natus, *sprung from a decent
family*

naufrăgĭŭm, -ī (n.), *shipwreck*

nāvālĭs, -ĕ, *naval;* proelĭum navāle, *a sea fight;* bellum navāle,
a sea war

nāvĭgātĭŏ, -ōnĭs (f.), *navigation,
a voyage*

nāvĭgĭŭm, -ī (n.), *a sailing vessel*

nāvĭgō, -ārĕ, -āvī, -ātŭm, *to sail*

nāvĭs, - (f.), *a ship;* navis longa,
a ship of war, a galley; navis
onerarĭa, *a ship of burden*

-nĕ, **interrogative particle** = ?

nĕ, *not, that not, lest;* ne quis, *lest
any one;* ne..quidem, *not even*

nĕc, *nor;* see neque

nĕcessĕ, *necessary*

nĕcessĭtās, -ātĭs (f.), *necessity*

nĕcessĭtūdŏ, -ĭnĭs (f.), *necessity;*
pl. *relatives*

nĕcō, -ārĕ, -āvī (nĕcŭī), -ātŭm,
to put to death, kill

nēfās, **indecl.**, *wrong*

neglĕgō, -ĕrĕ, neglexī, neglec-
tŭm, *to neglect, to pay no
heed to*

nĕgō, -ārĕ, -āvī, -ātŭm, *to declare that not*

nēmŏ (**Gen.** nullĭŭs), *no one, nobody*

nĕō, -ērĕ, nēvī, nētŭm, *to spin*

nĕpōs, -ōtĭs (m.), *a grandson*

nĕquāquăm, *in no wise*

nĕquĕ (nĕc), *nor, and not;* neque..neque, *neither..nor;* nec
non, *and besides;* nec solum..
verum etĭam, *not only..but
also;* neque enim, *for;* neque
modo..sed etĭam, *not only..
but also*

nĕquĕō, -īrĕ, -īvī, -ĭtŭm, *not
to be able*

nescĭō, -īrĕ, -īvī, -ītŭm, *not to
know*

nēvĕ, *or (that) not, and (that) not*

nex, nĕcĭs (f.), *murder; death*

nī, *if not*

Nĭcĭās, -ae (m.), *Nicias, an
Athenian general*

Nĭcoclēs, -ĭs (m.), *Nicocles,* tyrant of Sicily

nĭgĕr, -ră, -rŭm, *black*

nihĭl, **indecl.**, *nothing; not at all;*
pro nihĭlo habēre, *to regard as
nothing*

nīl = nihil

nĭmĭs, *too much, too;* non nimis,
not very

nĭmĭŭs, -ă, -ŭm, *too great, exces-
sive*

Nĭnŭs, -ī (m.), *Ninus,* king of
the Assyrians

Nĭnўās or Nĭnўă, -ae (m.), *Nin-
yas,* son of Ninus

nĭsĭ, *unless, except, without, if
not*

nĭtĕō, -ērĕ, -ŭī, (**no sup.**), *to be
sleek*

nĭtŏr, -ōrĭs (m.), *shine, sheen*

nix, nĭvĭs (f.), *snow*

nobĭlĭtās, -ātĭs (f.) *nobility*

noctū, *by night*

nōlō, nollĕ, nōlŭī, (**no sup.**), *to be
unwilling, not to want*

nōmĕn, -ĭnĭs (n.), *a name, a
word;* nomĭne, *by name*

nōmĭnō, -ārĕ, -āvī, -ātŭm, *to
[name*

nōn, *not*

nondŭm, *not yet*

nonnĕ, *not?*

nonnĭsĭ, *except*

nonnullī, -ae, -ă, *some*

nōnŭs, -ă, -ŭm, *the ninth*

noscō, -ĕrĕ, nōvī, nōtŭm, *to learn to know, become acquainted with*

nostĕr, -ră, -rŭm, *our;* nostri, *our men*

nŏtă, -ae (f.), *a sign, nod*

nōtŭs, -ă, -ŭm, *known; one who knows*

nŏvŭs, -ă, -ŭm, *new*

nox, noctĭs (f.), *the night;* medĭa nox, *midnight*

nūbō, -ĕrĕ, nupsī, nuptŭm, *to marry* (of the woman)

nullŭs, -ă, -ŭm, *none, no;* quam nullus, *how insignificant*

nūmĕn, -ĭnĭs (n.), *deity; divine will;* numĭne quodam, *by the will of the gods*

nŭmĕrō, -ārĕ, -āvī, -ātŭm, *to pay down*

nŭmĕrŭs, -ī (m.), *a number, amount;* in numĕro nullo esse, *to be of no consequence*

nummŭs, -ī (m.), *a coin, money*

numquăm, *never, not ever*

nunc, *now;* nunc..nunc, *now.. now*

nuncŭpō, -ārĕ, -āvī, -ātŭm, *to declare*

nuntĭō, -ārĕ, -āvī, -ātŭm, *to bring word, announce*

nuntĭŭs, -ī (m.), *news, message; a messenger*

nūpĕr, *(newly), lately, recently*

nusquăm, *nowhere*

nūtrĭmentŭm, -ī (n.), *nourishment;* of fire, *fuel*

nūtrĭō, -īrĕ, -īvī, -ītŭm, *to bring up;* ignem nutrīre, *to feed a fire*

nūtrix, -īcĭs (f.), *a nurse*

nūtŭs, -ūs (m.), *a nod, beck;* ad nutum, *at a beck*

O.

ŏb, **with acc.**, *for, on account of;* quam ob rem, *therefore*

obdūcō, -ĕrĕ, obduxī, obductŭm, *to cover over*

objĭcĭō, -ĕrĕ, objēcī, objectŭm, *to throw in the way of; to present*

oblĭgō, -ārĕ, -āvī, -ātŭm, *to bind*

oblīvĭō, -ōnĭs (f.), *forgetting*

oblīviscŏr, -ī, oblītŭs sŭm, *to forget*

obnoxĭŭs, -ă, -ŭm, *liable*

obruō, -ĕrĕ, obruī, obrŭtŭm, *to cover, bury*

obscūrŭs, -ă, -ŭm, *obscure*

obsĕquĭŭm, -ī (n.), *obedience*

obsĕquŏr, -ī, obsĕcūtŭs sŭm, *to obey*

obsĕrō, -ĕrĕ, obsĕvī, obsĭtŭm, *to sow, plant*

obsĕs, -ĭdĭs (m. & f.), *a hostage*

obsĭdĕō, -ĕrĕ, obsēdī, obsessŭm, *to beset, besiege*

obsĭdĭō, -ōnĭs (f.), *a siege, blockade*

obsistō, -ĕrĕ, obstĭtī, obstĭtŭm, *to oppose*

obtempĕrō, -ārĕ, -āvī, -ātŭm, *to submit to*

obtĭnĕō, -ĕrĕ, obtĭnŭī, obtentŭm, *to hold, obtain*

ŏbumbrō, -ārĕ, -āvī, -ātŭm, *to overshadow*

obvĭăm, *in the way;* obvĭam habēre, *to meet*

obvĭŭs, -ă, -ŭm, *in the way;* obvĭum habēre, *to meet*

— 161 —

occāsĭŏ, –ōnĭs (f.), *a favorable time, opportunity, chance*
occĭdens, –tĭs (m.), *the setting sun, West*
occīdĭŏ, –ōnĭs (f.), *a massacre;* occidiōne caedĕre, *to cut down completely*
occīdŏ, –ĕrĕ, occĭdī, occāsŭm, *to fall, set*
occīdŏ, –ĕrĕ, occīdī, occīsŭm, *to kill, slay*
occultē, *secretly*
occultŭs,–ă,–ŭm, *hidden, secret;* in occulto esse, *to remain hidden*
occumbŏ, –ĕrĕ, occŭbŭī, occŭbĭtŭm, *to go down;* occumbĕre mortem, *to die*
occŭpātĭŏ, –ōnĭs (f.), *an engagement*
occŭpātŭs, –ă, –ŭm, *surprised*
occŭpŏ, –ārĕ, –āvī, –ātŭm, *to take possession of, to occupy;* transĭtum occupāre, *to anticipate the passage*
occurrŏ, –ĕrĕ, occurrī (occŭcurrī), occursŭm, *to run up to, to meet;* obvĭam occurrĕre, *to run to meet;* ocŭlis occurrĕre, *to offer to the sight*
octōdĕcĭm, *eighteen*
octōgintă, *eighty*
ŏcŭlŭs, –ī (m.), *the eye;* sub ocŭlis, *in the sight of*
ŏdĭŭm, –ī (n.), *hatred;* odĭum regis, *hatred for the king*
ŏdŏr, –ōrĭs (m.), *perfumery*
offendŏ,–ĕrĕ, offendī, offensŭm, *to offend;* sibi offendĕre, *to injure one's self;* pontem offendĕre, *to hit upon the bridge*
offensă, –ae (f.), *enmity*

offĕrŏ, –rĕ, obtŭlī, oblātŭm, *to offer;* se offerre, *to offer, present one's self;* perĭcŭlis se offerre, *to oppose one's self to dangers*
offĭcĭŭm, –ī (n.), *duty* [*time*
ōlĭm, *in former times, once on a*
Ōlympĭăs, –ădĭs (f.), *Olympias,* Alexander's mother
Ōlympĭcŭs, –ă, –ŭm & Olympĭŭs, –ă, –ŭm, *Olympic*
Ōlynthŭs, –ī (f.), *Olynth,* a city of Thrace
ōmĕn, –ĭnĭs (n.), *an omen*
omnīnō, *entirely*
omnĭs, –ĕ, *all, whole*
ŏnĕrārĭŭs, –ă, –ŭm, *fit for burden;* navis onerarĭa, *a ship of burden*
ŏnŭs, –ĕrĭs (n.), *a burden, load*
ŏnustŭs, –ă, –ŭm, *loaded;* onusta navis, *a freighted vessel*
ŏpĕră,–ae (f.), *care, pains, help;* opĕram consumĕre, *to take pains*
ŏpĕrōsŭs, –ă, –ŭm, *sumptuous, costly*
ŏpīnĭŏ, –ōnĭs (f.), *expectation*
ŏportĕt, –ērĕ, –ŭĭt, (no sup.), *it behooves, one must, ought, is to be*
oppĭdŭm, –ī (n.), *a town*
oppōnŏ, –ĕrĕ, oppŏsŭī, oppŏsĭtŭm, *to oppose*
opportūnē, *opportunely*
opportūnŭs, –ă, –ŭm, *convenient, suitable, timely*
opprĭmŏ, –ĕrĕ, oppressī, oppressŭm, *to crush, oppress; to surprise*
(ops), ŏpĭs (f.), *help;* pl. *riches, power*

opsōnō, -ārĕ, -āvī, -ātŭm, (ὀψωνέω), to buy provisions; opsonārc famem, to get up an appetite

optātŭs, -ă, -ŭm, wished for, desirable

optĭmŭs, -ă, -ŭm, superl. of bonus, excellent; optĭme, very well

optō, -ārĕ, -āvī, -ātŭm, to wish

ŏpŭlentĭă, -ae (f.), wealth

ŏpŭlentĭŭs, more sumptuously

ŏpŭlentŭs, -ă, -ŭm, wealthy, rich

ŏpŭs, -ĕrĭs (n.), work; opus est, it is needful, wanted; opus tectorĭum, stucco

ōră, -ae (f.), a coast; ora maritĭma, a sea-shore

ōrācŭlŭm, -ī (n.), an oracle

ōrātĭō, -ōnĭs (f.), a speech, harangue; insignis oratĭo, extraordinary style of speech

ōrātŏr, -ōrĭs (m.), an orator

ōrātōrĭŭs, -ă, -ŭm, oratorical

orbĭs, - (m.), a circle; orbis (terrārum), the wide world, the world; imperĭum orbis, the empire of the world

orbĭtās, -ātĭs (f.), bereavement

ordō, -ĭnĭs (m.), order, rank, class; ordo successiōnis, regular succession; ordo nascendi, priority of birth

ŏrĭens, -tĭs, rising; sc. sōl, (m.), rising sun = East

ŏrīgō, -ĭnĭs (f.), origin

ŏrĭŏr, -īrī, ortŭs sŭm, to rise, arise

ornātŭs, -ūs (m.), adornment, beauty of style

ornō, -ārĕ, -āvī, -ātŭm, to adorn

ōrō, -ārĕ, -āvī, -ātŭm, to beg, beseech, entreat

ortŭs, -ūs (m.), a rising, birth

ōs, ōrĭs (n.), the mouth, face

ŏs, ossĭs (n.), a bone

oscŭlŏr, -ārī, -ātŭs sŭm, to kiss

ostendō, -ĕrĕ, ostendī, ostensŭm, to show

ōtĭōsŭs, -ă, -ŭm, at leisure

P.

păciscŏr, -ī, pactŭs sŭm, to stipulate

pactŭs, -ă, -ŭm, stipulated

paenĕ, almost

paenĭtentĭă, -ae (f.), repentance

paenĭtĕt, -ērŏ, -ŭĭt, (no sup.), to be sorry for, repent, regret

pāgŭs, -ī (m.), a district

pălăm, openly

pallĭŭm, -ī (n.), a cloak, robe

palmĕs, -ĭtĭs (m.), a branch

pălŭs, -ūdĭs (f.), a swamp

pānĭs, - (m.), bread

pannōsŭs, -ă, -ŭm, ragged

păr, părĭs, like, equal; same

părātŭs, -ă, -ŭm, ready

parcō, -ĕrĕ, pĕpercī, parsŭm, to spare

părens, -tĭs (m. & f.), a parent

părentō, -ārĕ, -āvī, -ātŭm, to bring funeral sacrifices, to do honor to the dead

părĕō, -ērĕ, -ŭī, (no sup.), to obey

părĭō, -ĕrĕ, pĕpĕrī, partŭm, to bear, bring forth

părĭtĕr, alike, equally

părō, -ārĕ, -āvī, -ātŭm, to make ready, prepare, get ready for; exercĭtum parāre, to get *ready an army;* naves parāre, *to equip ships;* latos fines parāre, *to acquire extensive possessions;* interītum parāre, *to bring destruction upon*

parrĭcīdĭŭm, -ī (n.), *foul murder, the murder of one's relative*

pars, -tĭs (f.), *a part, portion, side;* pl. *party;* in contrarīas partes, *in opposite directions*

parsĭmōnĭă, -ae (f.), *frugality*

partĭceps, -cĭpĭs, *sharing, partaking;* subst., *a sharer*

partĭm, *partly*

partĭō, -īrĕ, (-īvī) -ĭī, -ītŭm, *to distribute*

părŭm, *but little, too little, not enough*

parvŭlŭs, -ă, -ŭm, *very small;* as subst., *a little one*

parvŭs, -ă, -ŭm, *small*

passĭm, *at different places*

passŭs, -ūs (m.), *a pace;* mille passŭum, *1000 paces,* a Roman mile

pastŏr, -ōrĭs (m.), *a herdsman, shepherd*

pătĕfăcĭō, -ĕrĕ, pătĕfēcī, pătĕfactŭm, *to open; to bring to light*

pătĕō, -ērĕ, -ŭī, (no sup.), *to stand or be open*

pătĕr, -rĭs (m.), *a father*

pătĕră, -ae (f.), *a cup*

pătĕrnŭs, -ă, -ŭm, *paternal*

pătĭŏr, -ī, passŭs sŭm, *to suffer, endure, permit;* gravem pati, *to be indignant at*

pătrĭă, -ae (f.), *one's own country, native land*

pătrĭmōnĭŭm, -ī (n.), *an inheritance, property*

pătrŭŭs, -ī (m.), *an uncle*

paucĭtās, -ātĭs (f.), *fewness, small number*

paucŭs, -ă, -ŭm, *small;* pauci, *few, (but) few*

paulātĭm, *little by little, gradually*

paulŭlŭm, *a very little*

paulŭm, *a little;* abl. paulo; paulo ante, *a short while ago*

paupĕr, -ĭs, *poor*

păvens, -tĭs, *struck with fear*

păvĭdŭs, -ă, -ŭm, *timid*

pax, pācĭs (f.), *peace*

peccō, -ārĕ, -āvī, -ātŭm, *to do wrong, sin*

pĕcūnĭă, -ae (f.), *money*

pĕcŭs, -ŏrĭs (n.), *cattle, sheep*

pĕcŭs, -ŭdĭs (f.), *a head of cattle, an animal*

pĕdestĕr, -rĭs, -rĕ, *on foot, by land;* pedestres copĭae, *land forces;* proelĭum pedestre, *battle by land*

pĕlăgŭs, -ī (n.), *the sea*

pellō, -ĕrĕ, pĕpŭlī, pulsŭm, *to drive, to beat;* regno, imperĭo pellĕre, *to drive from the throne*

Pĕlŏponnēsĭŭs, -ī (m.), *a Peloponnesian*

Pĕlŏponnēsŭs, -ī (f.), *the Peloponnesus*

pĕnĕs, with acc., *with, in possession of*

pĕnĕtrābĭlĭs, -ĕ, *penetrable*

pĕnĭtŭs, *entirely, thoroughly*

pennă, -ae (f.), *a feather;* celerĭtas pennae, *swiftness of flight*

pensŭm, -ī (n.), *a task*

pĕr, with acc., *through, by means of; during;* per ordĭnem, *in order;* per somnum, *in his sleep* pĕrăgrō, -ārĕ, -āvī, -ātŭm, *to wander over*

percĭpĭō, -ĕrĕ, percēpī, percep-tŭm, *to receive, hear; to learn*

percontŏr, -ārī, -ātŭs sŭm, *to ask*

perculsŭs, -ă, -ŭm, *panic-stricken*

Perdiccās, -ae (m.), *Perdiccas, one of Alexander's officers*

perdĭtŭs, -ă, -ŭm, *ruined*

perdŏmō, -ārĕ, perdŏmŭī, per-dŏmĭtŭm, *to subjugate*

perdūcō, -ĕrĕ, perduxī, perduc-tŭm, *to bring, lead over*

pĕrĕgrīnŭs, -ă, -ŭm, *from a-broad, foreign;* subst., *a foreigner*

pĕrĕō, -īrĕ, -īī, -ĭtŭm, *to perish*

perfĕrō, -rĕ, pertŭlī, perlātŭm, *to get through, convey; to endure to the end*

perfĭcĭō, -ĕrĕ, perfēcī, perfec-tŭm, *to bring about, accom-plish*

perfĭdĭă, -ae (f.), *bad faith, per-fidy*

pergō, -ĕrĕ, perrexī, perrectŭm, *to go on*

pĕrīclŭm = pĕrīcŭlŭm

pĕrīcŭlōsŭs, -ă, -ŭm, *dangerous*

pĕrīcŭlŭm, -ī (n.), *a risk, dan-ger;* periculum facĕrĕ, *to make the experiment*

pĕrītŭs, -ă, -ŭm, *experienced, skilled;* peritissĭmus, *well versed*

perlĕgō, -ĕrĕ, perlēgī, perlec-tŭm, *to read to the end*

permănĕō, -ĕrĕ, permansī, per-mansŭm, *to persevere;* mos permănet, *the custom lasts*

permittō, -ĕrĕ, permīsī, permis-sŭm, *to permit, allow;* admi-nistratiōnem, potestātem per-mittĕrĕ, *to intrust the adminis-tration, power*

permōtŭs, -ă, -ŭm, *influenced*

permūtō, -ārĕ, -āvī, -ātŭm, *to interchange*

pernĭcĭēs, -ēī (f.), *ruin*

perpastŭs, -ă, -ŭm, *well-fed*

perpĕs, -ĕtĭs, *continuous*

perpĕtĭŏr, -ī, perpessŭs sŭm, *to endure*

perpĕtŭō, *forever*

perpĕtŭŭs, -ă, -ŭm, *continuous;* perpetŭum exsilĭum agĕrĕ, *to live in exile for life;* perpetŭus honor, *dignity for life*

Persă, -ae (m.), *a Persian*

perscrībō, -ĕrĕ, perscripsī, per-scriptŭm, *to report (in writ-ing)*

perscrūtŏr, -ārī, -ātŭs sŭm, *to examine*

Persĕpŏlĭs, - (f.), *Persepolis, cap-ital of the Persians*

persĕquŏr, -ī, persĕcūtŭs sŭm, *to pursue*

Persēs, -ae (m.), *a Persian*

persĕvērō, -ārĕ, -āvī, -ātŭm, *to persevere*

Persĭcŭs, -ă, -ŭm, *Persian*

perspĭcĭō, -ĕrĕ, perspexī, per-spectŭm, *to explore*

persŭādĕō, -ērĕ, persŭāsī, per-sŭāsŭm, *to persuade, convince*

perterrĭtŭs, -ă, -ŭm, *greatly frightened, alarmed*

pĕrūtĭlĭs, -ĕ, *very useful*

pervĕnĭō, -īrĕ, pervēnī, perven-tŭm, *to reach;* eōdem per-venīre, *to reach the same point* pēs, pědĭs (m.), *a foot*

pestĭs, – (f.), *a plague*

pětītŭs, –ă, –ŭm, *sought-for*

pětō, –ěrě, pětīvī, pětītŭm, *to make for; to beg, seek, ask;* petītum est, *they asked him;* pacem petěre, *to sue for peace;* Sicilĭam petěre, *to make for Sicily;* praetorĭum petěre, *to attack the headquarters;* auxilĭum petěre, *to ask for assistance*

pětŭlans, –tĭs, *impudent*

Phălēreūs, –ěī (m.), *Phalereus,* a ruler of Athens and a famous orator

Phălĕrĭcŭs, –ă, –ŭm, *Phalerian*

phĭdītĭă, –ōrŭm (n. pl.), *the public meals of the Lacedaemonians*

Phĭlippŭs, –ī (m.), *Philip,* king of Macedon

phĭlŏsŏphŭs, –ī (m.), *a philosopher*

Phintĭās, –ae (m.), *Phintias,* a Pythagorean

Phoenīcē, –ēs (f.), *Phoenice*

Phoenix, –īcĭs (m.), *a Phoenician*

Phthĭă, –ae (f.), *Phthia,* the birthplace of Achilles

pictŭs, –ă, –ŭm, *embroidered;* magnifĭcis operĭbus pictus, *magnificently embroidered*

pĭětās, –ātĭs (f.), *(filial) duty, affection, piety;* pietātis jura, *the rights of duty*

pĭlă, –ae (f.), *a ball*

pingō, –ěrě, pinxī, pictŭm, *to paint, embroider*

piscātŏrĭŭs, –ă, –ŭm, *of fishermen;* scapha piscatorĭa, *a fishing boat*

piscĭs, – (m.), *a fish*

Pīsistrătŭs, –ī (m.), *Pisistratus,* a tyrant of Athens

pĭŭs, –ă, –ŭm, *pious;* pia humanĭtas, *kind feelings*

plăcĕō, –ērě, –ŭī, –ĭtŭm, *to please;* mihi placet, *I am of opinion*

plăcĭdŭs, –ă, –ŭm, *gentle*

plānĕ, *absolutely, clearly;* bene planēque, *full well*

plānĭŭs, *more distinctly*

plănŭm, –ī (n.), *a plane*

plānŭs, –ă, –ŭm, *level*

Plătaeae, –ārŭm (f. pl.), *Plataea*

Plătaensēs, –ĭŭm (m. pl.), *the Plataeans,* inhabitants of Plataea

Plătō, –ōnĭs (m.), *Plato*

plaustrŭm, –ī (n.), *a wagon*

plebs, plēbĭs (f.), *the common people, commonalty*

plectō, –ěrě, (no perf.), plexŭm, *to punish*

plēnŭs, –ă, –ŭm, *full;* plenus artis, *richly wrought*

plērīquě, plēraequě, plērāquě, *most, the majority, many*

plērumquě, *for the greater part, generally*

plūrēs, –ă, *more; many, several*

plūrĭmŭs, –ă, –ŭm, *very much*

plūs, plūrĭs, *more*

pōcŭlŭm, –ī (n.), *a cup*

poenă, –ae (f.), *punishment;* poenas repetěre, *to demand satisfaction;* poenas dare, *to suffer punishment*

poenĭtentĭă, –ae (f.), *repentance;* also written paenitentĭa

pollĭcěŏr, –ērī, –ĭtŭs sŭm, *to promise*

Pŏlўdectēs, -ae (m.), *Polydectes,*
king of Sparta, Lycurgus'
brother

pondŭs, -ĕrĭs (n.), *weight*

pōnō, -ĕrĕ, pŏsŭī, pŏsĭtŭm, *to
put, place;* condĭtĭo ponĭtur, *a
choice is left;* tunĭcam ponĕrc,
to take off the tunic; timōrem
ponĕre, *to dismiss fear;* posĭ-
tum esse, *to depend*

pons, -tĭs (m.), *a bridge*

pontĭcŭlŭs, -ī (m.), *a little bridge*

pŏpŭlārĭs, -ĕ, *popular*

pŏpŭlŭs,-ī (m.), *a people, nation*

porrectŭs, -ă, -ŭm, *outstretched*

porrĭgō, -ĕrĕ, porrexī, porrec-
tŭm, *to put out*

porrō, *moreover*

portă, -ae (f.), *a gate*

portendō, -ĕrĕ, portendī, por-
tentŭm, *to portend*

portŭs, -ūs (m.), *a port, harbor*

pŏsĭtŭs, -ă, -ŭm, *placed;* posĭ-
tum esse, *to depend on*

possessĭŏ,-ōnĭs (f.), *a possession*

possĭdĕō, -ĕrĕ, possēdī, posses-
sŭm, *to hold, occupy*

possŭm, possĕ, pŏtŭī, (**no sup.**),
can, to be able; omnĭa posse, *to
be all-powerful*

pōst, **w. acc.**, *after, behind*

postĕă, *after that, afterwards;*
postĕa quam, *after*

postĕrŭs, -ă, -ŭm, *following,
next;* postĕrī, -ōrŭm (m. pl.),
the descendants, posterity

postquăm, postĕăquăm, *after*

postrēmŭs, -ă, -ŭm, *last;* postrēmo, ad postrēmum, *at last*

postrīdĭĕ, *next day, following day*

postŭlō, -ārĕ, -āvī, -ātŭm, *to
require, demand, claim*

postŭmŭs, -ă, -ŭm, *born after
the father's death, late-born*

pŏtens, -tĭs, *powerful*

pŏtentĭă,-ae (f.), *power, capacity*

pŏtestās, -ātĭs (f.), *power, command;* potestas bellōrum, *control of wars;* p. vitae necisque,
power of life and death

pŏtĭŏr, -īrī, -ītŭs sŭm, *to get or
hold possession of;* rerum potīri, *to gain dominion*

pŏtissĭmŭm, *chiefly;* if *possible*

pŏtĭŭs, *rather*

prae, **w. abl.**, *for, on account of;
in comparison with*

praebĕō, -ĕrĕ, -ŭī, -ĭtŭm, *to
offer;* ubĕra praebĕre,*to suckle;*
specĭem praebĕre, *to furnish
the appearance;* se praebĕre,
to offer one's self

praeceptŭm, -ī (n.). *an order*

praecĭpĭō, -ĕrĕ, praccēpī, praeceptŭm, *to order, enjoin, direct*

praeclārĕ, *very well*

praeclārŭs, -ă, -ŭm, *splendid,
illustrious;* praeclāra, *illustrious deeds*

praeclūdō, -ĕrĕ, praeclūsī, prae-
clūsŭm, *to shut up;* praeclūsa
voce, *his voice failing him*

praecō, -ōnĭs (m.), *a crier, her-
ald, proclaimer*

praedă, -ae (f.), *booty, plunder*

praedĭcō, -ārĕ, -āvī, -ātŭm, *to
declare; to praise, laud*

praedĭtŭs, -ă, -ŭm, *gifted, en-
dowed; possessed of*

praefectŭs, -ī (m.), *a prefect*

praefĕrō, -rĕ, praetŭlī, praelā-
tŭm, *to prefer;* omen praeferre,
to present an omen

praefĭcĭŏ, -ĕrĕ, praefēcī, prac-
fectŭm, *to put over, to appcint*
praemittō, -ĕrĕ, pracmīsī, prae-
missŭm, *to send ahead*
praemĭŭm, -ī (n.), *a reward*
pracmŏnĕŏ, -ĕrĕ, -ŭī, -ĭtŭm, *to
forewarn*
pracnuntĭŏ, -ārĕ, -āvī, -ātŭm,
to foretell
pracpărātŭs, -ă, -ŭm, *ready*
praepōnŏ, -ĕrĕ, praepŏsŭī, prac-
pŏsĭtŭm, *to place first, prefer;*
genti praeponĕre, *to set over a
tribe;* ducem praeponĕrc, *to
put in command;* praeposĭtus,
set over
praesăgĭens, -tĭs, *presaging;*
quiddam praesagĭens, *scme
touch of presage*
praesăgĭtĭŏ, -ōnĭs (f.), *presaging*
pracsens, -tĭs, *present;* ad praesens tempus, *for the moment;*
praesens mors, *imminent death*
pracsentĭens, -tĭs, *foreboding;*
quiddam pracsentĭens, *something like foreboding*
pracsĭdĭŭm, -ī (n.), *help, protection; a garrison*
praestō, *present, at hand, ready*
praestō, -ārĕ, pracstĭtī, (no sup.),
*to show, perform; fulfill (a
promise); to surpass;* officĭum
praestārc, *to perform, discharge a duty;* tutum pracstărc,
to keep safe; praestat, *it is better*
pracsŭm, pracessĕ, pracfŭī, (no
sup.), *to be at the head, to command;* rebus divīnis praeessc,
to preside over religious rites;
bello praecssc, *to have the command in war*
praetĕr, **w. acc.**, *except, beyond*

praetĕrĕă, *besides*
praetŏr, -ōrĭs (m.), *a general,
leader*
praetōrĭŭm, -ī (n.), *the general's
tent, headquarters*
prandĕŏ,-ĕrĕ, prandī, pransŭm,
to breakfast
prĕcēs, -ŭm (f. pl.), *prayers,
entreaty;* summis precĭbus,
with every entreaty
prĕcŏr,-ārī, -ātŭs sŭm, *to pray,
supplicate*
prĕmō, -ĕrĕ, pressī, pressŭm,
to press hard; vocem premĕrc,
to be silent
prĕtĭōsŭs, -ă, -ŭm, *precious,
costly*
prĕtĭŭm, -ī (n.), *a price*
prīdĕm, *long since*
prīmŭs, -ă, -ŭm, *first;* primo,
at first; primum, *first;* in primis, *especially;* primas dare,
to give the first place
princeps, -ĭpĭs (m.), *a prince,
chief; the first*
princĭpĭŭm, -ī (n.), *a beginning;*
principĭa, *the elements*
prĭŏr, -ŭs, *former, previous;
more excellent*
pristĭnŭs, -ă, -ŭm, *former, previous, original*
prĭŭs, *formerly*
prĭusquăm, *before that, sooner
than*
prīvătŭs,-ă,-ŭm, *private;* **subst.**,
a private citizen
prīvĭlēgĭŭm, -ī (n.), *a privilege*
prō, **w. abl.**, *for, instead of, in
proportion to; in behalf of*
prŏbātŭs, -ă, -ŭm, *of approved
goodness;* minus probātus, *not
so good*

prŏbŏ, -ārĕ, -āvī, -ātŭm, *to approve*

prŏcax, -ācĭs, *shameless*

prŏcēdŏ, -ĕrĕ, prŏcessī, prŏcessŭm, *to go on, proceed;* obvĭum procedĕre, *to proceed to meet*

prŏcellă, -ae (f.), *a storm*

prŏcrĕŏ, -ārĕ, -āvī, -ātŭm, *to bring forth;* pass., *to be born*

prŏcŭl, *at a distance, from afar*

prŏcūrātĭŏ, -ŏnĭs (f.), *a charge*

prŏcurrŏ, -ĕrĕ, prŏcurrī (prŏcŭcurrī), prŏcursŭm, *to rush forwards*

prōdĭgĭŭm, -ĭ (n.), *an omen*

prōdĭtŏr, -ōrĭs (m.), *a traitor*

prōdŏ, -ĕrĕ, prōdĭdī, prōdĭtŭm, *to disclose;* memorĭae prodĕre, *to record;* prodĭtum est, *it has been recorded, there is a tradition;* aquĭlam prodĕre, *to give up the standard*

proclĭŏr,-ārī,-ātŭs sŭm, *to fight*

proclĭŭm,-ĭ (n.), *a skirmish, battle*

prŏfectŏ, *really, indeed*

prŏfĕrŏ, -rĕ, prōtŭlī, prōlātŭm, *to bring forth, extend;* in locum edĭtum proferre, *to bring to an elevated spot;* artem proferre, *to bring out an art;* caput proferre, *to put out one's head;* in forum proferre, *to bring into the market*

prŏfĭciscŏr, -ī, prŏfectŭs sŭm, *to set out, to proceed, depart;* in bellum proficisci, *to go to war;* proficisci ad mortem, *to go to die*

prŏfĭtĕŏr, -ērī, prŏfessŭs sŭm, *to profess; give in one's name*

prŏfŭgĭŏ,-ĕrĕ, prŏfŭgī, prŏfŭgĭtŭm, *to flee away, escape*

prōgrĕdĭŏr, -ī, prōgressŭs sŭm, *to proceed, advance;* cultĭus progrĕdi, *to walk along more elegantly*

prŏhĭbĕŏ, -ērĕ, -ŭī, -ĭtŭm, *to keep from, hinder; to forbid;* prohibēre ab injurĭa, *to protect from injury;* prŏhĭbĭtă,-ōrŭm (n. pl.), *forbidden things*

prŏindĕ, *accordingly, therefore*

prōjĭcĭŏ, -ĕrĕ, prōjēcī, prōjectŭm,*to cast forth;* se projicĕre, *to rush*

prōlŏquŏr, -ī, prōlŏcūtŭs sŭm, *to speak out*

prōmissŭs, -ă, -ŭm, *long, flowing*

prōmittŏ, - ĕrĕ, prōmīsī, prōmissŭm, *to promise*

promptŭs, -ă, -ŭm, *forward, ready*

promuntōrĭŭm, -ĭ (n.), *a promontory*

prōnuntĭŏ, -ārĕ, -āvī, -ātŭm, *to denote, declaim*

prōnŭs, -ă, -ŭm, *sloping down*

prŏpĕ, with acc., *near, hard-by;* adv. *nearly, almost; near, nigh*

prōpĕdĭĕm, *at an early day*

prōpellŏ, -ĕrĕ, prōpŭlī, prōpulsŭm, *to repel*

prŏpinquŭs, -ă, -ŭm, *near;* propinquus, subst., *a relative*

prōpōnŏ, -ĕrĕ, prōpŏsŭī, prōpŏsĭtŭm, *to set before, to issue;* proposĭta fuga, *flight put before the eyes*

prŏprĭĕtăs, -ātĭs (f.), *possession*

prŏprĭŭs, -ă, -ŭm, *own;* proprĭum est, *it is the mark*

propter, w. acc., *on account of, in consequence of*

propterëä, *on that account*

prorsūs, *wholly, absolutely; precisely*

proscrībō, -ĕrĕ, proscripsī, proscriptŭm, *to write upon*

prōsĕquŏr, -ī, prōsĕcūtŭs sŭm, *to follow*

Prōserpīnă, -ae (f.), *Proserpine*

prospĕr, -ă, -ŭm, *favorable*

prospĭcĭō, -ĕrĕ, prospexī, prospectŭm, *to foresee*

prōsŭm, prōdessĕ, prōfŭī, (no sup.), *to be useful, to benefit, to do good*

prōtĭnŭs, *on the spot, immediately*

prōtrăhō, -ĕrĕ, prōtraxī, prōtractŭm, *to protract*

prōvĕhō, -ĕrĕ, prōvexī, prōvectŭm, *to promote;* provĕhi in altum, *to proceed to the deep water*

prōvĕnĭō, -īrĕ, prōvĕnī, prōventŭm, *to be born*

prōvĭdĕō, -ĕrĕ, prōvīdī, prōvīsŭm, *to foresee*

prōvŏcō, -ārĕ, -āvī, -ātŭm, *to call forth*

proxĭmŭs, -ă, -ŭm, *next;* proxĭma quaeque victorĭa, *every preceding victory;* proxĭma nocte, *last night;* proxĭmi (m. pl.), *the nearest relatives*

prūdens, -tĭs, *foreseeing, sensible, prudent*

prȳtănēŭm, -ī (n.), *the prytaneum, or town-hall*

Ptŏlĕmaeŭs, -ī (m.), *Ptolemy,* the name of the kings of Egypt after Alexander the Great

pūbĕr, -ĭs, } *of puberty, adult*
pūbēs, -ĕrĭs }

pūblĭcŭs, -ă, -ŭm, *public;* publice, *publicly, at the cost of the state, in behalf of the state;* in publĭco, *in the street;* in publĭcum, *in public*

Pūblĭŭs, -ī (m.), *Publius,* a Roman praenomen

pŭdŏr, -ōrĭs (m.), *shame*

pŭĕr, -ī (m.), *a boy, a slave;* admŏdum puer, *a mere boy*

pŭĕrītĭă, -ae (f.), *boyhood*

pugnă, -ae (f.), *a fight, battle*

pugnans, -tĭs (m.), *a fighting man*

pugnō, -ārĕ, -āvī, -ātŭm, *to fight;* pugnātum est, *the battle was fought*

pulchĕr, -ră, -rŭm, *fine*

pulchrītūdŏ, -ĭnĭs (f.), *beauty*

pulmentārĭŭm, -ī (n.), *a dainty*

pulmentŭm, -ī (n.), *delicate fare*

pulsō, -ārĕ, -āvī, -ātŭm, *to beat*

purpŭră, -ae (f.), *purple*

pūsĭŏ, -ōnĭs (m.), *an urchin*

pŭtāmĕn, -ĭnĭs (n.), *the shell of a nut*

pŭtō, -ārĕ, -āvī, -ātŭm, *to think, consider*

Pygmālĭōn, -ōnĭs (m.), *Pygmalion,* king of Tyre

pȳră, -ae (f.), *a funeral pile*

Pȳthăgŏrăs, -ae (m.), *Pythagoras*

Pȳthăgŏrēŭs, -ī (m.), *a Pythago-[rean*

Q.

quadrāgintă, *forty*

quadrātŭm, -ī (n.), *a square*

quadrĭdŭŭm, -ī (n.), *a space of four days*

quadrīgae, -ārŭm (f. pl.), *a team of four horses;* quadrigārum currus, *a chariot drawn by four horses* quaerō, -ĕrĕ, quaesīvī, quaesītŭm, *to ask, seek;* gratĭam quaerĕre, *to obtain favor;* sedes quaerĕre, *to search for settlements;* labor quaerendi, *acquisitive disposition;* quaesītus, *sought for*

quaesō, *I pray, prithee*

quaestĭō, -ōnĭs (f.), *a question, a subject of inquiry;* quaestiōni esse, *to be doubtful*

quaestŏr, -ōrĭs (m.), *a paymaster, quaestor*

quaestŭs, -ūs (m.), *gain;* quaestus divitiārum, *the way of making riches*

quālĭs,-ĕ, (such) as, of which sort

quālĭtercunquĕ, *howsoever*

quăm, *as, how, than;* quam.. tam, *as.. so;* quam primum, *as soon as possible;* quam w. superl., *as.. as possible*

quamquăm, *although;* neverthe-

quamvīs, *though* [*less*

quantŭs, -ă, -ŭm, *how much, as much as*

quārĕ, *wherefore, why*

quartŭs, -ă, -ŭm, *the fourth*

quăsī, *as if; as it were*

quattŭŏr, *four*

-quĕ, *and*

quĕmadmŏdŭm, *how*

quĕrellă, -ae (f.), *a complaint*

quĕrŏr, -ī, questŭs sŭm, *to complain*

quī, quae, quŏd, **rel.**, *who, which, that;* **interrog.**, *what (manner of)?* qui, qua, quod, **indef.**, *any, some* — quī, *how?*

quĭă, *because*

quīcumquĕ, quaecumquĕ, quodcumquĕ, *whoever, whatever*

quīdăm, quaedăm, quoddăm (quiddăm), *some one, a certain;* quodam modo, *in a certain measure;* quiddam praesentĭens, divīnans, *some touch of presage, divination;* divīnum quiddam, *a divine something*

quīdĕm, *true, indeed;* ne..quidem, *not..even*

quĭēs, -ētĭs (f.), *rest, sleep*

quiescō, -ĕrĕ, quĭēvī, quĭētŭm, *to rest, to be at rest, to keep quiet; to retire to rest*

quĭētŭs, -ă, -ŭm, *quiet*

quĭn, *(how not), so as not; why not;* quin etĭam, *yea indeed*

quindĕcĭm, *fifteen*

quingentī, -ae, -ă, *five hundred*

quinquāgintă, *fifty*

quinquĕ, *five*

quinquennĭŭm, -ī (n.), *a space of five years*

quintŭs, -ă, -ŭm, *the fifth*

Quintŭs,-ī (m.), *Quintus,* a Roman praenomen

quippĕ, *namely, for*

quĭs? — quĭd? *who? what?* quid? *why?*

quĭs, quă, quĭd, **indef.**, *some one, any one;* ne quis, *lest any one, that no one*

quisnăm? quidnăm? *who? what*

quisquăm, quidquăm, *any at all*

quisquĕ, quaequĕ, quidquĕ (quodquĕ), *each one*

quisquĭs, quidquĭd, *whoever, whatever*

quō, *whither, to whom, to which*

quō, with **compar.**, *that the*

quŏăd, *as long as, until*

quŏd, *that, in that, because;* quodsī, *if*

quŏmŏdō, *how*

quondăm, *formerly*

quŏnĭăm, *(now that)*, *since*, *as*

quŏquĕ, *also* [*indeed*

quŏtĭcns, *how often*

R.

răbĭdŭs, -ă, -ŭm, *savage*

rădĭcŭlă, -ae (f.), *a rootlet, root*

rādix, -ĭcĭs (f.), *a root;* radīces
Caucăsi, *the foot of the Caucasus*

rāmōsŭs, -ă, -ŭm, *branching;*
ramōsa cornŭa, *antlers*

rāmŭlŭs, -ī (m.), *a little twig*

rānă, -ae (f.), *a frog*

rapīnă, -ae (f.), *plunder*

răpĭō, -ĕrĕ, răpŭī, raptŭm, *to
carry off, rob, steal;* raptŭs,
-ă, -ŭm, *carried with, stolen;*
raptae virgīnes, *the captured
virgins*

raptŏr, -ōrĭs (m.), *a plunderer*

rārō, *seldom*

rătĭŏ, -ōnĭs (f.), *reasoning, account; a method, way;* ratĭo
rei militāris, *the principles of
military discipline*

rătĭs, – (f.), *a raft*

rĕātŭs, -ūs (m.), *an impeachment*

rĕbellō, -ārĕ, -āvī, -ātŭm, *to
revolt, rebel*

rĕcēdō, -ĕrĕ, rĕcessī, rĕcessŭm,
to retire

rĕcens, -tĭs, *fresh;* recens tabŭla,
a freshly written tablet

rĕcĭdō, -ĕrĕ, rĕcĭdī, rĕcăsŭm, *to
recoil*

rĕcĭpĭō, -ĕrĕ, rĕcēpī, rĕceptŭm,
to take back; to take in; in
fidem recipĕre, *to take under
protection;* se recipĕre, *to withdraw; to come back*

rĕcordātĭŏ, -ōnĭs (f.), *remembering*

rĕcordŏr, -ārī, -ātŭs sŭm, *to
remember*

rĕcumbō, -ĕrĕ, rĕcŭbŭī, rĕcŭ-
bĭtŭm, *to lie down again*

rĕcŭpĕrō, -ārĕ, -āvī, -ātŭm, *to
recover*

reddō, -ĕrĕ, reddĭdī, reddĭtŭm,
to give back; to make, render

rĕdĕō, -īrĕ, -ĭī, -ĭtŭm, *to return*

rĕdĭgō, -ĕrĕ, rĕdēgī, rĕdactŭm,
to bring back, reduce; in captivitātem redigĕre, *to reduce to
captivity*

rĕdĭtŭs, -ūs (m.), *return*

rĕfectŭs, -ă, -ŭm, *revived*

rĕfĕrō, -rĕ, rĕtŭlī (rettŭlī), rĕlā-
tŭm, *to bring back, report,
relate;* controversĭam referre,
to start a question; ad alĭquem
referre, *to refer to some one;*
pedem referre, *to retreat*

rĕfertŭs, -ă, -ŭm, *(choke-)full,
full to overflowing*

rĕfĭcĭō, -ĕrĕ, rĕfēcī, rĕfectŭm,
to repair; to refresh, recover

rĕfŭgĭŭm, -ī (n.), *a refuge*

rēgālĭs, -ĕ, *royal, regal*

rēgĭă, -ae (f.), *the king's palace*

rēgīnă, -ae (f.), *a queen*

Rēgīnī, -ōrŭm (m. pl.), *the Re-
gini, inhabitants of Regium*

rēgĭŏ, -ōnĭs (f.), *a country, re-
gion, province*

Rēgĭŭm, -ī (n.), *Regium, a town
on the Sicilian Straits*

rēgĭŭs, -ă, -ŭm, *of a king,
royal*

regnō, -ārĕ, -āvī, -ātŭm, *to be
king, to reign*

regnŭm, -ī (n.), *royal power, kingdom, realm, throne;* regnum agitāre,*to spend the reign;* regna exercēre, *to tyrannize*

rēgrēdĭŏr, -ī, rēgressŭs sŭm, *to step back, to return*

rĕlĭgĭŏ, -ōnĭs (f.), *religious feeling; divine service;* metus religiōnis, *religious awe;* religĭo juris jurandi, *the obligation of an oath;* cruenta sacrōrum religĭo, *bloody sacrifices*

rĕlinquō, -ĕrĕ, rĕlīquī, rĕlictŭm, *to leave*

rĕlĭquŭs, -ă, -ŭm, *(what is left), remaining, rest*

rĕmănĕō, -ĕrĕ, rĕmansī, rĕmansŭm, *to remain, stay behind*

rĕmĕdĭŭm, -ī (n.), *a remedy*

rĕmissĭŏ, -ōnĭs (f.), *a depression*

rĕmittō,-ĕrĕ, rĕmīsī, rĕmissŭm, *to send back, to slack*

rĕmŏvĕō, -ĕrĕ, rĕmōvī, rĕmōtŭm, *to move back, to remove*

rēmŭs, -ī (m.), *an oar;* inhibēre remis, *to row a ship backwards;* remis incitāre, *to set in rapid motion with the oars*

rĕnŏvō, -ārĕ, -āvī, -ātŭm, *to renew*

rĕnuntĭō, -ārĕ, -āvī, -ātŭm, *to report*

rĕŏr, -ērī, rātŭs sŭm, *to think, suppose*

rĕpărō, -ārĕ,-āvī, -ātŭm, *to renew*

rĕpellō, -ĕrĕ, rĕpŭlī, rĕpulsŭm, *to drive back, reject*

rĕpentĕ, *suddenly*

rĕpentīnŭs, -ă, -ŭm, *sudden*

rĕpĕrĭō,-īrĕ, reppĕrī, rĕpertŭm, *to discover, find*

rĕpĕtō, -ĕrĕ, rĕpĕtīvī, rĕpĕtītŭm, *to seek again, to discover;* poenas repetĕre, *to demand satisfaction;* altĭus repetĕre, *to begin further back;* Sicilĭam repetĕre, *to return to Sicily;* sacra repetĕre, *to recover the sacred vessels;* certāmen repetĕre, *to renew a contest*

rĕprĭmō, -ĕrĕ, rĕpressī, rĕpressŭm, *to keep back*

rĕpŭdĭō, -ārĕ, -āvī, -ātŭm, *to reject*

rĕquīrō, -ĕrĕ, rĕquīsīvī, rĕquīsītŭm, *to inquire after; to require*

rēs, rĕī (f.), *a thing, an event, a circumstance, an affair, a deed;* res gestae, *exploits, achievements;* res Tyriōrum, *the history of the Tyrians;* res publĭca, *a commonwealth;* res male acta, *a failure;* res marĭtĭmae, *naval operations;* res mīlitāris, *military affairs;* res divīnae, *religious rites;* res gerundae, *public business;* rerum abundantĭa, *riches.* (res is often to be translated by combination, often to be omitted.)

rĕservō, -ārĕ, -āvī, -ātŭm, *to preserve, spare*

rĕsīdō, -ĕrĕ, rĕsēdī, (no sup.), *to sit down, to perch*

rĕsistō, -ĕrĕ, restĭtī, (no sup.), *to make resistance, oppose, withstand; to stand still*

respectŭs, -ūs (m.), *consideration*

respĭcĭō, -ĕrĕ, respexī, respectŭm, *to regard*

respīrō, -ārĕ, -āvī, -ātŭm, *to recover breath;* spatĭum respirandi, *a breathing space*

respondĕō, -ērĕ, respondī, responsŭm, *to answer; to suit to;* responsum erat, *an answer was received*

responsŭm, -ī (n.), *an answer*

restaurō, -ārĕ, -āvī, -ātŭm, *to renew*

restĭtŭō, -ĕrĕ, restĭtŭī, restĭtŭtŭm, *to restore*

restĭtŭtĭŏ, -ōnĭs (f.), *rebuilding;* restitutĭo etĭam in majus, *rebuilding even on a larger scale*

rētĕ, -ĭs (n.), *a net*

rĕtentŭs, -ă, -ŭm, *entangled*

rĕtĭnĕō, -ērĕ, rĕtĭnŭī, rĕtentŭm, *to keep back*

rĕŭs, -ī (m.), *a defendant*

rĕvertō, -ĕrĕ, rĕvertī, rĕversŭm; rĕvertŏr, -ī, *to return*

rĕvŏcō, -ārĕ, -āvī, -ātŭm, *to recall*

rex, rēgĭs (m.), *a king, sovereign*

Rhŏdĭŭs, -ī (m.), *a Rhodian*

Rhŏdŭs, -ī (f.), *Rhodes,* an island in the Aegean Sea

rĭdĕō, -ērĕ, rīsī, rīsŭm, *to laugh,* rĭgens, -tĭs, *frozen* [*smile*

rīsŭs, -ūs (m.), *laughing*

rīvŭs, -ī (m.), *a brook*

rŏbustŭs, -ă, -ŭm, *strong*

rŏgō, -ārĕ, -āvī, -ātŭm, *to request, entreat, ask;* summis precĭbus rogārĕ, *to use every entreaty*

rŏgŭs, -ī (m.), *a funeral pile*

Roxānē, -ēs (f.), *Roxane,* wife of Alexander the Great

rŭdĭs, -ĕ, *ignorant, inexperienced*

Rūfŭs, -ī (m.), *Rufus,* a Roman surname

rumpō, -ĕrĕ, rūpī, ruptŭm, *to burst, break*

rŭō, -ĕrĕ, rŭī, rŭtŭm, *to rush*

rursŭm, rursŭs, *again*

rūs, rūrĭs (n.), *the country*

S.

Săbīnŭs, -ī (m.), *a Sabine;* also a Roman surname, *Sabinus*

saccŭs, -ī (m.), *a bag*

săcĕr, -ră, -rŭm, *sacred;* săcră, -ōrŭm, *sacred objects;* sacra Eleusinĭa, *the Eleusinian mysteries;* sacra Hercŭlis, *the sacred vessels of Hercules;* sacra facĕrĕ, *to sacrifice*

săcerdōs, -ōtĭs (m. & f.), *a priest, priestess*

săcerdōtĭŭm, -ī (n.), *priesthood*

săcrĭfĭcĭŭm, -ī (n.), *a sacrifice*

săcrĭlĕgŭs, -ī (m.), *a sacrilegist*

săcrō, -ārĕ, -āvī, -ātŭm, *to consecrate*

saecŭlŭm, -ī (n.), *a century*

saepĕ, *often*

saetă, -ae (f.), *a hair, bristle*

saevĭō, -īrĕ, -īvī, -ītŭm, *to rage*

saevĭtĭă, -ae (f.), *cruelty*

saevŭs, -ă, -ŭm, *furious, fierce*

săgittă, -ae (f.), *an arrow*

Salamīnĭŭs, -ă, -ŭm, *of Salamis*

Sălămĭs, -īnĭs (f.), *Salamis,* an island in the Saronic Gulf

sălĭō, -īrĕ, sălŭī, saltŭm, *to leap*

sălūs, -ūtĭs (f.), *safety;* salūti consulĕrĕ, *to have a care for safety*

sălūtārĭs, -ĕ, *advantageous*

sălūtō, -ārĕ, -āvī, -ātŭm, *to salute, greet*

sanciō, -īrĕ, sanxī, sancītŭm & sanctŭm, *to sanction, enact a law;* capĭte sancīre, *to enact capital punishment against;* lēge sancīre, *to constitute by law*

sanctissĭmē, *most purely*

sanctŭs, -ă, -ŭm, *inviolable,* sānē, *indeed* [*sacred*

sangŭĭs, -ĭnĭs (m.), *blood*

sānō, -ārĕ, -āvī, -ātŭm, *to heal*

sapĭens, -tĭs, *wise;* adv., sapĭen-ter, *wisely*

sapĭentĭă, -ae (f.), *wisdom*

sarcĭnă, -ae (f.), *a package*

Sardănăpallŭs. -ī (m.), *Sardana-pallus,* an effeminate king of Assyria

sarmentŭm, -ī (n.), *a fagot*

sătellĕs,-ĭtĭs (m.), *an attendant*

sătĭō, -ōnĭs (f.), *a planting*

sătĭō, -ārĕ, -āvī, -ātŭm, *to sat-isfy, fill*

sătĭs, *enough, sufficiently;* non satis fĭĕri, *to be without indem-nification*

sauciō, -ārĕ, -āvī, -ātŭm, *to wound*

saxŭm, -ī (n.), *a rock* [*skiff*

scăphă, -ae (f.), *a light boat, a*

scĕlŭs, -ĕrĭs (n.), *a crime*

scīlĭcĕt, *of course*

sciō, -īrĕ, -īvī, -ītŭm, *to know*

sciscĭtŏr, -ārī, -ātŭs sŭm, *to inquire*

scrībō, -ĕrĕ, scripsī, scriptŭm, *to write;* scriptus, *in writing;* scriptum est, *it has been com-municated*

scriptŏr, -ōrĭs (m.), *a writer;* scriptōres rerum suārum, *re-porters of his exploits*

scriptŭm, -ī (n.), *a writing*

scriptūră, -ae (f.), *a writing*

Scyllă, -ae (f.), *Scylla,* a rock between Italy and Sicily

sēclūsŭs, -ă, -ŭm, *separated*

sĕcō, -ārĕ, sĕcŭī, sectŭm, *to cut*

sĕcundŭm, w. acc., *after, accord-ing to, during*

sĕcundŭs, -ă, -ŭm, *following, second; favorable*

sĕcūrĭs, - (f.), *an axe*

sĕcūrĭtās, -ātĭs (f.), *security*

sĕcūrŭs, -ă, -ŭm, *without care, (feeling) safe*

sĕd, *but*

sĕdĕō,-ērĕ, sēdī, sessŭm, *to sit;* of birds, *to perch*

sēdēs, -ĭs (f.), *a seat, abode, set-tlement;* of a king, *throne;* au-spicāta sedes, *a lucky founda-tion*

sēdĭtĭō, -ōnĭs (f.), *a sedition*

sēdō,-ārĕ,-āvī,-ātŭm, *to bring to order;* dissensĭōnem sedāre, *to settle a difference*

sējungō, -ĕrĕ, sējunxī, sējunc-tŭm, *to disjoin*

Sĕmĭrămĭs,-ĭdĭs (f.), *Semiramis,* queen of Babylon

sĕnātŭs, -ūs (m.), *the senate*

sĕnectŭs, -ūtĭs (f.), *old age*

sĕnescō, -ĕrĕ, sĕnŭī, (no sup.), *to grow old*

sĕnex, -ĭs (m.), *an old man;* as adject., *old, aged*

sententĭă, -ae (f.), *an opinion, a vote, decision*

sentĭō, -īrĕ, sensī, sensŭm, *to become aware, think, feel; to notice*

sĕpĕlĭō,-īrĕ, sĕpĕlīvī, sĕpultŭm, *to bury*

septĕm, *seven*

septentrīōnēs, –ŭm (m. pl.), *(seven stars, Great Bear), North*

septingentī, –ae, –ă, *seven hun-*
septŭāgintă, *seventy* [*dred*

sĕpulcrŭm, –ī (n.), *a tomb, sepulcre*

sĕpultūră, –ae (f.), *a burial*

sĕquens, –tĭs, *following*

sĕquŏr, –ī, sĕcūtŭs sŭm, *to follow;* fidem popŭli Romānı sequi, *to seek the protection of the Roman people*

Sĕrīphĭŭs, –ī (m.), *a Seriphian*

Sĕrīphŭs, –ī (f.), *Seriphus,* a small island in the Aegean sea

sērĭŭs, –ă, –ŭm, *serious;* serīa, *serious matters*

sermō, –ōnĭs (m.), *a speech, talk*

sērŭs, –ă, –ŭm, *late, too late*

servīlĭs, –ĕ, *of a slave, servile;* servilĭbus verberĭbus adfici, *to be flogged by a slave;* servīlis ingenīi ratīo, *the reasoning of a servile mind*

servĭō, –īrĕ, –īvī, –ītŭm, *to serve*

servĭtŭs, –ūtĭs (f.), *slavery*

servō, –ārĕ, –āvī, –ātŭm, *to serve, preserve; rescue, save;* ı fidem servāre, *to keep a promise*

servŭs, –ī (m.), *a slave;* adject., *slavish, enslaved*

sescentī, –ae, –ă, *six hundred*

seu, *or;* seu..seu, *either..or*

sĕvĕrĭtās, –ātĭs (f.), *severity*

sĕvĕrŭs, –ă, –ŭm, *severe;* sevĕrīus, *more rigidly, carefully*

sĕvŏcō, –ārĕ, –āvī, –ātŭm, *to* sex, *six* [*remove*

sextŭs, –ă, –ŭm, *the sixth*

sexŭs, –ūs (m.), *sex*

sī, *if;* si modo, *if only;* si quidem, *as far as*

sīc, *so*

Sĭcānĭă, –ae (f.), = Sicilĭa, *Sicily*

siccō, –ārĕ, –āvī, –ātŭm, *to drain*

Sĭcĭlĭă, –ae (f.), *Sicily*

sīcŭbĭ, *wheresoever*

sīcŭt, sīcŭtī, *as;* sicut..ita, *as..so*

Sĭcўōn, –ōnĭs (f.), *Sicyon,* a city in the Peloponnesus

Sĭcўōnĭŭs, –ī (m.), *a Sicyonian*

Sīdōn, –ōnĭs (f.), *Sidon,* a Phoenician city

sīdōn, *fish*

sīdŭs, –ĕrĭs (n.), *a star, a group of stars*

Sīgēŭm, –ī (n.), *Sigeum,* a town in Troas where Achilles was buried

signĭfĭcō, –ārĕ, –āvī, –ātŭm, *to foretoken, to point out*

signŭm, –ī (n.), *a signal*

sīlentĭŭm, –ī (n.), *silence*

silvă, –ae (f.), *a wood, forest*

sĭmĭlĭs, –ĕ, *like, similar*

sĭmĭlĭtūdō, –ĭnĭs (f.), *resemblance*

Sĭmōnĭdēs, –ĭs (m.), *Simonides,* a famous lyric poet

simplĭcĭtĕr, *frankly, openly*

sĭmŭl, *at the same time*

sĭmŭlācrŭm, –ī (n.), *an image, a statue; a phantom*

sĭmŭlō, –ārĕ, –āvī, –ātŭm, *to make believe, feign*

sĭmultās, –ātĭs (f.), *a feud*

sīn, *but if*

sĭnĕ, w. abl., *without*

singŭlī, –ae, –ă, *each, individual, single, one by one;* singŭla emĕre, *to buy retail*

sĭnistĕr, –ră, –rŭm, *left*

sīnŭs,-ūs (m.), *the bosom; a gulf*,
sīquĭdĕm, *in as much as* [*bay*
sīquŏ, *if somewhere*
sistŏ, -ĕrĕ, stĭtī, stătŭm, *to
cause a person to appear in
court;* vas sistendi, *bail for his
appearing in court*
sītĭens, -tĭs, *thirsty*
sītĭs, – (f.), *thirst*
sītŭs, -ă, -ŭm, *situate;* situm
esse, *to depend upon*
sīvĕ, *or;* sivc..sivc, *either..or*
sŏcĭĕtās, -ātĭs (f.), *companion-
ship*
sŏcĭŭs, -ī (m.), *a companion, an
ally;* socĭa civĭtas, *a state in
alliance*
Sōcrătēs, -ĭs (m.), *Socrates*
Sōcrătĭcŭs, -ă, -ŭm, *Socratic*
Sochărĕs, -ĭs (m.), *Soebares,* Cyrus' companion
sōl, sōlĭs (m.), *the sun;* Sōl, *the
sun-god*
sŏlĕŏ, -ērĕ, sŏlĭtŭs sŭm, *to be
wont, accustomed, in the habit,
use*
sŏlĭdŭs, -ă, -ŭm, *whole, entire*
sōlĭtūdŏ, -ĭnĭs (f.), *a desert*
sōlĭtŭs,-ă,-ŭm, *usual, ordinary*
sollemnĭs, -c, *established*
sollers, -tĭs, *ingenious*
sollertĭă, -ae (f.), *skill*
sollĭcĭtātŭs, -ă, -ŭm, *stirred up,
allured*
sollĭcĭtŏ, -ārĕ, -āvī, -ātŭm, *to
induce, stir up; to allure;* in
amicitĭam sollicitāre, *to urge
to friendship;* sollicitāre in
partes suas, *to draw over to
one's side*
sollĭcĭtŭs, -ă, -ŭm, *anxious,
full of cares*

Sŏlōn, -ōnĭs (m.), *Solon,* the
lawgiver of the Athenians
sŏlŭm, -ī (n.), *the soil, ground*
sōlum, *only*
sōlŭs -ă, -ŭm, *alone*
sŏlūtŭs, -ă, -ŭm, *relaxed, loose;
let loose* (of a dog)
solvŏ, -ĕrĕ, solvī, sŏlūtŭm, *to
loosen;* solvĕre frenum, *to
slacken the reins;* pontem solvĕre, *to destroy a bridge;* religiōne solvĕre, *to free from an
obligation;* solvĕre (navem), *to
weigh anchor, set sail*
somnĭŭm, -ī (n.), *a dream*
somnŭs, -ī (m.), *sleep*
sonŭs, -ī (m.), *a sound, noise*
sorbĕŏ, -ērĕ, -ŭī, (no sup.), *to
suck up, swallow*
sordĭdŭs,-ă,-ŭm,*squalid, dirty;*
sordĭda veste, *by putting on
mourning*
sŏrŏr, -ōrĭs (f.), *a sister*
sors, -tĭs (f.), *a lot;* sors vitae,
condition of life
sortĭŏr, -īrī, -ītŭs sŭm, *to draw
lots;* in the perfect tenses, *to
obtain (by lot)*
sospĕs, -ĭtĭs, *safe and sound*
Spăcŏs, -ī (f.), *Spacos,* Cyrus'
nurse
Spartă, -ac (f.), *Sparta,* capital
of Laconia
Spartănŭs, -ī (m.), *a Spartan*
Spartĭātēs, -ae (m.), *a Spartan*
spătĭŭm, -ī (n.), *room, space,
time;* loci spatĭum, *extent of
space*
spĕcĭēs, -ēī (f.), *a show, appearance;* sub specĭe, *under the
mask;* specĭes navĭum, *the
shape of the ships*

spectācŭlŭm, -ī (n.), *a sight, view;* spectacŭlo dignus, *worth seeing*

spectātŏr, -ōrĭs (m.), *a beholder, spectator*

spectātŭs, -ă, -ŭm, *tried*

spectō, -ārĕ, -āvī, -ātŭm, *to look at; to observe*

spĕcŭlŏr, -ārī, -ātŭs sŭm, *to spy out*

spēs, spĕī (f.), *hope*

spīrāmentŭm, -ī (n.), *an airhole*

spīrĭtŭs, -ūs (m.), *a breath, a draught, (current of) air;* spirītum extrēmum trahĕre, *to breathe one's last*

splendĕō, -ērĕ, -ŭī, (no sup.), *to shine*

splendŏr, -ōrĭs (m.), *excellence*

spŏliātŭs, -ă, -ŭm, *spoiled, stripped*

spondĕō, -ērĕ, spŏpondī, sponsŭm, *to promise*

squālŏr, -ōrĭs (m.), *filthiness, squalor;* habītus squalōris, *the appearance of squalor*

stābŭlŭm, -ī (n.), *a stable*

stagnŭm,-ī (n.), *a swamp;* Assyrīum stagnum, *Lake Genesareth* in Palestine

stătĭm, *immediately*

stătŭō, -ĕrĕ, stătŭī, stătūtŭm, *to place; to resolve, decide;* sedem statuĕre, *to fix one's residence;* vectīgal statuĕre, *to fix a tax*

stătŭs,-ūs (m.), *a situation, condition*

stercŭs, -ŏrĭs (n.), *dung*

sternō, -ĕrĕ, strāvī, strătŭm, *to (strew),cover over,throw down*

stirps, -ĭs (f.), *offspring*

stō, -ārĕ, stĕtī, stătŭm, *to stand;* ex adverso stare, *to face*

strāgŭlŭm, -ī (n.), *a fabric*

Strătōn, -ōnĭs (m.), *Straton,* a chief of the Tyrians

strātŭs, -ă, -ŭm, *prostrate, spread;* stratus sulphŭre, *covered with sulphur*

strēnŭĕ, *strenuously*

strĕpĭtŭs, -ūs (m.), *a din, noise*

stŭdĕō, -ērĕ, -ŭī, (no sup.), *to pay attention to, to endeavor;* arti studĕre, *to devote one's self to an art;* sacrificiis studĕre, *to pay attention to sacrifices;* agricultūrae non studĕre, *not to care for agriculture*

stŭdĭōsŭs, -ă, -ŭm, *fond;* studiōse, *fondly*

stŭdĭŭm,-ī (n.), *zeal;* belli studĭa, *zeal for war;* studĭum majōris imperĭī, *endeavor to enlarge the dominion;* studĭum rei militāris, belli gerendi, *pursuit of military affairs, of warfare;* studĭa doctrīnae, *study and learning*

stultĭtĭă, -ae (f.), *folly*

stultŭs, -ă, -ŭm, *foolish*

stŭpŏr, -ōrĭs (m.), *stupidity*

sŭādĕō, -ērĕ, sŭāsī, sŭāsŭm, *to advise*

sŭāvĭs, -ĕ, *sweet*

sŭb, **with acc. & abl.,** *under;* sub ocŭlis, *before the eyes;* sub monte, *at the foot of a mountain*

subdŏlŭs, -ă, -ŭm, *deceitful*

subdūcō, -ĕrĕ, subduxī, subductŭm, *to haul ashore*

sŭbĭgō, -ĕrĕ, sŭbēgī, sŭbactŭm, *to subjugate*

sŭbĭtō, *suddenly*

sŭbĭtŭs, -ă, -ŭm, *sudden*

sublĕgō, -ĕrĕ, sublēgī, sublec-
tŭm, *to elect*

sublīmĭs, -ĕ, *aloft, high in the
air;* in sublīme, *high in the air*

submĭnistrō, -ārĕ, -āvī, -ātŭm,
to supply

submŏvĕō, -ĕrĕ, submōvī, sub-
mōtŭm, *to put out of the way*

sŭbŏlĕs, -ĭs (f.), *offspring*

subsĕquŏr, -ī, subsĕcūtŭs sŭm,
to follow closely

substernō, -ĕrĕ, substrāvī, sub-
strātŭm, *to lay under*

subtrăhō, -ĕrĕ, subtraxī, sub-
tractŭm, *to take away;* se subtrahĕre, *to retire*

subvĕnĭō, -īrĕ, subvēnī, subven-
tŭm, *to assist*

succēdō, -ĕrĕ, successī, succes-
sŭm, *to succeed; to follow,
march on*

successĭō, -ōnĭs (f.), *succession*

successŏr, -ōrĭs (m.), *a successor*

succurrō, -ĕrĕ, succurrī (succŭ-
currī), succursŭm, *to succor*

sūdŏr, -ōrĭs (m.), *sweat, perspi-
ration*

suffōcō, -ārĕ, -āvī, -ātŭm, *to
stifle*

suggestŭm, -ī (n.), *a platform*

sŭī, sĭbĭ, sē, *self*

sulphŭr, -ĭs (n.), *sulphur*

Sulpĭcĭŭs, -ī (m.), *Sulpicius,* the
name of a Roman gens

sŭm, essĕ, fŭī, (no sup.), *to be;* capillo sunt promisso, *they wear
their hair long*

summŭs, -ă, -ŭm, *highest,
greatest;* summis precĭbus,*with
every entreaty;* summa belli,

the command in chief; summa
voce, *at the top of one's voice;*
vir summus, *a very noble man;*
summis virĭbus, *with the utmost vigor;* summa fĭde, *conscientiously*

sūmō, -ĕrĕ, sumpsī, sumptŭm,
to take

sumptŭōsŭs, -ă, -ŭm, *expensive*

sumptŭs, -ūs (m.), *expense*

sŭpĕr, with acc., *over, above, besides*

sŭpĕrindūcō, -ĕrĕ, sŭpĕrinduxī,
sŭpĕrinductŭm, *to do over, to
coat*

sŭpĕrĭŏr, -ŭs, *upper, higher,
former; preceding, last;* super-
iōrem esse, *to have the advantage;* superior vita, *the former
life;* superior annus, *last year;*
superius tempus, *former time*

sŭpĕrō, -ārĕ, -āvī, -ātŭm, *to
subdue, to overcome, to beat*

sŭpersŭm, sŭpĕressĕ, sŭperfŭī,(no
sup.), *to be more than sufficient;
to remain, survive*

sŭpĕrŭs, -ă, -ŭm, *on high;* mare
supĕrum, *the upper,* i. e. *the
Adriatic and Ionian sea*

sŭpervĕnĭō, -īrĕ, sŭpervēnī, sŭ-
perventŭm, *to fall upon suddenly*

supplĕmentŭm, -ī (n.), *a supple-
ment;* supplementum copiārum,
reinforcements

supplex, -ĭcĭs, *on one's knees,
suppliant*

supplĭcĭŭm, -ī (n.), *punishment*

supprĭmō, -ĕrĕ, suppressī, sup-
pressŭm, *to sink*

sŭprā, with acc., *above, over;* adv.,
over

sŭprēmŭs, -ă, -ŭm, *highest, last*

surgō,-ĕrĕ, surrexī, surrectŭm, *to get up*

suscĭpĭō, -ĕrĕ, suscēpī, suscep-tŭm, *to take up;* of a child, *to bring up;* susceptus, *born;* bellum suscipĕre, *to undertake war*

suscĭtō, -ārĕ, -āvī, -ātŭm, *to lift up;* suscitāre e somno, *to awake*

suspĭcŏr, -ārī, -ātŭs sŭm, *to suppose*

sustĭnĕō, -ērĕ, sustĭnŭī, susten-tŭm, *to hold up; to hold out*

sŭsurrŭs, -ī (m.), *whispering*

sŭŭs, -ă, -ŭm, *his, her, its own;* sui, *his men;* sua, *their prop-erty*

symbŏlŭs,-ī (m.), *a sign* or *mark; a symbol*

Sȳrācūsae, -ārŭm (f. pl.), *Syra-cuse*

Sȳrācūsănŭs, -ī (m.), *a Syracu-*

Sȳrŭs, -ī (m.), *a Syrian*　　[*san*

T.

tăbellă, -ae (f.), *a tablet*

tăcĕō, -ērĕ, -ŭī, -ĭtŭm, *to be silent*

tăcĭtŭs, -ă, -ŭm, *silent;* tacīto, *secretly;* tacĭte, *silently*

taedĭŭm, -ī (n.), *trouble;* taedī-um belli, *disgust with war*

tālĭs, -ĕ, *such; such like*

tăm, *so*

tămĕn, *yet, nevertheless*

tandĕm, *at length; pray*

tangō, -ĕrĕ, tĕtĭgī, tactŭm, *to touch*

tantŭlŭs,-ă, -ŭm, *so small, triv-ial, insignificant*

tantŭm, *only*

tantŭs, -ă, -ŭm, *so great, so much;* tantus…quantus, *so much..as;* quod tanti est, *an equivalent*

tardŭs, -ă,-ŭm, *slow;* paulo tar-dius, *rather tardily*

taurŭs, -ī (m.), *a bull*

tectōrĭŭs, -ă, -ŭm, *that serves for covering;* opus tectorĭum, *stucco*

tectŭm, -ī (n.), *a roof; a house*

tegmĕn, -ĭnĭs (n.), *a cover*

tegō, -ĕrĕ, texī, tectŭm, *to cov-er, hide*

tēlŭm,-ī (n.), *a weapon, javelin*

tĕmĕrĕ, *rashly; commonly; with-out good reason*

tempĕrămentŭm, -ī (n.), *moder-ation*

tempĕrantĭă,-ae (f.), *moderation*

tempestās, -ātĭs (f.), *weather; storm; time;* tertĭa tempestas, *the third day*

templŭm, -ī (n.), *a temple*

temptō, -ārĕ, -āvī, -ātŭm, *to make an attempt upon*

tempŭs, -ŏrĭs (n.), *time;* ad tempus, *at the right time;* anni tempus, *a season;* post tempus, *hereafter*

tĕnĕō, -ērĕ, tĕnŭī, tentŭm, *to hold (in possession), keep; re-strain;* imperĭum tenēre, *to hold the supreme power;* te-nēri, *to be bound;* tenēre quo-mĭnus, *to detain from;* portum tenēre, *to guard the harbor;* cursum tenēre, *to hold on one's way;* vento tenēri quomĭnus, *to be prevented by the wind from*

tĕnŭĭs, -ĕ, *thin*

tĕnŭĭtās, -ātĭs (f.), *humble station; slenderness*

tergĭversŏr, -ārī, -ātŭs sŭm, *to turn one's back;* tergĭversantes, *deserters*

tergŭm,-ī (n.), *the back;* de tergo, post terga, *in the rear;* terga dare, *to turn the back*

termĭnŭs, -ī (m.), *a limit, bound*

terră, -ae (f.), *earth, land;* universae terrae, *the whole world*

terrĕō, -ĕrĕ, -ŭī, -ĭtŭm, *to frighten*

terrestĕr, -rĭs, -rĕ, *by land*

terrĭbĭlĭs, -ĕ, *terrible*

terrŏr, -ōrĭs (m.), *dread, terror*

tertĭŭs, -ă, -ŭm, *third*

testĭmōnĭŭm,-ī (n.), *a testimony, evidence*

textĭlĭs, -ĕ, *textile*   [tocles

Thĕmĭstŏclēs, -ĭs (m.), *Themis-*

Thermŏpўlae, -ārŭm (f. pl.), *Thermopylae,* the famous defile of Oeta, where Leonidas fell

Thēsēūs, -ĕī (m.), *Theseus,* king of Athens

Thespĭae, -ārŭm (f. pl.) , *Thespiae,* a town of Boeotia

Thessălĭă, -ae (f.), *Thessaly*

tĭgĭllŭm, -ī (n.), *a little log*

Tĭmaeŭs, -ī (m.), *Timaeus,* a Greek historian of Sicily

tĭmens, -tĭs, *timid(ly)*

tĭmĕō, -ĕrĕ, -ŭī, (no sup.), *to fear*

tĭmĭdŭs, -ă, -ŭm, *timid*

tĭmŏr, -ōrĭs (m.), *fear*

tintinnābŭlŭm, -ī (n.), *a bell*

Tĭtŭrĭŭs, -ī (m.), *Titurius,* a legate of Caesar in the Gallic war

tollō, -ĕrĕ, sustŭlī, sublātŭm, *to take up, to take away;* of a child, *to bring up;* of laws, *to abolish;* ancŏras tollĕre, *to weigh anchor;* tĭmōrem tollĕre, *to take away fear;* clamōrem tollĕre, *to set up a cry*

tondĕō, -ĕrĕ, tŏtondī, tonsŭm, *to shave*

tonsŏr, -ōrĭs (m.), *a barber*

tonstrĭcŭlă, -ae (f.), *a little barber*

tormentŭm, -ī (n.), *torture; a missile*

torrens,-tĭs, *rolling in a stream, rushing*

tŏt, (indecl.), *so many*

tōtŭs, -ă, -ŭm, *whole;* totis virĭbus, *with might and main*

tractō, -ārĕ, -āvī, -ātŭm, *to handle, treat;* bella tractāre, *to conduct war*

trādō, -ĕrĕ, trādĭdī, trādĭtŭm, *to hand over, deliver, report, relate;* in matrimonĭum tradĕre, *to marry;* epulandum tradĕre, *to set before to feast upon;* exercĭtum tradĕre, *to surrender an army;* quem biformem tradidĕre, *whom they said was two-shaped;* tradĭtur, *it is said;* regnum tradĕre, *to entrust a kingdom;* artem tradĕre, *to teach an art;* se tradĕre, *to give one's self up*

trăhō, -ĕrĕ, traxī, tractŭm, *to draw, derive;* proelĭum trahĕre, *to protract a battle;* spirĭtum extrēmum trahĕre, *to breathe one's last;* vitam trahĕre, *to drag one's life;* gratĭam trahĕre, *to gain favor*

trājectŭs, –ūs (m.), *a crossing,
passage*

trājĭcĭō,–ĕrĕ, trājēcī, trājectŭm,
to cross

transĕō,–īrĕ,–ĭī,–ĭtŭm, *to cross,
pass by, to pass;* transeuntes,
the passers-by

transfĕrō, –rĕ, transtŭlī, trarslā-
tŭm, *to transfer, to bring over;*
se transferre, *to betake one's
self;* se transferre a bello terrestri in navŭle, *to pass from
war by land to war by sea*

transĭtĭŏ, –ōnĭs (f.), *desertion*

transĭtŭs, –ūs (m.), *a crossing,
passage*

transportō, –ārĕ, –āvī, –ātŭm,
to transport, carry across

trēcentī, –ae, –ă, *three hundred*

trĕpĭdātĭŏ, –ōnĭs (f.), *confusion*

trĕpĭdŭs, –ă, –ŭm, *restless*

trēs, trĭă, *three*

trĭbūnŭs, –ī (m.), *a tribune;* tri-
būnus milītum, *a military tribune*

trĭbŭŏ, –ĕrĕ, trĭbŭī, trĭbūtŭm,
to attribute, give

trīdŭŭm, –ī (n.), *a space of three*
trīgintă, *thirty*   [*days*

Trīnăcrĭă, –ae (f.), *Trinacria,*
old name of the island of Sicily

Triptŏlĕmŭs, –ī (m.), *Triptole-
mus,* king of Eleusis, inventor
of agriculture

tristĭs,–ĕ, *sad, gloomy, disheart-
ening;* tristĭor mens, *deeper
affection*

trĭvĭŭm, –ī (n.), *a cross road*
Trōjānŭs, –ī (m.), *a Trojan*
trŏpaeŭm, –ī (n.), *a trophy*
trŭcīdō, –ārĕ, –āvī, –ātŭm *to
butcher, slay*

trūdō, –ĕrĕ, trūsī, trūsŭm, *to
drive*

truncŭs, –ī (m.), *the trunk*
trux, trŭcĭs, *fierce, wild*
tū, *thou*
tŭĕŏr, –ērī, (tŭĭtŭs, tūtŭs) tū-
tātŭs sŭm, *to protect*
tŭm, *then;* tum tempŏris, *at that
time*
tŭmens, –tĭs, *swollen*
tŭmultŭŏr, –ārī, –ātŭs sŭm, *to
be in confusion*
tŭmultŭs, –ūs (m.), *a tumult,
confusion*
tŭmŭlŭs, –ī (m.), *a mound*
tunc, *then, at that time*
tūnĭcă, –ae (f.), *a shirt, tunic*
turbă, –ae (f.), *a crowd*
turbĭdŭs, –ă, –ŭm, *muddy*
turbō, –ārĕ, –āvī, –ātŭm, *to
disturb*
turbŭlentŭs, –ă, –ŭm, *muddy*
turpĭs, –ĕ, *shameful, disgraceful,
dishonorable*
turrĭs, – (f.), *a tower*
tūtēlă, –ae (f.), *guardianship*
tūtŏr, –ārī, –ātŭs sŭm, *to pro-
tūtŭs, –ă, –ŭm, *safe*   [*tect*
tŭŭs, –ă, –ŭm, *thy*
tўrannĭs, –ĭdĭs (f.), *absolute
power, tyranny*
tўrannŭs, –ī (m.), *a tyrant*
Tўrĭŭs, –ī (m.), *a Tyrian*
Tўrŭs, –ī (f.), *Tyre,* a commer-
cial city of the Phoenicians

U.

ūbĕr, –ĭs (n.), *a dug;* ubĕra praebĕre, *to suckle*
ūbertās, –ātĭs (f.), *abundance*
ūbī, *where; when, as;* ubi primum, *as soon as*

ulciscŏr, -ī, ultŭs sŭm, *to avenge*

ullŭs, -ă, -ŭm, *any; in negative and conditional clauses*

ultĕrĭŏr, -ŭs, *remoter*

ultĭŏ, -ōnĭs (f.), *avenge; in ultiōnem, to avenge one's self*

ultŏr, -ōrĭs (m.), *an avenger*

ultrā, w. acc., *beyond;* adv., *further*

ultrō, *of one's own accord*

umbrā, -ac (f.), *a shade*

umquăm, *ever*

ūnā, *together*

undā, -ac (f.), *a wave*

undĕ, *whence*

undĭquĕ, *from all quarters*

ungŭentŭm, -ī (n.), *a perfume, ointment*

ungŭĭs, - (m.), *a claw, talon*

ūnĭcŭs, -ă, -ŭm, *only, sole*

ūnĭversŭs, -ă, -ŭm, *whole, all together*

ūnŭs, -ă, -ŭm, *one, sole, only*

urbs, -ĭs (f.), *a city*

urgĕŏ, -ērĕ, ursī, ursŭm, *to urge, press hard*

usquăm, *anywhere;* usque terrārum, *anywhere in the world*

usquĕ, *as far as, to*

ūsŭs, -ŭs (m.), *use, usefulness;* usūi esse, *to be of service or advantage;* usus belli, *experience in war*

ŭt, ŭtĭ, *how, as, when, that;* after verbs of *wishing* and *willing*, *to;* after verbs of *fearing, that not;* sic ut, *so as to;* ut..ita, *as..so*

ŭtĕr, -ră, -rŭm, *which of two*

ŭterquĕ, ŭträquĕ, ŭtrumquĕ, *either, both;* utrĭque, *both parties;* ex utrăque parte, *on both sides*

Ŭtĭcă, -ac (f.), *Utica, a very old town in Africa*

Ŭtĭcensĭs, - (m.), *an inhabitant of Utica*

ūtĭlĭs, -ĕ, *useful*

ūtĭlĭtās, -ātĭs (f.), *utility*

ūtŏr, -ī, ūsŭs sŭm, *to use, make use, enjoy, have;* legĭbus uti, *to obey the laws;* alacrĭtāte uti, *to show alacrity;* institūtis uti, *to have institutions*

ūtrŭm..ăn, *whether..or*

ūvă, -ac (f.), *a grape*

uxŏr, -ōrĭs (f.), *a wife*

V.

văcō, -ārĕ, -āvī, -ātŭm, *to be without*

văcŭŭs, -ă, -ŭm, *empty, wanting something;* vacŭus homĭnĭbus, *deserted*

vădŭm, -ī (n.), *a ford; the depths*

vaccors, -dĭs, *insane;* subst., *a madman*

văgŏr, -ārī, -ātŭs sŭm, *to roam about*

vălĕō, -ērĕ, -ŭī, -ĭtŭm, *to be strong, powerful;* plus valēre, *to have more influence*

vallĭs, - (f.), *a valley*

văpŏr, -ōrĭs (m.), *vapor*

vărĭĕ, *in various ways*

vărĭĕtās, -ātĭs (f.), *changeableness, fickleness, variety*

vărĭŭs, -ă, -ŭm, *various, varied*

văs, vădĭs (m.), *bail*

vastō, -ārĕ, -āvī, -ātŭm, *to devastate, lay waste*

vātēs, -ĭs (m.), *a prophet*

vātĭcĭnŏr, -ārī, -ātŭs sŭm, *to predict, prophecy*

vectĭgăl, -ālĭs (n.), *a tax*

věhěmens, -tǐs, *violent*
věhěmentěr, *very much*
věhō, -črě, vexī, vectūm, *to carry;* pass., *to be carried, borne; to ride, drive, sail*
vělōcǐtās, -ātǐs (f.), *speed*
vělǔt, vělǔtǐ, *as if, as it were*
věnālǐs, -ě, *for sale*
věnans, -tǐs, & věnātǒr, -ōrǐs (m.), *a hunter*
věnātǐǒ, -ǒnǐs, (f.), *hunting*
věnātǒr, -ōrǐs (m.), *a hunter*
věnātǔs, -ūs, (m.), *hunting*
vendō, -črě, vendǐdī, vendǐtǔm, *to sell*
věněnātǔs, -ǎ, -ǔm, *poisoned*
Věnětǐcǔs, -ǎ, -ǔm, *Venetian*
věnǐǎ, -ae (f.), *permission, pardon, pretext;* venǐam darě, *to forgive*
věnǐō, -īrě, věnī ventūm, *to come;* ventum est, *they came*
věnǒr, -ārī, -ātǔs sǔm, *to hunt*
ventěr, -rǐs (m.), *the belly*
ventǐtō, -ārě, -āvī, -ātǔm, *to keep coming; to be wont to come*
ventǔs, -ī (m.), *the wind*
verběr, -ǐs (n.), *a scourge*
verbǔm, -ī (n.), *a word;* verbis elevārě, *to cry down*
věrě, *truly*
věrěǒr, -ěrī, věrǐtǔs sǔm, *to fear*
vergō, -črě, (no perf. & sup.), *to incline, to lie*
věrǐtās, -ātǐs (f.), *truth*
věrō, *truly, indeed; but*
versǐcǔlǔs, -ī (m.), *a little verse*
versǔs, -ūs (m.), *a verse*
versūtǔs, -ǎ, -ǔm, *clever*
vertex, -ǐcǐs (m.), *a whirlpool*

vertō, -črě, vertī, versǔm, *to turn;* in fugam verti, *turn to flight;* versa vice, *reversedly*
věrǔm, *(true), but*
vescǒr,-ī, (no perf.), *to feed on, eat*
vespěr, -ī (m.), vespěrǎ, -ae (f.), *evening;* prima vespěra, *at the first appearance of dark*
vestěr, -rǎ, -rǔm, *your*
vestǐs, - (f.), *a garment*   [*bid*
větō,-ārě,větǔī, větǐtǔm, *to forvětěrānǔs, -ī (m.), *a veteran*
větǔs, -črǐs, *old; former*
větustās, -ātǐs (f.), *antiquity*
vexātǔs, -ǎ, -ǔm, *harassed*
vǐǎ, -ae (f.), *a road*
vǐcě, *turn; instead of;* versa vice, *reversedly*
vǐcīnǐtās, -ātǐs (f.), *vicinity*
vǐcīnǔs, -ǎ, -ǔm, *neighboring;* subst., *a neighbor*
victǐmǎ, -ae (f.), *a victim*
victǒr, -ōrǐs (m.), victrix, -īcǐs (f.), *a conqueror, winner; victorious, triumphant*
victōrǐǎ, -ae (f.), *victory*
Victōrǐǒlǎ, -ae (f.), *a little statue of Victory*
victǔs,-ǎ,-ǔm, *overcome;* subst., *a loser*
victǔs,-ūs (m.), *sustenance, food; living*
vǐděō, -črě, vīdī, vīsǔm, *to see;* viděri, *to seem, appear;* mihi vidětur, *it seems (good) to me*
vǐgěō, -črě, -ǔī, (no sup.), *to be in force*
vǐgǐlǐǎ, -ae (f.), *watch;* tertǐa vigilǐa, *at the beginning of the third watch*
vǐgǐlō, -ārě, -āvī, -ātǔm, *to watch, to be wakeful*

vīgintī, *twenty*

vīgŏr, -ōrĭs (m.), *liveliness*

vīlĭs, -ĕ, *vile*

vincō, -ĕrĕ, vīcī, victŭm, *to defeat, overcome, to win a victory;* in a lawsuit, *to gain the cause;* pass., vinci, *to be restrained;* consilĭo vincĕre, *to win over by one's opinion*

vindex,-ĭcĭs (m. & f.), *a protector*

vindīcō, -ārĕ, -āvī, -ātŭm, *to take revenge, avenge; to deliver, to claim;* regnum vindicāre, *to claim the kingdom;* se vindicāre a captivitāte, *to deliver one's self from captivity*

vindictă, -ae (f.), *vengeance*

vīnĕă, -ae (f.), *a vine-trellis*

vīnŭm, -ī (n.), *wine;* vini avīdus, *fond of the cup*

vĭŏlō,-ārĕ, -āvī, -ātŭm, *to offer violence,to violate; to mutilate;* respublĭca violanda, *betraying one's country*

vīr, -ī (m.), *a man*

virgŏ, -ĭnĭs (f.), *a virgin, maiden;* virgo regĭa, *a royal princess*

virīlĭs, -ĕ, *manly, suitable to a man*

virtūs, -ūtĭs (f.), *bravery, valor, virtue*

vīs, - (f.), *strength, power, force, violence;* summis virĭbus, *with the utmost vigor*

viscĕră, -ŭm (n. pl.), *entrails, vitals*

vīsō, -ĕrĕ, vīsī, vīsŭm, *to go to see, to look*

vīsŭm, -ī (n.), *a vision*

vītă, -ae (f.), *life*

vītĭs, - (f.), *a vine*

vītĭŭm, -ī (n.), *a vice;* vitĭa ebrietātis, *the injurious effects of drunkenness*

vītō, -ārĕ,-āvī, -ātŭm, *to avoid*

vĭtŭpĕrō, -ārĕ, -āvī, -ātŭm, *to find fault with*

vīvō, -ĕrĕ, vixī, victŭm, *to live*

vīvŭs, -ă, -ŭm, *living, alive*

vix, *hardly*

vŏcō, -ārĕ, -āvī, -ātŭm, *to call*

vŏlō, vellĕ, vŏlŭī, (no sup.), *to be willing, wish, want; to mean, be of opinion*

vŏluntās, -ātĭs (f.), *will*

vŏluntārĭŭs, -ă,-ŭm, *voluntary;* voluntarĭa mors, *suicide*

vŏluptās, -ātĭs (f.), *pleasure*

Vŏlŭsēnŭs, -ī (m.), *Volusenus*

vŏrāgŏ, -ĭnĭs (f.), *a whirlpool*

vōs, *you*

vox, vōcĭs (f.), *a voice, word, remark;* vocc, *by word of mouth;* magna voce, *with a loud voice;* vocem edĕre,*to exclaim;* vocem premĕre, *to be silent*

Vulcānŭs,-ī (m.), *Vulcan,* god of [fire

vulgŭs, -ī (n.), *the rabble, masses*

vulnĕrō, -ārĕ, -āvī, -ātŭm, *to wound*

vulnŭs, -ĕrĭs (n.), *a wound*

vulpēs, -ĭs (f.), *a fox*

vultŭs,-ūs (m.), *the countenance*

X.

Xĕnŏphŏn, -ontĭs (m.), *Xenophon,* a Grecian historian

Xerxēs, -ĭs (m.), *Xerxes,* king of Persia

Z.

Zŏrŏastrēs, -ĭs (m.), *Zoroaster,* the lawgiver of the Medes